THE FRENCH IN THE WEST INDIES

Books *by* W. ADOLPHE ROBERTS

BIOGRAPHY

Sir Henry Morgan: Buccaneer and Governor
Semmes of the Alabama

HISTORY

The Caribbean: The Story of Our Sea of Destiny
The French in the West Indies

NOVELS

The Mind Reader
The Moralist
The Top-Floor Killer
The Pomegranate

VERSE

Pierrot Wounded and Other Poems
Pan and Peacocks

JEAN-BAPTISTE DU CASSE
Great sea rover, Governor of Saint Domingue
and wearer of the Golden Fleece.

THE FRENCH IN THE WEST INDIES

by W. ADOLPHE ROBERTS

THE BOBBS-MERRILL COMPANY

PUBLISHERS

INDIANAPOLIS . . . NEW YORK

First Edition

Dedicated to

DAVID LAURANCE CHAMBERS

CONTENTS

LIST OF ILLUSTRATIONS

Whoever has made himself acquainted with the history of the West Indian islands cannot fail to have observed that, whenever the nations of Europe are engaged, from whatever cause, in war with each other, those unhappy countries are constantly made the theatre of its operations. Thither the combatants repair, as to the arena.

—BRYAN EDWARDS

CHAPTER I

Adam's Will

ALEXANDER VI, the Borgia Pope, divided the newly discovered Western Hemisphere between Spain and Portugal in his four bulls of 1493, clarified by the Treaty of Tordesillas. Barely thirty years later, Francis I of France began to launch expeditions against that domain, and when this was protested by Charles V, Holy Roman Emperor and King of Spain, Francis made his celebrated remark:

"The sun shines for me as for others. I should very much like to see the clause in Adam's will that excludes me from a share of the world."

The rulers of all the maritime nations of northern Europe felt as he did. The nascent Reformation had loosened their bonds of interest with Rome. But Francis was an extremely Catholic monarch, and his defiance would seem strange if we were not aware of the gap that separates spiritual from political Catholicism, and how wide this was in the turbulent first half of the sixteenth century. Francis never relaxed his rivalry with Charles, whom he hoped to replace as lord of Europe, world suzerain and the favored of the Vatican. The question was virtually settled at the Battle of Pavia, which ended with the French King a prisoner.

But he would not admit it. He was interested in the Northwest Passage, which he sent Verrazano the Florentine to discover in 1523. Tales from Brazil allured him, and his ships cruised along the limitless coast assigned to Portugal. The golden conquests of Mexico and Peru, however, undoubtedly proved most potent to sting him to envy. The Caribbean Sea

13

took on the character of lobby to these treasure houses, and the vague notion of geography that prevailed in the northern courts led the Antilles to be called the Peruvian islands.

Francis longed for a foothold there. He again commissioned Verrazano, and as the latter was financed by a group of Florentine bankers doing business at Lyons the King got his exploring for nothing. He would have been unable to find the money himself. The ransom paid after Pavia had been ruinous. Nothing came of the brilliant navigator's voyage, which cost him his life obscurely among cannibals, somewhere on the tropical mainland. And that is the last one hears of legitimate enterprises by Francis in America.

The truth was that this particular dream did not have sufficient dominion over the royal sensualist with the long nose, the curled black beard, and Italy stamped on his heart. His ambition to outdo in a military sense the Holy Roman Emperor and King of Spain shaped his public acts. Privately, he was a devotee of the Renaissance and did more than any other man to introduce it into France. He hired the services of Leonardo da Vinci and Benvenuto Cellini. He was a builder of châteaus, headed by superb Fontainebleau, and of many hunting lodges. The chase was a mania with him. He set an extravagant table at all times. His mistresses—Françoise de Foix, Anne de Pisseleu and the rest—though mentioned last, were by no means the least of his expenses.

Francis obtained his revenue by applying a crushing system of universal taxation, till then unknown in medieval Europe. He saw the New World chiefly as a source of wealth which could relieve the burdens of his people and enable him to wage greater wars against Charles V, the present beneficiary of all that gold. His deceptions were infinite. It was not for nothing that he had taken the salamander for his symbol. But he lacked the capital to become an interloper on the grand scale needed for success, nor would he sacrifice his pleasures in

order to amass it. So the project lost its aspect of glory and
degenerated into the merely mercenary.

A seafaring merchant class had sprung up in the Channel
ports, due to the stagnation of the Low Countries under the
Spaniards. Dieppe was notably prosperous. Francis, on the
initiative of Guillon le Roy, grandfather of Cardinal Richelieu, had founded Le Havre at the mouth of the Seine.
Though resented at first by Rouen up the river, the new
harbor soon demonstrated its value to all the cities of the
Seine valley, including Paris. The trading out of the ports
was largely piratical. Oppressed Flemings had shown the
way by robbing the Spaniards and bringing their loot to
French markets. Their imitators called themselves privateers
and claimed the right to plague Charles V only in time of
war. It was a fine distinction which they did not long observe.

In 1523, the year of Verrazano's first sally into the unknown, a squadron belonging to the affluent Jean d'Ango, of
Dieppe, had met ships off the Azores carrying samples of
Mexican treasure from Cortés—mainly gold ornaments, jewels
and feathered Aztec cloaks. The French had cut off two of
the galleons, and the completely novel booty had caused the
greatest sensation in Dieppe and Paris. The memory of it
lingered in the King's mind.

He had an inspiration about his pirates. Why should they
not become a vanguard in the Caribbean? He let it be known
that mariners who pushed enterprises deep into that region
would be well regarded by the Crown. This meant that their
title to the goods they brought would never be challenged, so
long as they paid the heavy imposts. The implication of a
national policy more lucrative than the wars to regain Milan
also had weight with the hard-headed merchants. Enthusiasm
for West Indian adventure swept the quays from Boulogne
to Le Havre. It fired men to embark on voyages from which
they had previously shrunk, seeing how small and ill-fitted

were their vessels for crossing three to four thousand miles of water and then operating without a home port.

The pirates of the early years can seldom be identified by name, and there are no records by which we may estimate their total gains. They were first reported by the Spaniards as a serious menace in 1537 and 1538 when the coasts of Hispaniola (then called Española), Cuba, Honduras, the Isthmus of Panama and the Main were scoured, villages plundered and ships at anchor seized. The Governor at Santo Domingo sent home a dispatch complaining that the presence of the French was "shameless, bold and continuous." The plate fleets were held to be in danger from them.

D'Ango, of Dieppe, still active and richer than ever, furnished the most considerable diversion, though he was too cautious to venture as far as the Caribbean. He equipped fast vessels which spied on the treasure ships as they approached Spain, and late in 1537 he intercepted nine units out of fifty. The magnitude of the prize may be judged by the value of 280,000,000 *maravédis* (some $2,000,000) placed on the cargoes delivered to the King of Spain's warehouses by the boats that escaped.

Though not within the compass of this narrative, it should be noted for the sake of perspective that there was simultaneous French action in the far north. Jacques Cartier left St. Malo in May, 1535, for the first exploration of Canada.

Formal war with Spain was declared in 1542, and the Antilles became the scene of larger French enterprises. Royal craft were among the six which raided the pearl island of Cubagua and the city of Santa Marta, Venezuela. Landing parties collected everything valuable, and then applied the torch. The island of Margarita was despoiled. Similar attempts the next year did not fare so well. The individual corsairs continued to perform actively. Swarms of them appeared, mostly French, with the sinister addition of some

Moslems from Algiers, at that time the very home of piracy.

But this turned out to be a shorter war than usual. Francis was prematurely old, tormented by a malady believed to have been syphilis, and financially unable to hold up his end against Charles. He made peace in 1544. By one of the clauses of the treaty, he acknowledged the supremacy of Spain in America and undertook to prevent his subjects from going to the Caribbean. Though he did not keep his promise strictly, he lost all personal interest in the matter. Francis died three years later, aged fifty-three, having accomplished little to justify his quip about the Pope's interpretation of Adam's will.

The next Valois, Henry II, nursed a darker rancor. As a child, he had been sent to Madrid as hostage to guarantee the payment of his father's ransom, had been shabbily treated during the years he spent there. He and Philip II of Spain came to their thrones almost simultaneously, and one of his hopes was to make life unpleasant for Philip. No weakling, he was hampered by the fierce ambitions of strong persons around him. His Queen was Catherine de Médicis. The rising Huguenot movement had produced the great Admiral of France, Gaspar de Coligny, and on the Catholic side towered the formidable Duc de Guise. Demanding harmony, the King obtained it at least against Spain, with whom a new war began in 1552. He resumed his father's American policy, with more efficiency.

There was a sturdy old sea-fighter named François le Clerc, who because of his peg-leg was known as Jambe-de-Bois and later by the Spaniards as Pié-de-Palo, which means the same thing. Henry issued letters of marque to him, gave him the command of ten ships in which the Crown had an interest, and dispatched him as the first officially recognized privateer to sail the Caribbean. Le Clerc was the true forerunner of Sir Francis Drake and other Elizabethan captains of this type.

Jacques de Sores, a Lutheran, went with him as lieutenant. The partnership was effective in maintaining discipline among the crews, which contained many Protestants. No one took account of the peculiar seeds of hatred it might sow.

The Le Clerc expedition sailed in 1553 and methodically went to work on the island colonies of the Spaniards before passing to the Main. Information gathered by previous raiders, or the shrewd reports of scouts, served to concentrate the attacks on poorly protected settlements. Two squadrons were formed. That under Jambe-de-Bois himself burned La Yaguana, a wretched hamlet, but interesting because it was the future Port-au-Prince; then circled Hispaniola and Puerto Rico in a huge figure eight, striking at will.

Sores was assigned Cuba and extracted a nice profit from that strugging colony not yet fifty years old. He sacked Santiago in the east, extorting 80,000 pesos. July, 1555, he stormed Havana, held it for eighteen days, looted and burned it. The fort and the church escaped total destruction. Sores admired the defense the military commander had made and treated him well. He was not so amiable with the priests, whose vestments and holy images he snatched for use in a wild Lutheran travesty. Pirates in churchly dress paraded through the ruins of Havana, bearing aloft the images at which they hurled insults and frequently stabbed with their bloody poniards. These sacrilegious antics were not easily forgotten by the Spaniards, and never forgiven.

Both Le Clerc and Sores feinted several times at Santo Domingo, Cartagena and Nombre de Dios, the key ports of the Caribbean proper in their day, but refrained from attacking. It suited their purpose better to keep the enemy warcraft immobilized at these points through fear of an assault. Spanish commercial shipping was decimated until 1559, when the long Valois-Hapsburg quarrel was patched up. The privateers returned home as heroes, those that were left of them. Le Clerc obtained a patent in one of the lower orders of nobility. History is silent regarding the end of Jacques de Sores.

The year 1559 marked the beginning of a period fatal to French projects of expansion abroad. As usual, the signs were obscure. The peace treaty ordinarily would have amounted to an armistice. Even the death of Henry II, accidentally killed in a tournament with the knight Montgomery, did not necessitate retreat. Catherine de Médicis, as Regent for the young Charles IX, promised a government that would be stronger and, if anything, more aggressive. Coligny persuaded Catherine to let him attempt a colony in Brazil and, this failing, to plant one composed of Huguenots on the southeastern coast of North America.

The element that destroyed all such plans was the growing bitterness between Catholics and Protestants in France. Civil war was on the point of breaking out, with the frightful result of eight conflagrations in thirty-six years. These were known as the Wars of Religion, a cumulative disaster which left room for no other activity.

The story of Coligny's abortive ventures overseas, which wound up in Florida under the heel of the ruthless Spanish Admiral Pedro Menéndez de Avilés, has been often told.* Motivation and aftermath are what interest us here. When Jean Ribault sailed early in 1562 with two ships, Coligny knew that the troubles in France were on the point of becoming .calamitous. The Huguenot leader was anxious to found an asylum in America for his co-religionists. He had foreseen the bloodshed that took place at Dreux later that year, the persecutions that followed the initial victory of the Catholics. But he was poorly served by Ribault's pioneers. They decided on Port Royal, South Carolina, an excellent

---

* For an account of the French attempt at colonization in Florida, see Chapter Twelve of *The Caribbean: The Story of Our Sea of Destiny*.

location well outside the zone of Spanish activity, failed to make a success of it through lack of tenacity, and straggled home.

It helped that there had been a truce in the sectarian strife. Coligny was able to prepare a larger expedition under René de la Laudonnière in 1564, and arrange for Ribault to follow with re-enforcements in a year's time. An imp of the perverse induced Laudonnière to drop anchor in the St. John's River, near the site of modern Jacksonville. The French called it the Rivière Mai. Unfortunately, this was within the area regarded by the Spaniards as an organized province since the discovery of Florida by Ponce de León and the subsequent explorations of Pánfilo de Narváez and Hernando de Soto.

On the heels of the Huguenots came Menéndez, the prime fanatic of his day, savage with memories of the Lutheran excesses in Havana ten years before, and inflamed by partisan feeling about the French Wars of Religion. He had vowed to tolerate no intruders in Florida, above all no Protestants. From the military standpoint, he held the sound view that any fortified settlement on the peninsula would endanger communications by sea with Mexico. Advancing with a powerful fleet, some 700 armed men, as well as ecclesiastics and colonists, Menéndez founded St. Augustine in September, 1565. Ribault, meanwhile, had arrived from France, and he took the rash initiative of moving to the attack. A hurricane destroyed the ships of both sides. But Menéndez made an astounding overland march through wind and rain, and seized Fort Caroline, as Laudonnière's settlement was called.

There followed a massacre along the coast, in which shipwrecked sailors received no mercy and promises of immunity for surrender were broken. Menéndez had announced that his mission was to "hang or behead all Lutherans," and he fulfilled it, except that he spared the women and children. He vaunted an implacable intolerance for the future. He and the Holy Inquisition took up the gage the Norman privateers had thrown down. He could not know that the Huguenots he so abhorred represented a losing cause, and that the heretics with staying powers in the New World would be the English and Dutch.

The French were not quite finished with Florida in 1565. A young nobleman and a Catholic at that, Dominque de Gourgues, was stirred by news of the massacre to one of those blind rages that seldom last, but are triply dynamic when they do. He could not bear the terse praise which Philip II of Spain had given Menéndez, "He has done well." Gourgues sold his small estate in Gascony and all his goods, borrowed from his friends, armed three small boats, enlisted 180 men and sailed without announcing his destination.

To mask his intention, he cruised and traded for some months on the African coast. Then he crossed the Atlantic, made a stealthy landing near the Rivière Mai in the spring of 1568, stormed and demolished the old fort and slew its garrison. He staged a symbolic vengeance. Spanish corpses were swung on the same trees where Frenchmen had been hanged, with placards that fiercely parodied the bigoted sentiments of Menéndez.

But Dominique de Gourgues was not equipped to found or to defend a colony. He went home financially ruined and told the Court that there was no place on earth more rich, more spacious or more easy to conquer than North America. He was none too warmly thanked. The second civil war of the eight had started. Frenchmen were killing Frenchmen over the prayer book. The Massacres of Nîmes were a fresh horror, and they made slaughter in Florida seem fairly trivial. St. Bartholomew's Eve was in the offing. A clash with Spain just then was about the last thing that the Queen Mother desired.

There was, in point of fact, to be no further challenge to

Spain for nearly forty years. The only Frenchmen the warm lands would see would be free-lance pirates, some of whom briefly associated themselves with the raids of Hawkins, Drake, Clifford and other Englishmen. Florida had been a mirage, dissipated by a red sun of battle. So far as the Valois line was concerned, it had proved impossible to set aside the dictum of Pope Alexander VI.

CHAPTER II

El Dorado

HENRY of Navarre came to the throne of France as Henry IV, observing cynically that Paris was well worth a mass. He, the leader of the Huguenots, had accepted a nominal conversion to Catholicism for the sake of national unity. Considerable fighting had still to be done before he brought the maniacal Wars of Religion to an end and, in 1598, issued the Edict of Nantes which guaranteed many rights to the Protestants. The same year he signed the Treaty of Vervins with Spain. This pact contained, on his insistence, a secret article canceling the general provisos south of the Tropic of Cancer and west of the Meridian of the Azores. Thence sprang the expression, "No peace beyond the Linc," and the very real state of affairs under which not only France and Spain but all the maritime nations strove in the Caribbean for a century, regardless of amity in Europe.

By fixing the Tropic as the northern limit of lawlessness, Henry IV left Florida out of his calculations. His leaning was toward South America, largely because he was beguiled by the legend of El Dorado, to which the adventures of Sir Walter Raleigh had given new and meretricious publicity. Delusions of the kind apart, the King had serious plans. He was one of the four strong personalities who made a colonizing nation of France in the seventeenth century, the others being the ministers Richelieu, Mazarin and Colbert. If the King accomplished least, this was due to the fact that he came first in point of time, and to his early death. The confused state of the realm retarded action, anyway, until 1604.

In a memorandum prepared for Henry's information, the fabulous capital city of Manoa, home of the Gilded One, where there were gold and silver statues "as large as giants," was located at several days' journey from the port of Canury on the Orinoco River. The surrounding territory for hundreds of miles was known as Guiana and was vaguely delimited. Neither the Spaniards nor Portuguese had laid effective claim to it, being uncertain whether it lay east or west of the degree of longitude the Pope had set as a frontier. Also, they were busy elsewhere. This accounts for the easy encroachments which created the modern British, Dutch and French Guianas, the only section of South America never held by Iberians.

But the beginnings were not easy. Henry's explorers miscalculated. Daniel de La Touche de La Ravardière made the pioneer voyage in April, 1604, and steered so far south that he entered the Amazon. This mighty river dazzled him for the rest of his life, and although on his home trip he touched at Cayenne, the predestined site, his report to the King was concerned only with the Amazon, which he declared to be the gateway to Guiana. He visited it a second time, discovered Maranhão at its mouth and ranged over that fertile island in the company of the naturalist Jean Mocquet. When these two displayed their collection of tropical curios at Court, La Ravardière was given the title of Lieutenant General of Guiana; Mocquet was appointed *garde des singularités du Roi* therein, an attractive distinction.

The assassination of Henry IV in 1610 did not halt the project for a colony. Marie de Médicis as Regent empowered La Ravardière to settle fifty leagues of coast, and under his unlucky guidance an expedition landed on Maranhão two years later and built a fort. Alphonse du Plessis, a young uncle of Richelieu, was in the party, as well as François de Razilly, a Knight of Malta and gentleman of the royal bed-chamber. They sent Razilly back to plead for re-enforcements. He took with him half a dozen tattooed Para Indians, coiffed with parakeet feathers, who caused a sensation by dancing in the Louvre. Invited to become Christians, three of the savages agreed cheerfully and were baptized with the Queen Regent as godmother. The boy King, Louis XIII, hung collars of St. Louis about their necks to mark the relationship. The incident so edified the Parisians and stirred their enthusiasm that 300, including women, enlisted for the colony, which had been named La France Equinoxiale.

Unluckily, the island of Maranhão was within the domain mapped out by the Portuguese, who were keenly aware of the importance of controlling the Amazon. Their warships reconnoitered in the slow manner of the times, warned the French to depart and committed an occasional hostile act. La Ravardière thought so little of it that he went into the wilderness in search of the mythical female warriors after whom the river had been called. There is reason to believe that he took Mocquet with him, to record the "singularities." This estimable naturalist rounded out his career as a curator at the palace of the Tuileries.

The Portuguese attacked while La Ravardière was away. Desultory fighting continued for a couple of years, with the foe increasing his strength and no aid from home arriving for the French. The fort was reduced at last in 1616, the survivors expelled. The ferocious inhumanity that had been shown in Florida by the Spaniards was not duplicated, despite the killing of 115 men, including the astronomer Vanet. Many colonists returned to France. A few drifted along the coast in a northwesterly direction, as if dimly aware that Cayenne which La Ravardière had found on his first voyage constituted a goal.

Space has been given to the Brazilian misadventure because it was definitely the prelude to the stable Guiana settlement ten years afterward. The latter may thus be considered the first French colony in the neighborhood of the Caribbean Sea. Landings were indeed made on West Indian islands just before the occupation of Cayenne and these were part of a more widespread, more successful movement. But the forms taken by the lesser enterprise have unique interest.

Hollanders had shown the way while the French were still entangled in the delta of the Amazon. They had obtained the right, in one of the clauses of the truce of 1609 by which Spain acknowledged the freedom of the Netherlands, to trade for nine years in New World territory as yet unorganized. The Guiana coast below Trinidad met the conditions, and the Dutch merchants were soon doing business at the mouths of the Demerara and Essequibo Rivers. They sold cheap knives, iron pots, beads and other gewgaws, taking raw materials in exchange. Gold was coveted by them, of course. They got a modicum of it that trickled down from a hinterland the mining possibilities of which have not been developed to this day. But their shopkeepers' instinct, their hard-headedness, safeguarded them from the lures of El Dorado.

Accounts of these activities reached Europe, and as they grew in importance they fell under the scrutiny of the greatest statesman in Europe. Cardinal de Richelieu had become Premier of France in 1624. He could not be indifferent, since his uncle had been to Maranhão. La Ravardière, who had maintained some slight contact with the region, had the wit to go to the Cardinal immediately after the latter's accession to power and get his patents renewed. But Richelieu quickly saw through La Ravardière's visionary character, brushed him aside and in 1626 encouraged a native of Lyons, one Chantail, to begin the colonization of Cayenne. A cluster of shacks was built on the flat island of that name lying close offshore between two rivers. Frenchmen refused to go and live there, and the effort drooped.

So a mercantile company directed by Jacob Bontemps was formed in Rouen. It obtained from Richelieu the concession of all the land between the Amazon and the Orinoco, which was proclaimed to be the French principality of Guiana. This was a large order. It defied Portuguese claims to the south, and northward it ran afoul of the nominal sovereignty of Spain, the vested interests of the Dutch, who had not left the coast when their nine-year concession expired, and the recent interloping of British adventurers.

Bontemps had agricultural projects. He ended by vying commercially with the two peoples last named. His associates copied the Dutch and set up trading posts. Dyewoods were then in demand. The aborigines were much astonished to learn that trees felled would be used not to build ships, but to stain cloth. Eventually, French farmers came out, and some flourishing plantations were established on the riverbanks.

Richelieu did not rate high the possibilities of this new France Equinoxiale. His eyes were on Canada and the Antilles. His clear, cold brain foresaw the difficulties of a mainland colony wedged in between Spaniards and Portuguese* and unsupported by adequate sea power. Canada was a remote, harsh region that did not interest Spain. In the islands, a game of hide-and-seek could be played, the intricacies of which will be studied in the next chapter.

The Cardinal believed, however, that the Guiana foothold should be kept as a gamble for the future, unless the cost grew excessive. Even his realism was not proof against the seduction of a country about which such wonderful things were told. Sir Walter Raleigh, who had made two voyages up the Orinoco, in 1595 and 1617, wrote a best-seller in his *Discoveries of the large and bewtiful Empire of Guiana,* which was translated contemporaneously into several languages, in-

---

* From 1581 to 1640, Spain and Portugal were under the same crown.

cluding French. Richelieu had read descriptions such as this one by the English knight:

"I never saw a more bewtiful country, nor more lively prospects, hills so raised here and there over the valleys, the river winding into divers branches, the plains adjoining without bush or stubble, all fair green grass, the ground of hard sand easy to march on, either for horses or foot, the deer crossing in every path, the birds towards the evening singing on every tree with a thousand several tunes, cranes and herons of white, crimson and carnation perching in the river's side, the air fresh with a gentle Easterly wind, and every stone we picked up promised either gold or silver by his complexion."

Again, Raleigh described Guiana as a land "that hath yet her maidenhead, never sacked, turned, nor wrought, the face of the earth hath not been torn, nor the virtue and salt of the soil spent by manurance; the graves have not been opened for gold, the mines not broken with sledges, nor their Images pulled down out of their temples. It hath never been entered by any army of strength, and never conquered or possessed by any Christian Prince."

What lush romancing. Raleigh had not found a single elaborate temple, much more one in which unviolated statues stood. He was embroidering the tales of hearsay, as when he blandly affirmed that the courtiers of Manoa gathered for an annual feast "stripped naked, and their bodies annointed all over with a kind of white balsamum . . . when certain servants of the Emperor, having prepared gold made into fine powder, blow it thorow hollow canes upon their naked bodies, until they be all shining from the foot to the head; and in this sort they sit drinking by twenties, and hundreds."

The conquistador Jiménez de Quesada, subduer of the Chibcha realm on the plateau of Bogotá, had been the first European to spread that myth. In his version, none but the grand cacique had been gilded, in a ceremony that called for an immediate plunge into a sacred lake where the gold was washed from his person.

Manoa, a vivid though unseen reality in the sixteenth century, never was rated as quite imaginary until the end of the seventeenth. So Guiana was valued over and above its visible wealth. The country has never been a unit, except in the broadest geographical sense. Guiana as the name of the coast from the Orinoco to the Amazon was imposed by the French, and it has stuck. No one ever pretended to draw an approximate western border in the heart of the equatorial jungle. Today there are five Guianas, three of them European colonies, one a Venezuelan state renamed Bolívar in honor of the Liberator, and one a Brazilian territory. As in the times of the first white settlers, they have no common political aspirations, no sense even of racial oneness.

Let us finish with the early phase of French colonization. The death of Richelieu was followed by a new impulse toward Cayenne. In September, 1643, Charles Poncet de Brétigny sailed from Dieppe with 300 soldiers and settlers. A chevalier of some pretensions, he was accompanied by a chancellor, a maître d'hôtel, a personal squire and a secretary. He displayed a staff ornamented with a viceregal shield. All this show rallied to him at Cayenne what was left of previous expeditions on the coast.

But Brétigny was a megalomaniac tyrant, who perhaps consciously imitated in his small way the early Spanish bullies like Pizarro. He maltreated the Indians shamefully and lorded it over his own people with eccentric cruelty, so that they called him the "Nero of Guiana." His regime was short. The natives plotted against him, and it is plausible that the whites put few obstacles in their way. Brétigny perished, an arrow between his eyes.

The colony knew hard times after that. It had acquired a

bad name, and all support from France was withheld until the disorders of the Fronde (1648-1653)—still another civil war, and for trivial reasons—produced what the chroniclers termed a "nausea with life" in exalted circles. The Grand Condé, victor in many battles, declared himself disgusted with everything and willing to live in some unspoiled land, preferably an island. He took no such step, of course. But he did select Guiana and dream of a feudal republic there.

Condé sponsored a company which undertook to carry out his plans, issued a glowing prospectus and "sold" investors on the idea that their profits would be at least 300 per cent. The Parisians who embarked gave proof of being convinced utopians. On the voyage, one of their number tried to get himself accepted as "Perpetual General," and was run through the heart to the cry of *Vive la liberté!*

Republican projects, however, did not then have the stamina for survival. Conditions in Guiana were soon those of an ordinary seventeenth-century colony off the beaten track. The King's officials made the laws. Trade languished because there was no dependable shipping. That bonus of plunder which privateers and buccaneers gained for the West Indian plantations was lacking here.

The Dutch, more contentedly installed on the alluvial plains toward the Orinoco, saw advantages in French Guiana. They began to filter in, with a certain number of Jews. A galvanic effort was made and they were expelled. There ensued a long period of somnolence which nevertheless was fertile. The seeds of a permanent, if small, community germinated in the heat.

We have run far ahead of the story of expansion elsewhere in tropical America. As it was generations before Cayenne again played a significant role and its connection with Caribbean ventures was fairly remote, this procedure has seemed the logical one.

Chapter III

In the Lesser Antilles

THE French and English decided at virtually the same time to seize footholds in the Caribbean, and by a curious coincidence they fixed on the same island for their debut. We have seen that both nationalities had been represented in the Sea by valiant privateers during the second half of the sixteenth century. These men had brought home word of a glaring weakness in Spanish policy. The discoverers and claimants of the entire region were entrenched solidly in the Greater Antilles and on the mainland, but they had failed even to make a pretense of occupying the Lesser Antilles between Puerto Rico and Trinidad. If their arrogant conception of the Caribbean as a private lake was to be maintained, these small islands were indispensable as fortresses. The Spaniards, however, had raised no defenses there. They had shirked the task of subduing the warlike Caribs who inhabited them, particularly as there was no gold to be had and the empire won by the conquistadores offered vast agricultural chances elsewhere.

Barbados and St. Lucia were visited and nominally annexed by the English as early as 1607, a point that is interesting for the record. The first real attempt at a settlement was made by Sir Thomas Warner and a group of followers, an offshoot of Raleigh's "Company of Noblemen and Gentlemen of England for the Plantation of Guiana." They landed in 1623 on the island of St. Christopher, commonly called St. Kitts, bringing with them a good equipment of tools, seeds

31

and other farming necessities. The Caribs at once began to harass the newcomers.

A few months later, a small French ship under the command of Pierre Belain d'Esnambuc got into a fight with a Spanish galleon near the Cayman Islands. The business on which Esnambuc was engaged was probably some form of piracy. He was a younger son of a noble house whom the law of primogeniture had left without an income. Blades of his sort in that day turned to the Indies, East or West, for the making of a fortune. They were seldom squeamish about the means employed. On this occasion, the Frenchman had encountered too formidable an adversary. His vessel being badly damaged, he fled and was lucky to beach it in a sinking condition on the coast of St. Christopher.

Warner received the castaways hospitably. He was having a difficult time with the Caribs, and he proposed a combination of forces to defeat the tenacious savages. Esnambuc, who had saved most of his men and all his arms, agreed cheerfully. He and Warner became good friends in the course of a campaign which drove the enemy to the mountainous, wooded interior. The Caribs soon were slipping down to the sea at night and departing in their canoes for other islands. They were a nomadic people whose conquest of the Lesser Antilles from the mild Arawâks had occurred only a short while before the coming of Columbus.

St. Christopher, roughly oval-shaped, lies at an angle from northwest to southeast, and at the latter end narrows to a peninsula with a round head bearing a lagoon in the middle like an eye. The total area is sixty-eight square miles, about twenty-three miles long by six wide. Mount Misery, its greatest elevation, towers 4,330 feet. The aboriginal name was Liamuiga, which means fertile. The island, poorly watered, is not actually among the more fertile of the chain. But it seemed a paradise to Esnambuc.

He repaired his ship, got together a cargo of local produce on which he set a high valuation and sailed back to France in 1625, after signing a pact of friendship with Warner. It is hard to tell what he could have obtained in bulk, except tobacco, pineapples, coconuts and tropical timber. He would have had a certain number of parakeets and other exotic birds. At all events, his sales were extremely profitable. The merchants of the Channel ports thought well of him, and he attracted the favorable attention of Richelieu.

More easily persuaded now than he had been by those who believed in Guiana, the Cardinal authorized the colonizing and trading Compagnie de Saint-Christophe. The company signed a contract in October, 1626, with Esnambuc and Urbain de Roissey, who had been selected as co-commander. These men were obligated to seize and develop as French possessions the "unoccupied islands" between the eleventh and eighteenth degrees of latitude, also identified in the document as the "islands situated at the entrance of Peru." The area specified embraced the Lesser Antilles in toto. No one considered the Caribs as occupants with a status that any Christian need worry about.

The expedition, 300 strong, set out promptly and arrived at St. Christopher early in 1627. The feelings of Warner had not changed toward his recent ally, and when Esnambuc urged that they formally divide the island the proposition was accepted. By a most singular arrangement, the English took the center and the French the two ends. In place of boundary posts, cactus hedges were planted. Warner's headquarters was at Fort Charles. On the southwest shore, Esnambuc built the town of Basse-Terre.

A word about names. There are several Basse-Terres in the West Indies, all of them on the inner or Caribbean side. The word means low land, but the French sailors used it in the sense of "protected," as well as southerly, whereas they

called stations on the Atlantic and northerly side Capesterre,
or headland, with the implication that they were whipped by
the wind. This has led to some odd misnomers, as in Guadeloupe where the most mountainous section of the twin island
is called Basse-Terre. All nationalities have fantastically
twisted the pronunciation of names alien to them. Thus, the
favored British West Indian rendering of Basse-Terre, the
original spelling retained, is Baa-Star. Warner was a puzzler
to the early French historians. One finds him set down as
Waërnard, Woërnare and Woërner; while Elias Watts, a
canny old promoter of filibustering at Tortuga, becomes
Eliazouard.

After Esnambuc and Warner had lived amicably as neigh-
bors for longer than a year, the news arrived that King
Charles I of England had granted "all the Caribbees" to the
Earl of Carlisle. This piece of effrontery outdid Richelieu's
project, since the Cardinal had merely ordered the agents of
the French Crown to take what could be had. Carlisle succeeded in "planting" Barbados, as the term went, and he now
required Sir Thomas Warner to treat the French as tres-
passers under arms. What move, if any, the reluctant knight
made is not clear. But Esnambuc struck at Fort Charles and
with a minimum loss of life captured part of the squadron in
port there. Warner interpreted this as a good reason for re-
newing the pact of friendship, then sailed for England to explain. He was a tolerant man whose methods, if generally
adopted, would have eliminated much of the bloodshed from
Caribbean history and simplified the founding of colonies.

These events had not passed unnoticed by the Spaniards.
They remained uninterested in occupying the small islands,
but they knew that it was a danger to allow others to do so.
Their superiority complex led them to suppose that a puni-
tive expedition now and then would be all that was necessary.
As an exponent of the heavy hand without a policy to back it

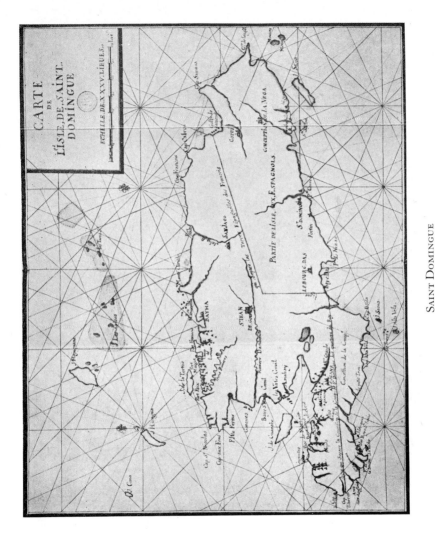

SAINT DOMINGUE

An old map showing extravagant French territorial claims.

up, Don Fadrique de Toledo descended on St. Christopher in 1629 with a strong fleet. He was resisted by the combined French and English, but the latter were weakened by the absence of Warner. We read, also, that the defenders included some buccaneer craft, the occasion being the first on which those extraordinary sea-rovers figured in a major action.

The military superiority of Toledo's force was overwhelming. The settlements were devastated. A better resistance could have been offered if Urbain de Roissey had not fallen into a panic, deserted Esnambuc and fled to Barbados, where he and his men were imprisoned by the Earl of Carlisle's officials. Even so, Toledo neither killed nor captured the numbers that should have fallen to him, and he was content to leave with the colonies theoretically destroyed. Esnambuc and most of the English had simply put to sea and found hiding places among the lonely bays of the Virgins, Antigua and Anguilla. Some had gone with the buccaneers to the western end of Hispaniola.

Esnambuc came back in three months, and not long afterward was followed by Warner. The old partition of territory was renewed, the crops replanted. St. Christopher entered upon what French chroniclers have expansively called an age of gold, and we shall see that in the next decade it did enjoy a certain primitive splendor, with both nationalities calling it their "mother colony of the West Indies."

The immediate problem in 1629 was war with the Caribs. The Caribs understood that they would not be left in peaceful possession of any of the Lesser Antilles, and being energetic warriors they took the offensive. Dominica was their rallying point, a spectacularly mountainous island which they held securely from its opalescent bays to its remotest valleys, and where there was a head cacique obeyed in emergencies by all the seafaring tribesmen. Great canoes now launched to the attack. Bows and arrows could not compete

with firearms, but the fierce, cunning natives equalized matters in part by night raids and ambushes. They were sure to
be beaten when they met the whites in a pitched engagement.
As guerillas by land or sea, they commanded respect.

Père Dutertre, the historian, described the Caribs as being
well-formed and robust, resembling "cooked shrimps" in
color. They were avid cannibals, and although they declared
that of all the Christians the French made the best eating,
their flesh being the tenderest, the blind detestation of them
shown by the Spaniards and English was not shared by the
French. A flair for getting along with the Caribs became at
last a potent aid to France in her colonial ventures.

After a few years of skirmishing, while the English expanded to Antigua, Nevis and Montserrat, it was concluded in
Paris that there must be new conquests. Charles de l'Olive
and a partner were assigned by Richelieu to take over Guadeloupe. Esnambuc at St. Christopher was encouraged to proceed to Martinique. Definitely included in the claim of
annexation would be Dominica, St. Lucia, St. Vincent and
Grenada, the military action against these to be pushed later.
The five units and near-by islets are what the French have
always called Les Iles du Vent, or Windward Islands, a term
used also by the English and Spanish, but with a rearrange-
ment of the grouping.

The expeditions of Olive and Esnambuc landed within a
month or so of each other in 1635. Both marked the beginnings of successful colonies, at the cost of bloody warfare
with the natives. The memory of Olive, a cruel oppressor, is
not honored. Esnambuc was assisted by able lieutenants, and
he did his job well—so well that the long preponderance of
Martinique over Guadeloupe, governmentally and from a
social standpoint, has been ascribed to the start he made.

But we need not linger over the early phase in these two
islands, which were to be of such economic value to France

and so important in the spreading of French culture. Esnambuc is at best a shadowy figure. He had come by accident
upon the stage he strode. He did not have the color and magnetism to stamp his personality on the roll of heroes. His
pioneering work finished in Martinique, he passed. It is of
interest that the Empress Josephine was directly descended
from his sister.

The grand manner appeared in the history of the colonies
when Richelieu appointed as Governor-General, with his
capital in St. Christopher, a truly remarkable man, Philippe
de Lonvilliers de Poincy, aged fifty-six, grand cross and bailiff
of the Order of the Knights of Malta. He was characterized
not long afterward as "an accomplished soldier, a leading
politician, a person strong in wealth and friends, and one of
the sound heads of Europe." He knew the power of theatrical
effects. Greeted by planters gone ragged or dressed in make-
shifts, Poincy debarked on a tropical beach February 20, 1639,
wearing the full robes of his order, the red cassock with a
white cross on the breast, the flat velvet cap. A bodyguard
of squires attended him, but he had dispensed with the maître
d'hôtel and other palace officials who had made Brétigny in
Guiana ridiculous. These could wait until he had built a
palace. He brought carpenters, stone trimmers, brick mak-
ers, locksmiths and lime-kiln burners, describing them as
workmen of the callings that would be most needed.

Poincy was to spend twenty-one years, the rest of his turbulent, effective life, in the Antilles. His name figures in the
chronicles of his foes with a persistency and exaggeration of
his prowess that is flattering. His admirers attached it to
various imposing things, not least of which was the poinciana
tree, or flamboyant, a solid blaze of scarlet at blossoming
time.

The Governor-General's first act was to form the colonists
of St. Christopher into twelve military companies, which he

drilled thoroughly and armed in up-to-date fashion. He then sailed for St. Croix, previously divided by the English and Dutch, seized it without difficulty from the few whites who were struggling to maintain themselves there, and beat back Spanish troops that came from Puerto Rico. He extended control from Martinique and Guadeloupe over Marie Ga- lante, La Désirade and Les Saintes; felt out the Caribs in St. Lucia and Grenada, but decided that, along with those of Dominica and St. Vincent, they had best be left undisturbed for a while.

A curious problem engaged his attention early. The phe- nomenon of the buccaneers was about to reach its peak. As the writer has pointed out in other works, this was one of the most important movements of the seventeenth century. It would be unthinkable to survey any phase of Caribbean history in that century and not give special consideration to the buccaneers. But whereas their relations with the English, Dutch and Spaniards are pretty clearly understood, many stu- dents have confused them with the legitimate colonists of France. Poincy himself has been referred to as a sort of buc- caneer leader.

The fact is, he grasped for a new island to add to his do- main. Learning that Tortuga, off Hispaniola, had become the headquarters of the sea-robbers and that many of them were Frenchmen, he was eager to annex it. Whatever his agents may have done, he saw the buccaneers as prospective subjects and not as irregulars to whose misdeeds it would be good business to close an eye. Poincy was by temperament an imperialist, too formal a one perhaps for his times.

Only a year after his arrival, he sent a small detachment of men under Captain Levasseur to assert the rights of the Crown and the Compagnie de Saint-Christophe at Tortuga. His choice of a commander was dictated by prejudice, as well as craft. Levasseur, a native of Dieppe, had served from the

beginning under Esnambuc and had risen to be the acknowledged leader of the Huguenot faction in St. Christopher. It
was not tolerable to so earnest and eminent a son of the
Church as Poincy, naïvely explains Père Dutertre, to be in
daily association with a heretic lieutenant, and he welcomed
the chance to give Levasseur an independent commission.
But the Knight of Malta had a still better reason. He knew
that the majority of the buccaneers were Protestants, including a quota of political refugees from France. They were
more likely to be persuaded by a Huguenot than even by
his distinguished self.

Quick results were not expected of Levasseur. Word came
back that he was meeting with success. That was enough for
Poincy, who temporarily put him out of his mind and drove
ahead with his conquests. By 1642, he was established in fourteen islands, including the very small ones, and scattered
through them were 5,000 French inhabitants—an unusually
good showing when we recall how slow a business it was to
transport colonists and supply their needs by sail.

Poincy felt justified in erecting a château. Old drawings
picture it as a grand affair of three storeys in stone and brick.
It had an exterior stair with a double flight of steps leading
to the second floor. The main building was square, with a
flat roof which was used as a platform for the enjoyment of
a magnificent view of the encompassing hills and the palm-
studded slope leading down to Basse-Terre. A high wall enclosed the château and its gardens. Cannon and a well-
stocked arsenal gave it the strength of a fortress. One glowing
account says that Poincy was the master of 100 servants, in
addition to 300 slaves, but it is improbable that that many
freemen could have been spared from the general work of
the colony. The slaves had their own village outside the
walls, called Angola in memory of the African territory from
which they had been brought.

Poincy also built churches. He set up courts of justice. Very rapidly, in short, he introduced civilization. The most piquant evidence of this was the success obtained by a pamphlet in verse, written on the spot by a Breton gentleman named Kerroland and directed at the Governor-General. It was entitled *La Prosopopée de la Nymphe Christophorine*, an amusing satire on the knight's weakness for a local beauty. Contemporaries refer to it as having been the first published work of the kind in the French West Indies. But as no printing press was available, manuscript copies must have been circulated. It was too much for Poincy. He forced Kerroland to flee and later deported one of the Breton's friends.

Describing the comfortable, self-sustaining life of the colony when there were few mouths to feed, Maurile de St. Michel wrote home:

"Here, instead of bread made from wheat, we eat bread made from the cassava plant which is very common and abundant. Instead of beef, we eat lamentin [the manatee], which is a sort of sea cow caught along the shore. Instead of chicken, we eat lizards, from which a very good soup is made and the meat of which is very delicate. . . . I have often eaten them. . . . One of the principal articles of food is peas, which grow here in abundance. . . . The ordinary dinner of the average man consists of pea soup, cassava bread seasoned with red pepper, lemon juice and a small piece of bacon."

But comfort among the settlers stopped short of their furniture. A bed, a table, a chest or two and some benches usually completed the equipment of a house, according to an observer who saw Martinique, Guadeloupe and St. Christopher. Often the bed was a hammock, without pillows or coverings. Ordinary dwellings were thatched like those of the Caribs. Only the houses of the Governors had glass windows.

In 1643, the Company sent out a general inspector to report on the state of the islands. Poincy obstructed him, did not attempt to conceal his resentment of any form of supervision. Criticisms of his regime accumulated, mainly on the grounds that he was too rigid a disciplinarian. As a gesture, he offered to resign. No one was more astonished than he when he was taken at his word and ordered to return to France on the same boat that brought Patrocles de Thoissy, in November, 1645, to succeed him.

Poincy thereupon manifested the egotism and daring which set him apart from other men. He refused to allow Thoissy to land, trained guns on his ship and drove him off to Guadeloupe, where he formed a rival administration. War raged between the two for longer than a year. Thoissy could not win over a sufficient number of the colonists to tip the balance, and when he finally attacked St. Christopher he was defeated and taken prisoner. All the islands, including Guadeloupe, applauded.

Poincy had defied the Company that employed him, rather than the Crown to which he owed his selection in the first place. He based his action on what he declared to be the common good. Loyalties in these colonial ventures by concessionnaires were strangely mixed. It is significant that Cardinal Mazarin, successor of Richelieu, upheld the result, issuing a statement in the name of the minor, Louis XIV, that Poincy had "spared nothing to maintain our authority and the dignity of the French name." Mazarin knew what he was about. The Company was on the verge of bankruptcy. It was liquidated in 1647 and its possessions distributed in lots. The new holders, be it understood, were to enjoy somewhat more exclusive rights.

Acting for the Knights of Malta, Poincy acquired the French part of St. Christopher, St. Croix, St. Bartholomew, Tortuga, and half of St. Martin, the other half being held by the Dutch. The Marquis de Boisseret and Charles Houël du Petit-Pré, the inspector with whom Poincy had quarreled, got Guadeloupe and its dependencies. Jacques Dyel du Parquet, a nephew of Esnambuc, took over Martinique, with the privilege of conquering St. Lucia and Grenada. Unofficially, Poincy was still recognized as the chief, an elder statesman and military oracle to whom all deferred.

CHAPTER IV

Tortuga and the Buccaneers

BUCCANEERING has been romanticized to the point where the average person has a false perspective on it and imagines it to have been what it was not. Notably obscured is the way the different nations turned it to account, rejected it and at the last absorbed it into the stream of empire. The process was not uniform. France had a longer, more complicated relationship with buccaneering than did her rivals against Spain. The solid holdings of the freebooters all passed under the French flag, and as a result the idea has prevailed that every French colony in the Caribbean had a similar origin. The work of Esnambuc, Poincy and their successors has been less publicized than the lurid exploits of the men of Tortuga.

In order to be quite clear about the matter, let us repeat that the buccaneers were outlaws of many nationalities who drifted together in the semi-deserted northwestern peninsula of Hispaniola. They comprised fugitives from the religious wars of Europe, military deserters and escaped criminals. They asked at first only to be left alone. They made their living by hunting wild cattle and hogs, smoking meat and selling it to passing ships. The Indian word *boucan* was applied indiscriminately to the meat and to the thatched sheds in which it was cured, so the practitioners became *boucaniers,* or in English buccaneers. The Spaniards, advancing from Santo Domingo, commenced attempts to exterminate them around 1620, but succeeded only in driving them back to coastal strongholds. The chief of these was Tortuga, a small island opposite Port Margot and Port-de-Paix.

43

The buccaneers took to building ships and were soon the most formidable corsairs that the Caribbean has ever known. Their organization was unique, and their methods were not those of sheer piracy. They tended to fall into groups dominated by Frenchmen, Englishmen or Hollanders, each group retaining some national sentiment and preaching, though they did not always practice, the exemption of their countrymen from rapine. The Spaniard was the common enemy, to whom no mercy was shown. In time they were strong enough to assemble fleets. They recognized a central authority at Tortuga. Anthony Hilton, an Englishman, was their Governor in 1629, but the claim that that made an English colony of the place is flimsy. Men of various races filled his shoes. The fact that another Englishman, one Captain Willis, happened to be in charge in 1640 served the ends of Levasseur, the agent of Poincy. It was a still more fortunate chance that that year the buccaneers had formed themselves into the Confederacy of the Brethren of the Coast, with an ambitious program but no outstanding leader.

A volume would be required to do justice to their history. It is the intention here to trace briefly the maneuvers that ended by bringing their territory under the control of the French Crown.

Levasseur approached his problem with a cool head. He landed at Port Margot, where he proclaimed that he meant the wild sea-thieves no harm whatsoever. They did not know whether to believe him, and the situation remained ticklish for some weeks. Then Levasseur spread the word that he and his followers were themselves would-be buccaneers, a statement not far from truth, as the event proved. He had seen that there was no hope of his capturing Tortuga unless he could sow dissension among its inhabitants and gain allies. He seized on the governorship of Willis to stir the rancor of the French outlaws. Why should they be ruled by an Eng-

lishman? he asked. Why not let him aid them to throw out
Willis and elect a chief of their own race?

The proposition was accepted by a sufficient number to
put Levasseur's party in the majority. His experience as a
commander both on land and sea caused him to be chosen
as leader of the attack. He crossed to Tortuga and without
great difficulty defeated and expelled Willis. The English
and Dutch, accustomed to such overturns, were not particularly resentful. They assumed that Levasseur was now Governor, the end toward which he had been working. The French
had liked the way he conducted himself in battle. There
were no candidates against him. But when he announced
annexation to France as a dependency of St. Christopher, all
the buccaneers laughed at him. He passed off his statement
as a pleasantry and busied himself with improving the defenses of Tortuga. He built the famout Fort du Rocher on
the heights above the beach of the safest roadstead, Basse-
Terre. It was reached by a footway with steps cut in the rock.
When this was barricaded in time of danger, a movable ladder
and a knotted cord as a guide and safety device were used.

Before long, Levasseur was an accomplished director of the
activities of the "sweet trade," as its practitioners called it.
He does not appear to have sailed on piratical enterprises.
His role as executive and unifier was more efficacious—and
more profitable. The crews of the raiding ships selected an
admiral by ballot. In the first decade after the founding of
the Brethren of the Coast, admirals followed one another in
rapid succession. Levasseur is said to have promoted this
system, because it enhanced his power as the one stable chief.

He sent reports off and on to Poincy, in which he gave the
impression that he was organizing Tortuga as a colony. Nothing could have been further from the truth. The island was
independent and he was its uncrowned monarch. When
Poincy suggested that he visit St. Christopher to give an

accounting, he made evasive answers. He declared that he did not need re-enforcements of soldiery.

Finally Poincy grew suspicious and ordered him to turn over his command to a successor. This Levasseur declined to do. He undoubtedly had heard about Poincy's resistance of Thoissy, and he took a leaf from that book. His motives were hardly such as would win the King's favor. Levasseur was enjoying his power and living luxuriously on the plunder the Brethren brought in. He turned back the envoy from St. Christopher and maintained an attitude of defiance for years. Conquering his buccaneers was known by the Mazarin ministry to be a task for a strong fleet, nor in view of their services in plaguing the Spaniards was it thought to be good policy. The occasional loss of a French merchantman at their hands could be endured.

But when the West Indian colonies were broken up into lots between 1647 and 1649 and Tortuga nominally was transferred to the Knights of Malta, Poincy as representative of that churchly order found Lavasseur intolerable. He appointed the Chevalier de Fontenay Governor, requiring him to get results at no matter what cost. How he went about it has not been clearly recorded. He operated from the Hispaniola mainland, and it is probable that he intrigued with malcontents against Levasseur, much as the latter had previously conspired. The finale took a different form. Levasseur was assassinated by two of the men who had been closest to him. In the confusion that followed, Fontenay seized control and was accepted by acclamation. This was in 1652. It does not appear that he was able to enforce French law, or was in any real sense a viceroy for Poincy.

Only two years later, the Spaniards heavily assaulted Tortuga, clearing the roadstead of ships, landing artillery and investing the Fort du Rocher on three sides. Fontenay made a gallant defense. "Traitor!" he cried to one of his lieutenants who spoke of capitulation. "If I am forced to it, you will not be here as a witness!" And he laid the man dead at his feet.

Compelled to give up the position, the buccaneers retired through the broken interior and put off in rowboats to Hispaniola. They lurked in the bays they had known from old times, while the Spaniards devastated Tortuga. We hear no more of Fontenay, who considered the check decisive and did not await the chance to return to the little rocky island. The freebooters began to seep back in 1655, and for the next ten years were ruled in succession by the Englishman Elias Watts, the Frenchmen Du Rausset and the Sieur de la Place. Jerome Deschamps du Rausset, the most important of the three, had been a buccaneer and an intimate of Levasseur. He was an unprincipled schemer, who tried on one occasion to sell Tortuga to England for 6,000 pounds sterling. Actually commissioned to deliver the goods by D'Oyley, the first English Governor of Jamaica, he was unable to do so and the cash was not paid. He visited France, when the fact that he had negotiated with a foreign power was remembered and he was thrown into the Bastille.

The twenty-five years beginning with Levasseur and the forming of the Confederacy was a period of great activity by the buccaneers, their heyday in a sense. The formidable exploits of commanders of fleets, often in league with European governments, came just afterward. But the earlier period was marked by a swift, dynamic upsurge of individualistic fighting men who took their world by surprise. They swarmed over the Caribbean collecting toll by the most unorthodox means. No captain among them was so poor-spirited as to doubt his ability to capture the largest galleon with a one-masted barque. Reliance was on the technique of boarding parties composed of desperadoes beside whom professional sailors were weaklings.

Family names were not fashionable in that life, and if used

were generally false. Roche, called the Brazilian, often defeated the Spaniards when he was outnumbered five to one. His delight in showing off once led him to cruise in a fishing smack under the guns of Campeche, Yucatan. He was taken, condemned to death and placed on a galleon with the idea of transferring him to Spain for the execution of his sentence. Roche induced his jailors to gamble and drink with him, won not only their money but their admiration of his icy nerve, turned them into followers and seized the ship.

Alexandre, known as Bras-de-Fer, was wrecked on one of the islands off the eastern end of the Spanish Main. He and his small band made friends with the Indians and got their help to start work on a sea-going canoe. Then a Spanish barque approached and sent men ashore to look for water. Bras-de-Fer met them alone, told them an extravagant tale about himself as an honest castaway, drew them into an ambush. Growing suspicious at the last moment, they set upon and wounded him. His filibusters swarmed from the bushes and killed every one of the Spaniards. There had been gunfire, which would alarm the enemy craft. Bras-de-Fer took advantage of this by having his men dress in the costumes of their dead foes and hasten to the beach, shouting triumphantly in Spanish. The ruse enabled them to row out to the barque unsuspected. When they had completed the massacre, they had no need of the unfinished canoe. It was a good example of the buccaneer tradition that armaments should be improved at the expense of the other side.

The celebrated Exterminator belonged to this period. His true name was too distinguished to be concealed. He was the Sieur de Montbars, of Languedoc, a romantic with an obsession of vengeance against the Spaniards for their cruelties, particularly their butchery of the Indians as told by Las Casas, and the fury of the Holy Inquisition. He decided that the buccaneers' way would be the most effective, so he went to Tortuga handsomely equipped and with money in his pocket. He made such an impression on the inhabitants that they broke their rules and accepted him at once as the leader of a foray, a confidence which he justified brilliantly. He then formed a band of his own and made the islet of St. Bartholomew his headquarters.

The Exterminator once led a small boarding party on to the deck of a Spanish vessel. Passing twice from bow to stern, he carved his way through the enemy, his example so animating his comrades that the ship was taken.

Montbars was wildfire that flamed briefly and disappeared, leaving no trace. It is not known how he perished. But his memory was long-lived. For this unique robber cared so little about the booty he won that he generally refused the commander's share, leaving all to his men. His interest was in killing as many Spaniards as possible and devising unheard-of tortures for those who fell into his hands alive. He said, this Exterminator who did not give the impression of being a sadist, that he was simply squaring old accounts.

Before the period ended, the buccaneers were firmly entrenched at many points in Hispaniola. The northwestern peninsula belonged to them, and an impulse toward the mastery of the rest of the island became noticeable. The year 1655 was a turning point. In that year, the English conquered Jamaica and founded Port Royal, destined to be the greatest of buccaneer cities. The freebooters of British blood began almost at once to desert Tortuga in favor of Port Royal. French influence was predominant among those left behind. With the desire to avenge the recent spoliation of Tortuga by the Spaniards went an eagerness to emulate the English. If the latter could have the solid support of a colony like Jamaica, why should not the French do as well for themselves in Hispaniola?

These were the considerations behind the bold attack on

the inland city of Santiago de los Caballeros in 1659. A force
of 400 men was assembled, divided into four troops, each
with its own captain. The commander-in-chief may have
been Edward Mansvelt, then Admiral of the Brethren of the
Coast. Transportation was lacking, because there were no
seaworthy craft of sufficient capacity in Basse-Terre roadstead.
But a large frigate arrived opportunely from France and was
commandeered. The raiders sailed aboard her, dropped down
the coast, made a successful landing near Puerto de Plata on
Palm Sunday, and immediately marched south through the
woods.

Santiago de los Caballeros lay in a wide, fertile savanna near
the north-center of the island. It had a population of between
one and two thousand, several churches, an administration
building, and a fair showing of merchants' stalls. Such towns
thought themselves safe from buccaneers. Indeed, this affair
was the first of its kind. The expedition reached the environs
of Santiago in three days. Before dawn on Holy Wednesday,
the attackers charged into the streets, shooting the citizens as
they rushed to the doors and windows to see what was happening. They surprised the provincial Governor in his bed,
were about to kill him, but decided to hold him in ransom for
60,000 pieces of eight. Other prominent men were made
prisoners before the fighting ended, but it is refreshing to
know that this was one occasion when women and children
escaped unmolested.

The buccaneers proceeded to pillage for twenty-four hours,
stripping the homes and shops of all portable valuables,
robbing the churches of their ornaments and sacred vessels,
and taking even the bronze bells. Some think that they intended to hang the bells in their own church in Tortuga, and
others that they planned to melt them for bullets. Stolen food
and wines for a huge banquet were spread in an open field,

and after the victors had gorged themselves they commenced the return journey, dragging the captives along.

Meanwhile, an alarm had been sounded all over the savanna. Planters rode in pell-mell from the Cibao. A thousand or more men were mobilized, including fugitives from Santiago. This force took a shortcut through the woods, got in front of the buccaneers and engaged them from cover at close quarters.

The French and their polyglot associates had already suffered some losses and were now outnumbered three to one. But they stood their ground, without abandoning a single sack of loot. There is something familiar about old Père Dutertre's testimony that it was marksmanship that counted and that every freebooter's shot told. The Spaniards shouted incessantly for the blood of the Lutherans, as they then called European opponents in the New World, presuming them to be heretics. The others retorted with menaces to cut the throats of the Governor and the rest of the prisoners. What with harquebus and cutlass, the desperate skirmishing from tree to tree, it must have been a pretty bit of frontier deviltry.

We are informed that at last the Spaniards "took counsel and retired to their homes." They had lost interest in the Governor, for they sent only a small amount of his ransom after the bucaneers had reached the coast and were preparing to sail. The renewal of dire threats loosened no purse strings. Nevertheless, all the captives were released, unharmed save for kicks and curses, and the expedition returned to Tortuga. Each man's share in the booty was figured at 300 crowns.

It had been a trial of strength and a portent. Official France had nothing whatever to do with it. But both Mazarin at home and West Indian colonial authorities such as the aging Poincy grasped its significance for the future of French interests. Spain was more vulnerable in the Greater Antilles than had been thought. Her hold on the pioneer colony, Hispaniola, was manifestly weakening. The English had taken Jamaica from her with ridiculous ease. On the other hand, the buccaneers were developing cohesion and showing respectable prowess by land as well as by sea. They had possibilities as a national weapon. The French began to call them *forbans* and *flibustiers* rather than buccaneers. From *flibustier* the modern term "filibuster" is derived.

It can safely be stated that at this time the ambition to control little Tortuga commenced to be replaced by an imperial dream that was destined to come true—the dream of Saint Domingue.

CHAPTER V

From Poincy to Ogeron

THE Knights of Malta, or Order of Saint John of Jerusalem, was the oldest and most famous of the religious and military fraternities produced by the Crusades. It had been stalwart in its opposition to the Moslem world. During the previous century it had endured the bitter sieges of Rhodes and Valletta, and had taken part as a sovereign power in the great naval victory of Lepanto. A slow decline of vigor and idealism began shortly afterward. Its international character was impaired by the admission of too many French members. Very old men were chosen in succession for the office of Grand Master, which thus became an honorary one. Distinguished knights, like Poincy, accepted commissions from mundane lords. But the Order still preserved a façade of spiritual severity.

An authority declares that its character around 1648 "became more exclusively aristocratic, and its wealth, partly acquired by commerce, partly derived from the contributions of the commanderies scattered throughout Europe, was enormous."

What was it doing in America? It could find no opportunity there to fight for the redemption of the Holy Sepulchre. Missionary work among savages had never been on its program. A foe of Spain it assuredly was not, for in the Mediterranean it had counted on the support of that Catholic monarchy against the Turk. We must conclude that the Order was looking mainly for commercial profits. In that it re-

53

sembled other European interests. But because of old crusading ties it did expect—and obtain—a certain immunity from Spanish vengeful anger at interlopers.

The five holdings that fell to the Knights after the division of 1649 were of unequal value. It has been shown that Tortuga was not brought under their sway by the Chevalier de Fontenay and the French adventurers who followed him. The islet of St. Bartholomew, eight rocky and timberless square miles, also remained to all intents and purposes a buccaneer stronghold. The French half of St. Martin, twenty square miles to eighteen for the Dutch, was too limited and remote to become a successful plantation, though beginnings were made. But St. Christopher and St. Croix were estates of some consequence, as administered by the Knights, the first specializing in tobacco and the second in sugar.

Poincy, nearing sixty-seven when he closed the deal for his Order, survived for a decade during which he gave his best energies to directing the war against the Caribs. He saw this as a matter of establishing French supremacy, had no wish to exterminate the aborigines, and indeed sought them as allies wherever possible. The records are scant. It is evident, however, that the proprietors of Martinique and other islands heeded his counsel, and that the foe had a wholesome respect for him. A delegation of Caribs went to St. Christopher and asked him a natural question. In view of the French greed for land, they inquired, where were the natives expected to go, where could they exist in peace? The reply of a Spanish Governor, had he consented to such an interview, would have been, in effect, that he saw no reason for their survival except as slaves. But Poincy said that he would think about the problem.

On his death bed in the château he had built, he signed a treaty dated March 31, 1660, guaranteeing possession of Dominica and St. Vincent to the Caribs, who thereafter often fought beside the French in their struggles with other European Powers. The treaty was the basis of subsequent neutrality agreements in which England and Holland joined. The savages gained full protection from none of them. At least Poincy's intent was sincere, and a brave people gained a respite. It was time. There had been a terrible massacre in Grenada, where an expedition from Martinique had triumphed. The episode of the Morne des Sauteurs, or as the English call it the Caribs' Leap, is material for the as yet unwritten epic poetry of the Caribbean. Herded to a promontory on the northern coast, the last surviving islanders had thrown themselves into the sea rather than submit.

Poincy willed his possessions to the Commandeur de Sales, a nephew of Saint François de Sales, particularly assigning to him the island of St. Croix. This knight was subsequently given the St. Christopher governorship.

Martinique and Guadeloupe, meanwhile, had been making only fair progress. Their lords-proprietor were less efficient than the agents of the trading companies had been. Planting was confined at first to cotton and tobacco, under conditions of strife with the Caribs and an oppressive political administration which militated against prosperity. Then the sugar cane was introduced by some fifty Hollanders who had been chased from Brazil by the Portuguese. They brought from 1,000 to 1,200 African slaves. The mills they erected, chiefly in Guadeloupe, were a vast improvement over any operated by the English or Spaniards. An early start in the impending fabulous sugar bonanza was thus made by the French islands. It would have helped them little, had the crimes of petty tyrants been allowed to continue.

The natural obstacles to subduing and cultivating these mountainous, heavily wooded islands may be judged from the following description by a Martinique writer of later days, Dr. E. Rufz:

"The forest, what an inextricable chaos it is! The sands of the sea are not more closely pressed together than the trees are here: some straight, some curved, some upright, some toppling—fallen, or leaning against one another, or heaped high one upon the other. Climbing withes which cross from one tree to the next, like ropes passing from mast to mast, help to fill up the gaps in this maze. Parasites—not timid parasites like ivy or moss, but parasites which are trees self-grafted on trees—dominate the primitive trunks, overwhelm them, usurp the place of their foliage, and fall back to the ground, forming factitious weeping-willows. You do not find here, as in the great forests of the North, the eternal monotony of birch and fir. This is the kingdom of infinite variety. Species the most diverse elbow one another, interlace, strangle and devour one another. All ranks and orders are confounded, as in a human mob."

To the primeval setting Europeans brought their crafts—and their superstitions. At the early date of 1657 there was a witch trial in Martinique which must have edified the Caribs. A married Frenchwoman was accused of causing children to wither away under her touch. She also sent caterpillars to devour the contents of houses. The judge examined her person to see if she had any of the marks the Devil imprints on sorcerers, but could find none. Then he recalled that he had heard witches never wept while in the hands of justice. He commissioned a priest to tell her the most heartrending things. Nothing happened, in the way of tears. So the judge had the priest try again in his presence—and lo, she wept a flood! A test to discover whether she reacted normally to immersion in a pool gave equally contradictory results. She was finally beaten with rods, and died under the torture without confessing. Dutertre says that public opinion condemned the judge's zeal as excessive.

To understand the next development, it is necessary to return to Europe. National enterprises were then conducted in an intensely personal manner, and nowhere more so than in France. The importance of nurturing colonies did not loom large compared with the endless intricacies of continental policy, the diplomatic juggling among the courts, the brusque and often-invoked argument of war. If King and Prime Minister believed in colonies, these got their proper share of attention. Otherwise, the exploiters who held them as concessions were left to do as they pleased.

The great Richelieu had been colonial-minded. Mazarin was less so, but would have enlarged the program if he had not been hampered by the rebellions of the Fronde and other difficulties. He may be said to have done what he could. Both he and Richelieu had the advantage of comparative freedom from royal interference. Mazarin's power lasted for ten years after Louis XIV attained his majority, so towering was the Italian Cardinal's prestige and so potent the influence exerted in his behalf by the Queen Mother, Anne of Austria, reputedly his mistress. He honestly believed that the farming out of the West Indian islands was the best solution, and when he realized the contrary his health was failing. More intimate problems harassed the last breath of this artist of politics, as he justly rated himself to be.

Mazarin died in 1661. Louis, then twenty-three, embarked on the unparalleled personal regime that made him the Roi Soleil. He was his own Prime Minister until the end. But he could not get along without a cabinet, and fortunately for him he inherited a genius from the entourage of Mazarin. Jean-Baptiste Colbert was made controller general of finances, promptly exposed irregularities in the accounts of his immediate predecessor in that post, Fouquet, and was allowed to extend his influence over all the commercial, industrial and maritime departments.

Colbert stood for colonial expansion. A zealous reformer, he declined to tolerate the old concessionnaires in the Antilles and notified them that they must sell their holdings to the Crown. Generous prices were paid. However, the theory of shifting the expenses to a private concern that would recoup from revenue was not yet exploded. Colbert founded the Compagnie des Indes Occidentales, granting it a monopoly of navigation and trade in the Caribbean for forty years. The business management of all the colonies was turned over to it in 1664. More than half its total capital, be it said, was subscribed by the Crown. The same year, the Marquis de Tracy was sent out to travel from island to island, sit as a judge where there had been flagrant abuses, and install new Governors named by the King on the Company's recommendation. Of these appointees, the only one of lasting historical significance was Bertrand d'Ogeron, made Governor of Tortuga. He utilized the Hispaniola buccaneers with exceptional shrewdness, succeeded in attaching them to France and laid the foundations of Saint Domingue.

Before reviewing the career of Ogeron, let us take note of the war which saw the first juggling of colonies between France and England, an interchange that was to grow frenzied in the next century and a half. Louis XIV took the side of the Dutch against Charles II in 1666. Fighting spread to the Caribbean. The friendly settlements on St. Christopher were at each other's throats, and although the French gained the upper hand at first, English re-enforcements arrived and they were subdued. Martinique repulsed a naval attack. The French ships there proceeded to the capture of Antigua and Montserrat, but a stronger English squadron defeated them and chased them to the Guiana coast, sending landing parties to seize an islet or two on the way. In 1668, the Treaty of Breda canceled these results by restoring all the colonies to their original owners.

Bertrand d'Ogeron meanwhile had been busy grasping for success at the end of a life of failure. This free-lance soldier had been a member of an unofficial company in France which had schemed to establish a colony on the Spanish Main. He had gone to the West Indies as its advance agent in 1656, had daringly investigated several possibilities under the noses of the Dons, had traveled as far as Cayenne and then doubled back to Martinique. He was forced to conclude that his company's project was visionary. He drifted to western Hispaniola on his own account in 1659, and during the next few years he made mysterious trips to the Bahamas, to Jamaica, and back and forth to France. An empty concession to exploit the salt ponds of the Caicos Islands disillusioned him. At this stage, or a little earlier, he undoubtedly sailed as a buccaneer. But in 1663 he found himself in Hispaniola for the third time, stranded at Port Margot and surrounded, as he expressed it, by the debris of his unfortunate enterprises.

Ogeron wrote an unsolicited report on the work of Du Rausset, whose overlordship of Tortuga he had perhaps envied. He had the inspiration to praise his subject's energy, while pointing out that Du Rausset could have gone further with official backing, and outlining the results that could be obtained. He did not know that his man had landed in the Bastille. The report surprised and convinced the new Compagnie des Indes Occidentales. But Du Rausset's patriotism, rather than his ability, was doubted. He was a dead cock in the pit. It was decided to award the post to the apparently disinterested author of the report. Ogeron learned of it when the Marquis de Tracy came on his mission to the Caribbean. He could hardly believe that fortune at last was on his side.

The ceremony with which he was conducted to Tortuga on June 6, 1665, impressed the buccaneers. Indeed, the ancient historians marvel over the way that these rough men allowed him to be "imposed" on them as a Governor. He found 400 armed seafarers and a score of ships. Others were away on predatory voyages. Organizing them was not his immediate worry. They could take care of themselves. Within a few weeks, however, we find him writing to Colbert about the meat-hunters on the mainland:

"There are 700 or 800 Frenchmen scattered along the coasts of the island of Hispaniola in inaccessible places, surrounded by mountains or great rocks of the sea, by which alone they can pass from place to place in their little boats. They are three, or four, or six, or ten together, separated from one another by six, eight or fifteen leagues according as they find convenient places. They live like savages without recognizing any one's authority and without any chief, and they commit a thousand brigandages. They have robbed many Dutch and English vessels, which has caused much disorder. They live on the meat of wild swine and cattle and make a little tobacco which they barter for arms, provisions and clothes. So it is very necessary for His Majesty to give an order to cause these people to leave the said island of Hispaniola and betake themselves in two months into Tortuga, which they would do without doubt if it were fortified. And it would bring in a great revenue to the King if all captains of merchant ships and other vessels were forbidden to buy or sell anything to these Frenchmen along the coasts of Hispaniola, but rather here."

Ogeron did not really want the mainland deserted for Tortuga. But he was anxious to get the meat-hunters under his hand for a while. He believed that a royal order would have moral effect, unenforceable though it might be in a material way. Colbert obtained the proclamation for him, and it worked. Most of the wild men came in. Ogeron then arranged for new settlers to be sent from France at his personal expense and that of friends. Within two or three years, some 2,000 colonists had arrived.

His way of inducing certain buccaneers to establish homes has been often cited. The tradition of the Brethren was all against that. They had never allowed mistresses to live with them, but had shared their sketchy housekeeping with male companions, in pairs or in groups up to five. The members of such groups called one another *matelots,* meaning by this use of the French word for sailor a special companionship. A man's *matelot* fought beside him in battle and nursed him in times of sickness. Finding the system disorderly, Ogeron exclaimed:

"*Corbleu,* I shall fetch chains from France for these rascals!"

He chartered a ship, which brought back to him the novel cargo of 150 women, freely enlisted for the life ahead of them. Ogeron put them on the auction block, with dramatic success. The bidder was not forced to marry his purchase, for whom he paid the price of her transportation, but undertook to live with her as a partner, not a slave. The opportunity to have European women broke down the ancient prejudice of the freebooters. All contemporary accounts agree that these concubines had been harlots and pickpockets, the sweepings of the ports of France. Yet they embraced domesticity and bore some children. Should a woman's mate be killed at sea or fail to return within a few months, she was free to adopt another protector.

Tortuga was no sooner better populated and its life stabilized than Ogeron began the systematic settlement of the peninsula opposite. He placed families on the land, encouraging them to cultivate cocoa in addition to the standard crops such as maize and tobacco. He developed the town of Port-de-Paix which had been started by Du Rausset, and fostered the growth of Léogane a future capital. On Tortuga he built La Tour, a more effective fortress than the old one on the heights above the beach. He was a born colonizer and had all the instincts of an executive.

Ogeron's greatest triumph, given the morals of the times, was that he had not alienated the fighting buccaneers. Asking them to become peaceful citizens or to abandon their lurking-places on the mainland peninsula was not on his agenda. Instead, he encouraged them to embark on more and more ambitious exploits, and he provided them with a market at Basse-Terre, Tortuga, which could absorb their plunder. He did just what the English had done at Port Royal. His middlemen paid derisory prices, to be sure, but they were always ready with the cash, whereas in days gone by dependence had been on chance comers. It looked like good business to the buccaneers.

He had caught them during the short period of their greatest effectiveness. Mansvelt, a Hollander, was still their admiral in 1665. He died two years later, poisoned according to some accounts, and was succeeded by Henry Morgan, easily the supreme talent in the annals of the "sweet trade." Mansvelt had operated from Tortuga, while Morgan made his headquarters at Port Royal. The point was unimportant. Both these leaders maintained a co-ordination between the French and English corsairs, planned joint enterprises and divided the loot fairly.

There were also a number of French captains who preferred to act independently. Chief among these was l'Olonnois, probably the worst all-around fiend that ever followed the calling, but an able commander. His real name was Jean David Nau, l'Olonnois being a *nom-de-guerre* derived from his birthplace, Sables-d'Olonne, France. He once stationed himself off Havana with two barques and only twenty-one men. A well-armed frigate came out to destroy him. His little craft darted to starboard and port simultaneously, the grappling irons were used and the Spaniard captured. When l'Olonnois learned that she had brought along a hangman to execute the buccaneers, he flew into one of his characteristic rages, ordered the prisoners up from below and as they came through the hatchway he lopped off their heads. He licked the blade after each stroke. A single messenger was spared to return to Havana and tell the Governor of this vengeance. Subsequently, he committed the dreadful deed of slashing open the breast of a prisoner who had defied him, wrenching out the heart and gnawing at it before he dashed it to the ground.

With Moïse Vauclin as his vice-captain and Michel le Basque in command of a landing force, l'Olonnois took several ships to Maracaibo Lagoon in 1666 and captured the towns of Maracaibo and Gibraltar. The most ruthless cruelty was shown the inhabitants and substantial booty extorted. Not long afterward, l'Olonnois was ambushed by Indians on the Central American coast. Even they knew him by reputation as the worst of men, and they made a ceremony of putting him to death by slow torture.

Very different was the brave Sieur de la Mothe, a Parisian gentleman who had been an army officer. He arrived at Tortuga with a number of Dutch prizes he had taken on the voyage out, and was accepted as a leader. He habitually signed himself, "A well-intentioned subject of the King."

In 1668, Henry Morgan led some 700 buccaneers, about a third of whom were French, to the south coast of Cuba, marched forty miles inland and pillaged the city of Puerto Principe (now Camaguey). The band retired to the Isle des Vaches, or Ile à Vache, a rocky cay off the southwestern end of Hispaniola, where they counted the spoils, and according to John Esquemeling, the buccaneer historian, "the sum being known, it caused a general grief to see such a small purchase." The French departed mutinously. They did not participate as a group in Morgan's next two famous exploits, the storming of Porto Bello and Maracaibo, where rich loot was obtained.

But in 1670, the men of Tortuga rallied eight ships, with fifty-nine guns and 520 men to take part in Morgan's great expedition against the city of Panama. The Admiral had twenty-eight English ships, many of them small, with 180 guns and 1,326 men. The combined force was the largest that had ever been assembled by a buccaneer chief. It concentrated at the Isle des Vaches, sailed in mid-December, seized Old Providence Island on the way, and debarked at the mouth of the Chagres River about the first of the year. The castle of San Lorenzo there was taken by frontal assault.

Morgan advanced through the jungle at the head of 1,200 men, including most of the French. Following roughly the course of the present canal as far as Venta Cruces, and after that the gold road between the Pacific and Porto Bello, he crossed the Isthmus in ten days, an astounding achievement in view of the difficulties of the terrain. Upon the savanna of Matasnillo outside Panama, he routed the Spaniards in a pitched battle. Just as the buccaneers were about to enter the city, its powder magazines were touched off by order of the Governor and a calamitous fire resulted. The ruins were occupied for twenty-eight days and systematically combed, to the tune of some 750,000 pieces of eight. When Morgan left, the city was transferred to its present site.

This affair was the last in which the French and English freebooters co-operated. It marked, in fact, the end of English buccaneering under the protection of the Government of Jamaica. The Treaty of Madrid between England and Spain had been negotiated in 1670, before the attack on Panama. It recognized English sovereignty over Jamaica and other islands, and although several months had been allowed for ratification the Spaniards were furious at the flagrant mockery of its spirit. To save the treaty, Charles II put Henry Morgan on trial, only to acquit him, give him a knighthood and raise him to the governorship of Jamaica. But the King did agree to suppress the "sweet trade" from Port Royal, a work to which Sir Henry set his hand with his usual energy.

The French corsairs had official support, off and on, for more than twenty years longer. Following the outbreak of war between France and Holland in 1672, Ogeron decided to see action himself. He sailed at the head of 300 Tortuga veterans to seize Curaçao. A storm drove his flagship out of its course and he fell into the hands of the Spaniards. They condemned him and some of his officers to hard labor in the mines of Peru. He had the luck to escape during an assault by English filibusters on the Isthmian fort where he was being held for transfer. Back at his seat of government, Ogeron planned for the conquest of the whole island of Hispaniola, but succumbed in 1675 before he had had time to strike. His nephew the Sieur Jacques de Pouancey was appointed Governor in his place.

The Dutch war ended without far-reaching consequences in the Windward Islands. The famous Admiral de Ruyter was repulsed at Martinique. The French commander, the Comte Jean d'Estrées, Admiral of France, chased the enemy from Cayenne, which they had occupied, wrested Tobago from them after a hard struggle, but failed at Curaçao. Tobago was the only unit that changed hands at the peace.

In 1674, however, while the war raged, a vastly important step was taken. Acting on the advice of Colbert, Louis XIV abolished the Compagnie des Indes Occidentales and all other concessionnaires. The possessions were at last made outright colonies under the Crown.

Chapter VI

The Colonies Take Form

FRANCE as a colonizing nation has never received due credit from the English-speaking world. The average person has an impression, derived from his schoolbooks, that French methods have been slovenly and on the whole incompetent compared with those of her rivals. It is true that defeat in war bereft France of vast prizes, such as Hindustan and Canada. She failed to obtain the grip on Middle America which was once her dream. But there are other standards by which colonial effort may be judged. The Gallic concept of overseas territory resembled that of Ancient Greece. It sought to make each holding an integral part culturally, politically and commercially of the home land. Britain and Spain followed the Roman plan of establishing preserves that would enrich the conqueror. Though these peoples laid the foundations of future democracies, the process was fortuitous. In New England itself, where a mass migration for libertarian reasons occurred, divergence from the Old World character was soon a point of pride, and resentment of the tax collector's greed was soon a stimulus to revolution.

But France had extraordinary success in transferring her spirit to the lands she founded. From that viewpoint, there probably never has been in the whole history of colonization so outstanding an achievement as Quebec. Not only have French manners, customs and language survived annexation of the province by England, but the clannishness of the people, their fertility, their purposeful Gallicism, bid fair to give them in time complete control of the Dominion of Canada.

The record has been almost as remarkable in tropical colonies, old ones particularly, like those that concern us here. It was impossible for Saint Domingue or Martinique to become Nouvelle France in the sense that Quebec was and is, for labor conditions caused the importation of Negro slaves until the whites were greatly outnumbered. But the plantation way of life became an extension of the capacities of France. The colonists so loved their traditions that no new civilization sprang up. The antique culture was sympathetically absorbed by subject natives, even by the more intelligent slaves. The writer has said elsewhere that he believes French culture to be peculiarly suited to the Negro race. Yet the latter would not have accepted it as a thing imposed. Intellectual tolerance by the masters, no matter how unjust their economic system, was what made it agreeable. Consequently, we find colonies that have grown to be ninety-five per cent negroid still passionately devoted to the country that shaped them, and more esthetically alert than other Africanized communities.

France introduced Catholicism as the state religion wherever she went. But her officials and priests, unlike the Spaniards, were not fanatical about it. The intensity of the form it took seems to have been largely a question of climate. In Quebec the peasantry always have been devoted to the Church, a fact which gives them cohesion and political strength today. A more formal practice of the faith marked the people of Louisiana. In the islands, a tropical insouciance demanded pageantry and little else, while among the slaves the Romish ritual was grafted naïvely upon voodooism.

Erroneous theories of the wealth of nations and of how trade should be conducted were general at the time the West Indian colonies were founded. A prophetic wisdom could not be expected of France. She negligently allowed Dutch merchants to monopolize the provisioning of St. Christopher, Martinique and Guadeloupe at the start. The Hollanders took their payment in kind, leaving little in the way of crops for the holding companies to ship to France. Then Colbert decided to do as rival nations were doing.

According to the strict regulations drawn by him, commodities grown in the colonies could be handled only through home markets, where middlemen forwarded those destined for sale abroad. Taxes were levied on exports as well as imports. The cramping effect of having to sell at low prices and purchase at abnormally high ones was regarded as an ill inseparable from having one's interests far from the heart of the kingdom. A resident of Paris, it was argued, had no choice but to do business within the framework of the national economy. Why, just because his plantation lay beyond the ocean, should a colonial claim different rights? The metropolis was everything, and financially speaking it could not allow subsidiaries overseas.

Colbert, indeed, regarded the building up of French trade as the *raison d'être* of colonies. They should contribute to this end by furnishing raw products and becoming customers for manufactured articles. Being the exclusive property of the home land, colonies should not be a source of profit to foreigners, who must not be allowed to furnish even such goods as France could not supply, or take away even the surplus colonial products for which there was no market in France.

This was the extreme theory exemplified by the practice of Spain, who applied it rigidly for 300 years. It was soon liberalized by the successors of Colbert. But it continued to affect the colonial policies of all the competing Powers until the revolutionary era at the end of the eighteenth century.

France proved wiser than England in the tropics on at least three counts. She discouraged absentee landlordism, she promoted the diversification of crops, and she was quick to adopt improved methods of agriculture. This is not to say that the policy involved was uniformly successful among the French, or that the English were blind to it. Jamaica and Barbados grew into colonies which compared favorably with Saint Dominigue and Martinique. But France had a clearer perception of how tropical holdings could be made happy and self-sustaining as well as profitable, and so she got impressive results in a shorter time. On one count—insistence that proprietors should live on the land and direct the work themselves— she was always definitely ahead. Her rich sugar planters did at a certain juncture waste their substance scandalously in Paris. Those of Saint Domingue were the worst offenders. It was understood to be an evil and was disfavored, whereas England never seemed to understand that absentee landlordism was a folly dangerous to the economic life of even the most golden of geese.

It would have been fortunate for the West Indian islands if they had all come under the sway of France during the empire-building period. The advantages of unity, which they lack today, are obvious. Cuba and Puerto Rico would have known a swifter progress. Everywhere, but especially in the British islands, the proletariat springing from slavery would have been shaped more subtly for citizenship. It was not to be. In the Caribbean scramble that became increasingly bitter after the middle of the seventeenth century, France could have taken what she desired from Spain, had she not been thwarted by a virtually ceaseless naval contest with England. That she held her own as well as she did redounds to her credit, for England was the maritime genius of the age.

Pouancey, the successor of Ogeron in Hispaniola, found his task simplified by the fact that the Compagnie des Indes Occidentales had just been suppressed and that he was responsible only to the Crown. During his governorship, Tortuga began to lose its prestige as the cradle of the colony. This small island was not valuable except as a stronghold, and its

capital Basse-Terre had been outdistanced by many ports on
the mainland. Port-de-Paix was growing fast. Under both
Ogeron and Pouancey, it was where the government functioned most of the time. The excellent harbor of Cap Français a little farther east had been occupied, and the township
there was on its way to becoming the leading city of the
north. Gonaïves at the upper end of the western gulf had
acquired importance. There was a small settlement at Yaguana, also called the Cul-de-Sac, the site of Port-au-Prince. On
the lower peninsula, Léogane and Petit Goave had developed
as municipalities, the bays of Jérémie and Jacmel were in use,
while the buccaneers had a private port at Aux Cayes behind
their Isle des Vaches.

From now on, it is wrong to think of the French settlements
as being dependent on Tortuga, or to regard them as piratical
enterprises. Thousands of immigrants had come from Europe
and devoted themselves to planting. A colonial status had
been accepted even by the buccaneers, whose attitude was that
of privileged gangsters willing to give and take under an
easy administration, but prepared to revolt against a harsh
one. The name Saint Domingue was current. The French
applied it to roughly half of Hispaniola. Neither they nor
the Spaniards controlled the mountainous interior through
which the supposed frontier ran, and a flat denial of the
claim was of course maintained by the Spaniards. The French
colony was none the less a reality.

Louis XIV hoped that the Treaties of Nymwegen, which
ended his war with the Dutch in 1678 and his much greater
conflict with Spain, the Holy Roman Empire and Sweden the
following year, would include recognition of his right to Saint
Domingue. This appeared to be on the cards, since by conceding Jamaica to England in 1670 Spain had at last tolerated
a breach of the Papal grant. It was not to be—not yet. Though
Louis got duchies, cities and fortresses that made him the

arbiter of Europe, Saint Domingue was omitted from the roll of prizes. "No peace beyond the Line" was still the watchword in Caribbean rivalry.

Pouancey's governorship was undistinguished. He did not have the ability of his uncle, Ogeron. He coped badly with popular resentment of the activities of private individuals to whom Colbert had farmed out the tax on tobacco. Riots swept the colony. When they died down, many planters uprooted their tobacco in pique and substituted sugar cane. The transition was made too rapidly, and Pouancey failed to guide it. Considerable suffering resulted. Yet the instinct of the planters had been sound. Saint Domingue was about to become the greatest sugar bowl of them all.

As in the past, the buccaneers furnished the melodrama of sudden forays and dubious returns with shiploads of plunder. New leaders had appeared since Morgan had left the game, and for the moment the best of these were Netherlanders. Laurens de Graff, a Dutchman, and Van Horne, a Fleming from Ostend, had remarkable success. The first is described as "a superb man with gold-blond hair." He had served in the Spanish Navy as a gunner, and upon being captured had joined the corsairs. His long career ended, as we shall see, in an aura of semi-respectability under the French. Van Horne was a blustering exhibitionist, of whom it is recorded that he "commonly wore a great collar of pearls with a magnificent ruby."

These two set out from Hispaniola in 1683 with ten vessels, reputedly carrying the large force of 1,200 men, to attack Vera Cruz, Mexico. This rich port, starting point of one of the Spanish plate fleets, had never been taken by buccaneers. It was guarded by the powerful castle of San Juan Ulúa and it maintained a garrison of more than 3,000. Yet with Van Horne as first in command, the nut was cracked.

The raiders landed during the night some three leagues

from Vera Cruz and marched to the walls by dawn, effecting a surprise. They made a headlong assault, battering down one of the gates and terrifying the guards into opening others to them. A ruthless massacre in the streets quickly reduced the city to impotence. Before starting to pillage, the buccaneers herded the chief inhabitants into the cathedral against the walls of which they stacked barrels of gunpowder. They threatened to blow it up unless the prisoners paid a ransom of 2,000,000 pieces of eight. Half the sum was almost at once produced. A general looting of the city, accompanied by the classic cruelties, went on for three days. The plunder amassed was enormous.

The fourth day, a fleet of seventeen Spanish vessels was reported to be approaching, while in the foothills to the west an army had mobilized. The order to evacuate was given, and it is pleasant to know that the powder barrels at the cathedral were not touched off. The freebooters brawled on the docks as they embarked, mistrusting one another so much that they fought over which ships should carry certain precious loot. Van Horne argued over the possession of a casket of jewels, and in the scrimmage that resulted he was run through the body, some accounts say by Graff himself. The latter, at all events, seized the dead man's command and led the way out of the harbor. He steered between two incoming galleons, giving them simultaneous broadsides and disabling them both. The rest of the buccaneer craft took advantage of the confusion, and all escaped. It was one of the most dazzling feats in the history of the trade, worthy to be compared with those of Sir Henry Morgan. The fate of Van Horne became a matter of indifference, and Graff was elected Admiral.

He got back to Saint Domingue on the eve of momentous changes. Pouancey had died and Paul Tarin de Cussy had been appointed in his place. Louis XIV was about to sign the Truce of Ratisbon, to run for twenty years, and by the

terms of which all the leading countries agreed to refrain
from wars and to be virtuous generally. Buccaneering spe-
cifically was to be suppressed. When Cussy arrived he published an ordinance forbidding Frenchmen to sail as irregulars
under penalty of the confiscation of goods and corporal
punishment. He set up special courts of justice at Petit
Goave to pass on this type of offense.

Cussy was not enthusiastic about the new policy. He
winked at an early violation when Laurens de Graff and François Grammont ravaged Campeche. He memorialized the
King several times to the effect that the buccaneers were
needed to hold back the Spaniards on the unrecognized
frontier in Hispaniola, and that they would rebel if deprived
of their perquisites. Cussy may have realized how insincere
was the Truce of Ratisbon and how short a time it would
last. But the King insisted, and for three or four years there
was genuine suppression.

In 1689, England and Holland joined Spain in attacking
France over the succession of the Palatinate. The truce had
become a jest in barely five years. Incidentally, it was the
first time since the discovery of America that warfare spreading to the Caribbean found England and Spain on the same
side. Cussy immediately reported:

"I have crushed filibustering, because the Court wished it,
and I obtained that result with much difficulty. I wish now
that I had not succeeded, for there should be on this coast ten
or twelve good ships manned by many brave fellows who
would assure the safety of this colony."

The response was at last to his liking. In view of the war
with Spain, he was permitted to employ the buccaneers, especially in the conquest of Spanish Hispaniola. Royal commissions were issued to Graff and a few other captains. This
plan to militarize the sea-rovers did not have to be too strictly
interpreted, Cussy knew. His first call rallied 250 of them.

Then he ordered out the colonial militia which had recently been formed. He soon had a force of a thousand men, which he led to the capture of Santiago de los Caballeros in 1690. Few or no restrictions were placed upon the looting that followed. Cussy burned the town before he retired.

There was savage fighting for a year along the north coast, where an English fleet had aided the landing of Spanish soldiers. Cap Français was destroyed. In that neighborhood Cussy fell in battle honorably enough. He was a second-rate leader whose disappearance was an indirect contribution to the French cause. For it cleared the way for Jean-Baptiste du Casse, a star whose magnitude sets it apart. The year, 1691, though midway of a war, marked the beginning of a new period.

Compared with Saint Domingue and its ever-theatrical buccaneers, the Windward Islands and Guiana had been out of the spotlight after the pacts of Nymwegen. There had been a growth in prosperity to which Colbert's commercial policy had at least done no serious harm. The minister died in 1683. Little Martinique was rated in 1681 as being fifty per cent richer than Saint Domingue. It had replaced St. Christopher as the seat of government of all the West Indian possessions, though but slight control could be exercised from this point over Saint Domingue and distant Guiana. The first Governor-General appointed to Martinique was Jean Charles de Baas, Marquis de Castelmore, a brother of the Chevalier d'Artagnan-Montesquiou, Dumas' hero. A Superior Council enjoyed a few of the lesser prerogatives of a legislature; its power would grow.

In 1680, the King forbade a projected war against the Caribs of St. Vincent, one of the islands which had been relinquished to the aborigines by Poincy. Five years later, Protestants whether French or no were debarred from the colonies, thus foreshadowing the imminent revocation of the

Edict of Nantes in France. Jews had previously been expelled.

But the most important act of the period was the promulgation of the first Code Noir, for the protection of slaves who were arriving in the islands ruled by the French at the rate of about 2,000 a year, and the guidance of the whites in their human relations with them. The Code was several times modified. A chapter will be given to this document.

As the period closed, the population of the colonies was estimated at 52,000 souls, excluding the wild Indians of the woods. Roughly, there were 16,500 in Martinique, 11,000 in Guadeloupe, 10,250 in St. Christopher, 10,000 in Saint Domingue and the rest scattered. Golden Guiana of the early part of the century accounted for only 800. The Martinique total has been broken down to 5,000 whites as against 11,000 Negroes and 500 classed as either mulattoes or Caribs. It was probably typical.

Chapter VII

Illustrious Du Casse

IN PRESENTING a hero forgotten except by his own people, the most effective way is to draw comparisons with contemporary or almost contemporary figures whom the world does remember. Jean-Baptiste du Casse served France as a privateer and slave trader, as Sir John Hawkins and Sir Francis Drake had served England in the previous century. He was a brilliant leader of buccaneers, who rose to a political career like Sir Henry Morgan. He became an admiral in the regular navy, met tough opponents like John Benbow and generally defeated them, and reached the end of his life loaded with honors. Du Casse was on the whole a greater man than any who have been mentioned. He may not have matched the genius in battle of Drake and Morgan. As a colonial builder he clearly outshone them, Queen Elizabeth's knight being but an exponent of the hit-and-run school, and the Port Royal buccaneer's statesmanship of a naïve order when all was said and done.

Du Casse was born in 1646 near Bayonne in the south of France. We first hear of him in the employ of the Compagnie de Sénégal, a venture promoted under the auspices of Colbert to exploit the West Coast of Africa. Admiral the Comte d'Estrées, following his attacks on the Dutch in the West Indies, came to Sénégal and took possession of the island of Gorée, a slaving headquarters of the Netherlanders. Du Casse, then thirty-one, immediately pressed the advantage, placing the Company's agents at Gorée and continuing the work of conquest south of Cape Verde. He forced the native princes to sign treaties by which full trade privileges were extended to the French. The gains obtained were sanctioned by the first Treaty of Nymwegen.

Huguenots then had little chance to build a career except in the colonies, and Du Casse was of Huguenot parentage. His personal interest in the reformed church appears to have been slight. After making a trip with slaves to Saint Domingue in 1680, he investigated with rare open-mindedness the standing quarrel between his company and the colonists regarding what types of Negroes were best suited to plantation work, how many were needed each year, and under what conditions they should be sold. He promised Governor Pouancey to straighten the matter out, returned to France for that purpose and effected a compromise. He equipped a boat at his own expense, took a specially chosen cargo of slaves from Africa to the Antilles and sold at a great profit. This financed him to go privateering. He captured a large Dutch merchantman, which was so pleasing to Louis XIV that the King commissioned him at the age of forty a lieutenant in the Royal Navy. Other semi-official exploits followed.

The buccaneers saw in Du Casse a greater fighting man than Laurens de Graff, and a leader such as they had not had since Sir Henry Morgan. Many of them notified him that they were at his disposal. He used them to organize an expedition against the Dutch in the Guianas. It was unsuccessful, in that he failed to eject them from their chief settlement, Surinam, but he relieved pressure on half-strangled Cayenne. Passing to St. Christopher, which had been overrun by the English, he reversed the situation after a struggle of exceptional ferocity.

While these events were in progress, Cussy had been waging his unfortunate campaign in Saint Domingue ending with his death at Cap Français. Du Casse did not learn the details until he reached France to make a report on his own activities. He at once wrote a letter to Pontchartrain, Minister of Marine, in which he said:

"The question of Saint Domingue is the most important facing His Majesty, outside his kingdom, from the standpoint of the advantages of America, that island's location and the enterprises which can be fashioned there against Spain."

The Minister is not known to have made a direct reply, but Du Casse was promoted to be captain of a frigate, given two other ships as auxiliaries and ordered back to active duty in the islands. He was barely on the scene when he forced the English naval commander Codrington to raise the blockade of Guadeloupe. He attended to some minor unfinished business of a privateering nature and proceeded to Léogane, where mail awaited him. The first document he unfolded was his appointment to the governorship of Saint Domingue. This was in August, 1691, at the height of the war against both England and Spain.

"He was one of the best citizens and one of the best and most generous men I have known," wrote the Duc de Saint-Simon in his celebrated *Memoires,* portraying Du Casse, it is true, in the mellow years of the latter's presence at Court. "He was a tall, thin man who, with his corsair's manner and much fire and vivacity, was gentle, polite, respectful, and who was never false to himself. He was very obliging and had a good deal of wit, with a certain natural eloquence; and, even as to matters outside his calling, pleasure and profit were to be had in hearing him expound. He loved the State and good for the sake of good, which has become an extremely rare thing."

On taking over the administration at Port-de-Paix, Du Casse found public business in a condition of utter disorder. He could easily have blamed this on his dead predecessor, a chronicler asserts, but he made a point of doing honor to the memory of Cussy and punishing his traducers. In a few weeks, he had established an authority such as even Ogeron had never enjoyed. Saint Domingue at last became a French colony with none of the mental reservations inspired by the buccaneers. Warning the lawless elements that he would treat them as subjects of the King, neither more nor less, he at the same time let it be known that freebooting would continue under his protection.

A sharp message to the Spanish Governor at the city of Santo Domingo demanded humane treatment for prisoners, under the threat of pitiless reprisals. The Spaniards, who had little stomach for this war in which they found themselves strangely allied with England, mended their ways with alacrity. Feeling that he had not much to fear from them for the moment, Du Casse turned his attention to the British.

In June, 1692, one of the most violent earthquakes on record destroyed Port Royal, Jamaica, and did immense damage to other parts of the island. The news reached Saint Domingue quickly. It was not a compassionate age. The first thought of the French was that the calamity was a godsend to them. It weakened their foe and made an easy prey of his strong places. A buccaneer named Daviot lost no time in darting with a stout vessel and 290 men to the coasts of Jamaica, where he raked plunder from the ruins of smoking villages and plantation houses. Others flocked in his track. Du Casse employed Laurens de Graff on the business. For a while, the raiders landed almost weekly.

But Daviot encountered nemesis in circumstances that stimulated larger events. His ship laden with treasure and captured slaves was cruising near the southeastern end of Cuba, with what new object in view we do not know, when four English craft closed in on him. He put up a stiff fight until his adversaries were boarding him from both sides. He thrust a torch into the powder magazine and blew himself up, killing most of his men and scores on the other side.

Du Casse grudged the English their expensive coup. He was annoyed at the destruction of the considerable booty which had been lost with Daviot. The incident had been spectacular enough to sting the whole buccaneering fraternity into an eagerness for vengeance. He decided to set forward the date for a project he had long had in mind: the conquest and annexation of Jamaica. This accomplished, it was his hope to eject the Spaniards from their half of Hispaniola, fix his capital at Santo Domingo and develop a splendid French colony, to consist of the two islands, the second and third in size of all the Antilles.

Preparing a serious expedition in those days was a complicated business, subject to the caprices of rumor and the weather. There were no real warships, but only vessels specially armed for war. Men were cheap, but before risking afloat such valuable property as cannon one weighed the dubious reports that came from all quarters.

Du Casse fretted through 1693. Then three powerful craft belonging to the King arrived in Saint Domingue and he attached them to his fleet. He personally reconnoitered in the direction of Jamaica and satisfied himself that English naval strength there was negligible for the moment. Two Irishmen, serving against their will as soldiers in the Port Royal garrison, made their escape to Saint Domingue and told the Governor that "the fortifications at Port Royal were out of order and few men there, so that two hundred men could take that place." Encouraged, Du Casse set out early in June, 1694, with twenty-two sail and at least 1,500 men; some accounts declare that the armed force was much larger. About 800 of them were buccaneers, led by Graff.

English histories make light of the ensuing episode, averring that an attempt at invasion was repulsed easily. The truth is, the French landed some twenty-five miles east of Port Royal and plundered almost at will. On proceeding by sea to the earthquake-shattered city, Du Casse found that surprising progress had been made in restoring the defenses. It transpired that an English captain of a barque, who had been a prisoner in Saint Domingue, had paddled to Jamaica in a small canoe and warned his people before it was too late. Du Casse decided against a frontal attack. He sailed west to Carlisle Bay, where he put his full strength ashore without opposition. A breastwork had been thrown up a short distance away, and this the French under a Major Beauregard carried after a bloody action. Militia companies of planters with Negro bodyguards came up, charged the invaders gallantly and halted their advance.

The next few days were spent in skirmishing and in fruitful looting. The French advantage in swords was not less than two to one, and their control of the situation must have been fairly complete. They burned sugar mills and plantation houses, and raised the number of slaves captured to 1,300. It seemed inevitable that they would drive through to St. Jago de la Vega, the capital. Yet suddenly they loaded their ships, spiked the guns that had fallen into their hands at Carlisle Bay and returned to Saint Domingue. The Jamaican historian Cundall's remark that they had lost several of their best officers, and that they found "they could not penetrate further into the country," must be rejected as an explanation.

Du Casse's true motive for giving up a campaign which he had planned for over a year remains a mystery. It is perhaps significant that he gave the officers of the royal vessels under him an equal share with his colonials and buccaneers of the valuable booty obtained, and that the King in return bestowed a small pension on him. The Court's policy, for reasons now utterly obscure, may have been opposed to taking Jamaica, though not to its scourging. At all events, Du Casse concentrated on repelling the counterattacks which the English launched with Spanish aid.

A determined effort against Graff at Cap Français came to naught. But Port-de-Paix was seized, raids effected at many points on the coast and prisoners taken. An old chronicler remarks drily that "the English took the men, while the Spanish took the women." The allies were not on good terms for long. Partly for this reason and partly out of exhaustion, they failed to tackle Du Casse himself at Léogane. The private war among the colonies fizzled out. Hostilities continued to rage elsewhere in the Caribbean, but Du Casse reserved his strength for a few years in the expectation of conquering all Hispaniola. He diligently improved the civil administration of his charge.

One of his early acts was to bring all the remaining inhabitants of Tortuga to the mainland. He had found only seventy men capable of bearing arms on the little island shaped like a turtle's back, and some women and children. The place had outlived its usefulness, he urged, and plantations on its inferior soil would simply be a temptation to raiders. His view was sound. Even under tranquil conditions, Tortuga was never considered worth exploiting again. It is occupied now by a handful of Negro peasants and fishermen.

The Governor had sterner problems than Tortuga in that closing decade of the seventeenth century. Councillors, judges and petty officials had to be drawn from the raw material of adventurers and cutthroats, whose willingness to concede any merit to legal restraints was of yesterday. Culture virtually was non-existent. When Du Casse had to fill three seats on the council of Petit Goave, he complained that he "could hardly find persons who could read and write," and that "to tell the truth, the said Boisseau [retiring president of the council] was unable to do either one or the other."

He remarked about the Ministry's appointees in 1698: "It

seems that they are trying to make America a land of chicanery [legal] like Normandy. It would be better to banish that spirit like a contagion, for all that I see in 'justice' is rapine and sordid interests."

The pungency of the letters and reports written by Du Casse mirror the man. He described the colony as being "composed of the refuse of all the kingdom, men of the sack and cord, without honor and without virtue." Again, he spoke of it as having been "shaped only by the caprice of each individual, and therefore it has matured in disorder. . . . Men bear arms here as if they were at a carnival, without the least principle of discipline." He denounced the buccaneers as rascals who some day would have to be suppressed, and he did not hesitate to tell them so to their faces. But he knew how to handle them, and they always respected him as a leader.

"When some filibuster," recounts Le Pers, "sought out Du Casse to demand money which he pretended was due him: 'I know well,' the chief would say to him, 'that behind my back you call me a dog, a rogue and a thief. But I do not care. If you are not satisfied with me, take my sword and run it through my body! As for money, I have none, and you will not get any.' "

Late in 1696, Du Casse received a letter from Pontchartrain ordering him to assist Jean Bernard Desjeans, Baron de Pointis, who had obtained the King's patronage for an assault on the city of Cartagena de las Indias, the chief port of the Spanish Main. This project, fated to have a dazzling finale, had germinated in an unlikely manner. A Huguenot, the Sieur Petit, had been thrown into the Bastille to punish him for having resided in Holland and showing enmity to the Catholic religion among his friends there. As a bid for a pardon, he had sent the King a detailed plan of military operations against Cartagena, where he had sojourned and which he knew well. Prisoners in all ages have been given to thinking up such schemes. This one was examined by the King's experts and pronounced to be of small merit. The Baron de Pointis, however, sub-commander of a fleet, who had distinguished himself in the Barbary States, was impressed by it and persuaded Louis XIV to let him lead an expedition and form a syndicate to finance it.

A second letter from Pontchartrain required Du Casse to enlist for the venture all the buccaneers who frequented Saint Domingue, and suggested that he take part in it himself, if he felt that he could be spared from the colony. The date of Pointis' arrival was set at about February 15, 1697.

The Governor answered the Minister of Marine with a protest. He stated that in his opinion it would be more sensible to let him use his forces to drive the Spaniards out of Hispaniola. For this he was rebuked. The Court was then in the grip of a fallacy which rated money as a commodity, the true source of wealth. It was actually being maintained that gold was more important than crops, and that robbing Cartagena would be a larger gain than expanding a colony.

Du Casse prepared to obey, like a good soldier. He had difficulty with the buccaneers, especially as the coming of Pointis was delayed. He succeeded, nevertheless, in mobilizing 715 freebooters in seven frigates and some smaller boats, to which force was added 170 soldiers and a handful of volunteers.

The capture and sacking of Cartagena by Pointis and Du Casse is one of the best known incidents of that period of West Indian history. It need not be repeated here in detail. The sharply contrasted personalities of the leaders, the role of Du Casse and the eminence to which it raised him had a bearing on French colonial fortunes which has often been underestimated.

Pointis, sixty-two years of age, was noted for his arrogance, insolent presumption, vanity, selfishness, contempt for inferiors and even those whom he deigned to consider his equals. An able commander in battle, he exasperated his followers at other times by being a martinet. He came to Saint Domingue with nine frigates, four corvettes, transports and 4,000 men. This gave him a heavy preponderance in the council of war, but his domineering nature grasped for more. He hectored the buccaneers, informing them that "they must submit themselves to the same rules as the men on the King's ships." He loftily notified Du Casse that he did not propose to use him except as the captain of a vessel.

The Governor replied calmly that the buccaneers would observe their own customs, or pull out of the campaign. Pointis could take his choice. Furthermore, not one of them would consent to fight unless he, Du Casse, were with them. He offered to suppress his office and his naval rank and join as a volunteer. It would then be seen whether the buccaneers elected him their chief.

Pointis was astute enough to understand what that meant. He accepted Du Casse as a collaborator with semi-independent authority. But from that moment he was bitterly jealous of him. When the fleet reached Cartagena, Pointis conducted the siege operations efficiently. Du Casse landed at the head of the Saint Domingue brigade and captured the fortified hill of La Popa. He directed the taking of Fort San Lázaro and led the way through the first breach made by cannon in the walls of Getsémani suburb. The fall of the city occurred four days later. Pointis had a *Te Deum* sung in the Cathedral, and then collected a gigantic ransom running into the tens of millions of dollars—some accounts say $100,000,000. It was the most profitable grab ever accomplished by the French in America.

But in the division of the spoils, Pointis cheated the buccaneers. They had been promised an equal share with the men from France, and consequently they expected around one-fifth of the whole. By deducting first the costs of equipping the expedition, the King's share and bonuses for royal officers—and by other chicaneries—the sum awarded to the fighting men was cut down to a point that left only 40,000 crowns for the surviving Brethren of the Coast. They fiercely protested the ruling, which was made known at the last moment when Pointis, ready to depart, practically flung their pittance at them and would listen to no arguments. They threatened to attack the flagship, changed their minds and announced that they would remain in Cartagena, where they would know how to recoup themselves. Du Casse, who had zealously taken their part, issued a proclamation:

"I agree that you have been made the victims of an unexampled perfidy, but you must believe that after winning glory in the service of the King his justice will hear your complaints and will punish those who have violated his faith. I command you to retire under penalty of being adjudged mutinous, and I promise you to go and present your claims to the King."

This dignified appeal had some effect, but it was too much to hope that Cartagena could be spared a second plundering at the hands of the frenzied buccaneers. The fleet sailed in two sections, but all the freebooters did not leave with it and others turned back at sea. They extorted a large residue of treasure, most of which was taken from them by English and Dutch warships that intercepted them as they straggled toward their rendezvous, the Isle des Vaches.

Du Casse arrived in Saint Domingue just in time to repulse an English naval attack on Petit Goave. It proved to be the last action of the war in the Caribbean. Definitely influenced by the Cartagena disaster, Spain acquiesced in the Peace of Ryswick, one of the terms of which gave the western end of

Hispaniola to France. Du Casse thought it a poor compromise, but he returned to France to place his personal knowledge at the disposal of the statesmen engaged in delimiting the frontier across the island.

He was greeted with an acclaim that exceeded the flattering reception given the Baron de Pointis and his gorgeous loot. The King made Du Casse a knight of the Order of St. Louis, and promoted him to be an admiral. Pontchartrain had notified him that the buccaneers would receive their due and that "His Majesty is as satisfied with your conduct as you could possibly desire." Louis XIV now showed that the promises of monarchs are not always empty by giving him outright the equivalent of half a million gold dollars for the Saint Domingue irregulars. When these men were paid off, buccaneering may be said to have ended. Du Casse had promised that it would be so, and his authority was sufficiently great to accomplish what up till then had seemed impossible.

The last phase of this illustrious chief's career was a pure romance of the fabulous and paradoxical, such as few other ages could have produced. The Peace of Ryswick did not long endure in Europe. But as between France and Spain, it was the prelude to a dynastic alliance that put the American interests of the two Powers on a friendly basis for almost a century. Charles II, "the Bewitched," died in 1700 leaving no direct heir to the Spanish Crown. He had designated a Bourbon, a grandson of Louis XIV, to succeed him, and although several European nations objected so strenuously that the War of the Spanish Succession was soon under way, the Bourbon prince did mount the throne as Philip V and in the end retained it.

Looking about him for naval talent with which to combat the English, Philip V gave Du Casse an admiral's commission and persuaded Louis XIV to lend him for service in the Caribbean. He commanded a French fleet, but had Spanish

units under him when, in 1702, he met Benbow in an indecisive engagement off Santa Marta. The English admiral,
suffering from a wound of which he died two months later,
was forced to pull out of the fight. We hear of Du Casse commanding squadrons in various battles during the next five
years.

But stranger assignments were in store for him. He, who
had plundered Spanish ships as a privateer, was entrusted in
1708 with convoying the plate fleet from Vera Cruz. Some of
the galleons were cut off by English raiders. The showing,
nevertheless, was better than the average, and Madrid asked
Du Casse to bring through the plate fleet carrying Peruvian
treasure which had been transported across the Isthmus of
Panama. He joined it at Cartagena of all places, the scene of
his recent sanguinary exploit, and by the use of adroit strategy
he delivered it intact at Corunna.

Then came the rewards that astonished his world. The
King of Spain decorated him with the Order of the Golden
Fleece, a distinction rarely accorded to any but princes. The
King of France raised him to the highest military rank and
endowed him with a large pension. Saint-Simon, who admired him, thought it a scandal that an ex-buccaneer should
wear the Fleece. Less aristocratic critics were unanimous in
declaring that nothing was too good for him.

A symbol of the glory that could be won in the colonies,
Du Casse died peacefully at the age of sixty-nine, "more
broken by his fatigues and his old wounds than by his years,"
as a memoirist of the times romantically puts it.

CHAPTER VIII

Père Dutertre and Père Labat

THE Peace of Ryswick left each belligerent in possession of the colonies it had held at the outset of the war. In addition to Saint Domingue, now formally hers, France owned Martinique, Guadeloupe, St. Christopher, St. Croix, Grenada, Tobago and various dependent islets. She had an unchallenged foothold in St. Lucia and exercised a sort of suzerainty over Carib Dominica. The Dutch had ceased to encroach on Cayenne; about this time, indeed, they signed a special "provisional" treaty which served to fix the Guiana frontier for two centuries.

Of the holdings in the Lesser Antilles, St. Christopher was declining and Grenada just beginning to be of agricultural importance. The plantations of St. Croix had failed, because of droughts, and the colonists were transferred to Saint Domingue during the governorship of Du Casse. No serious attempt to develop Tobago had been made. Martinique and Guadeloupe constituted the center of interest. They had had an early start, had improved on it, and through all the vicissitudes of battle these two islands were to be France's permanent stake in the archipelago.

They were fortunate in not having been settled by outlaws. Their planters were Europeans with a solid ambition to create a larger life for themselves on virgin soil. Curiously, more gentlemen went to Martinique and more peasant farmers to Guadeloupe, so that a distinction was soon noted: *Les Messieurs de la Martinique* and *Les bonnes gens de la Guadeloupe.* Pioneer life in such isolated colonies might well have gone unchronicled, however, if it had not been for two priestly historians whose duties took them there. They were Père Dutertre and Père Labat, the first in the middle of the seventeenth century, and the second at its close. The given name of both was Jean-Baptiste, and both belonged to the Dominican Order. What the general reader gleans from disconnected works that mention the French islands at this period derives in almost every case from Dutertre and Labat. The colorful and discursive histories themselves remain little known in English. It seems pertinent to the writer to consider them briefly here.

Jean-Baptiste Dutertre was born in Calais in 1610. He was an adventurous spirit, eager to explore the wild places of the world, and with this in view he turned to the career of arms. He enlisted on a Dutch ship which made a voyage to Greenland, but that Arctic sub-continent did not have the kind of charm the youth sought. Transferring to the service of France, he saw military action in 1632. Shortly afterward, his religious feeling became intense and he joined the Dominicans. He was sent to the West Indies as a missionary in 1640, when thirty years of age, and except for trips home to report to his superiors he spent sixteen years there. His last assignment was to Grenada at the time of the conquest of that island from the Caribs. The difficulties of founding a mission proved too great and he was recalled to Paris, where he completed his book, the *Histoire Générale des Antilles Habitées par les Français,* published in four volumes and later reissued in two. He died in 1687.

The first half is a meticulous chronicle from the debut of Esnambuc in St. Christopher to and including the regime of the proprietors after Cardinal Mazarin had distributed the holdings in lots. Dutertre quotes documents, reports the sayings of the leading actors and is prodigal of anecdotes. Along broad lines he is a trustworthy historian, but the details

are often inaccurate. The worthy Father was credulous in an
age that loved to dispense wonders. We must admit, however,
that there were only a few authorities—most of them hostile
Spaniards—against whose work he could check his own, and
that he delayed assembling his material until he was forced
to rely largely on memory.

The second half of the *Histoire Générale* is a survey of
manners and customs, agriculture, the flora and fauna of the
islands. In this field, too, Dutertre accepted many superstitions as facts, and for an old soldier he was highly romantic.
The following sample of his attitude is translated from the
chapter entitled, "Of the Savages in General":

"Even as I have shown that the air of the Torrid Zone is the
purest, the most wholesome and the most temperate of all
airs, and that the land is a little Paradise perpetually verdant
and watered by the most lovely streams in the world: so it is
suitable to bring out in this treatise that the savages of these
isles are the most satisfied, the most happy, the least vicious,
the most sociable, the least artificial and the least tormented
by maladies of all the nations on earth. For they are what
Nature has made of them; that is to say, they have a great
simplicity and natural naïveté.

"They are all equal, recognizing almost no sort of superiority or of servitude, and one can scarcely even perceive any
sort of respect, even between relatives, as of the son to the
father. No one is richer and no one is poorer than his companion, and all of them unanimously limit their desires to
what is useful and really necessary to them, while they despise
all that is superfluous as being things unworthy to be possessed. They wear no clothes save those with which Nature
covers them. One observes no sort of police among them. . . .

"They are great dreamers and wear a sad, a melancholy
expression on their faces. They pass half-days on end seated
on a rock, or on a bank, their eyes fixed on the earth, or on
the sea, without uttering a single word. They do not know
what it means to stroll for pleasure, and they laugh loudly
when they see us pass several times from one spot to another

without going anywhere; for they look upon this as one of the greatest follies they have remarked in us. . . . They are by nature benign, soft, affable. They are sympathetic, sometimes, even to the point of tears, over the ills of us French; for they are not cruel, except to their sworn enemies."

The above paragraphs anticipate by a hundred years the conception of the noble savage which appears in the work of Jean Jacques Rousseau. There is also the same idealization of nature. That Dutertre was one of the many sources drawn upon by Rousseau is fairly evident. The dreamer of Geneva could not have guessed the strange falseness of the missionary's view. Père Dutertre's contacts were wholly with Caribs, to whom he ascribed not only the vigorous characteristics which were theirs, but also the kindly virtues of the Arawâks whom they had exterminated in the Lesser Antilles. It is improbable that Dutertre ever saw an Arawâk, even in Saint Domingue, for this gentle people had perished there under the oppression of the Spaniards. But he would have read Las Casas, their fiery champion of the previous century.

The Caribs assuredly were not "benign, soft," though their proud courtesy might have been so interpreted by a sentimentalist. They had cause enough for melancholy. If they wept, it would have been over their own sorrows. The best that can be said is that they did hate the French less than any other of their white conquerors.

Jean-Baptiste Labat was a more earthy, cosmopolitan priest than Dutertre, and a better writer. He was born in Paris, in 1664. The Church was his vocation from the start. He attracted favorable notice as a preaching Dominican, and when he expressed special interest in the New World his Order gave him a mission in Martinique, where he landed in 1693 and rose to be Superior. His thirteen years' service was divided among that island, Guadeloupe and Saint Domingue, with visits to the less important possessions. It was a stirring period. Labat encountered buccaneers fresh from bloody deeds, and he once sailed a few days on a corsair craft. He played more than a clerical part in opposing the enemies of France. He reported in Rome in 1706, and for reasons now obscure he was not allowed to return to the West Indies. Labat then wrote his best-known work, the *Nouveau Voyage aux Iles de l'Amérique*. It had an immediate success, and he followed it with studies, derived from documents, of other French colonies. His death occurred in Paris in 1738.

Shrewdly critical of the historians who had preceded him, Labat asserts in his preface:

"My confrère, Père Dutertre, was the first of our Frenchmen to make known the islands of America. His work was admirable at the time it was written. . . . But, as obviously he did not see everything for himself, he wrote on many matters from the reports of others and was deceived by them. . . .

"The Minister Rochefort, who never saw the islands of America with his own eyes, did not hesitate to write a history which would be tolerable enough, since he copied from Père Dutertre; but he entirely spoiled his narration with descriptions far removed from truth, his idea being to make things seem more agreeable, and the better to conceal his theft."

Labat then promises to record all matters precisely as he "saw, learned or practiced them." Although himself accused of plagiarism and careless handling of material by a modern author, P. Cultru, it may be said that he did extremely well. He produced the one contemporary account the lucid, undated style of which makes it fully as readable as in the year it was published.

He begins with a lively description of the voyage from Europe and an encounter with an English frigate close to his destination. A sharp exchange of cannonballs merely warmed his blood for the adventures in store for him. On landing, he was entertained by both churchmen and the laity, receiving impressions of colonial life which he conveys vividly. He was soon appointed to charge of the parish of Macouba at the northwestern tip of Martinique. His bonhomie and tolerance appear in the relation of one of his early contacts.

"On Thursday, March 4 [1694], I went to pay a visit to our neighbor M. Pinel, captain of filibusters, commander of a corvette of six guns. He had arrived the day before with two English vessels which he had taken to the windward of Barbados, one of twelve guns and the other of eighteen, coming directly from England very richly cargoed.

"He received me with a thousand civilities, and having learned that I had established myself in the parish he said he wished to contribute toward setting up my household, and he presented me with six fine bottles and twelve crystal glasses, as well as two English cheeses. Thus was begun the friendship he had for me right up to his death. I bought other provisions which I needed. . . .

"My intention was to return the next day to my parish, but our Father Superior halted me to take part in a great Mass which M. Pinel's filibusters desired said the next day and at which they would take communion in fulfillment of a vow they had made during their fight with the two English ships. On Friday we were busy all morning confessing the filibusters. We said the Mass of the Virgin with all the solemnity possible; I celebrated it and I blessed three large loaves of bread which were presented by the Captain, accompanied by his officers to the sound of drums and trumpets.

"The corvette and the two prizes, which were moored in front of the church, discharged all their guns at the beginning of the Mass, at the elevation of the Host, at the benediction, and at the end of the *Te Deum* which was sung after the Mass. All the filibusters took part in the offering, each giving a candle with a piece of thirty *sols* or an *écu*. Those who took communion did it with much piety and modesty."

Far from finding their calling reprehensible, Labat was

keenly interested in the technique of capturing merchant-men. He dined aboard the corvette, visited and examined the prizes. It amazed him that Pinel's little boat had dared to attack two that outmatched her in every way. How had it been done? The story he elicited is one of the most zestful accounts of a buccaneering feat that ever found its way into print. Labat sniffs the breeze and slyly conveys the impression that he would have given much to be there as he tells that the larger Englishman was boarded, demoralized by the throwing of grenades with sputtering wicks, carried at the point of the cutlass. The other craft, which had been exchanging shots with the corvette, struck her colors when she saw that her companion had been taken.

There follows a careful statement of the rules framed by the sea-rovers for the division of their plunder, including bonuses to the wounded—600 écus for the loss of a limb; 300 écus for a thumb, the index finger of the right hand, or an eye; 100 écus for any other finger. John Esquemeling, the buccaneer historian, had given similar figures about twenty years before, and it is piquant to note that the French irregulars were paying slightly better indemnities for mutilation than had been paid under Sir Henry Morgan.

When Labat had satisfied his curiosity, he chose some additional supplies for purchase, notably a keg of butter and a box of candles. On trying to pay for them, he was told that the booty had been so large the filibusters could easily make him a gift of these trifles—that it was, indeed, the least they could do to reward him for saying the Mass, and for the place they hoped to have in his prayers.

Such an attitude, such generosity and regard for religion, the Father observes, was not so unusual among filibusters as people in Europe might think.

His treatment of ethnology, social behavior, agriculture and natural history is markedly superior to that of Père

Dutertre. He describes the Caribs realistically, for example, and adds:

"Their physiognomy is melancholic. It is said that they make good folk, but one should take care not to offend them, for they are very vindictive."

The maladies of the tropics received his close attention. He was gullible about the supernatural and not immune to current medical fallacies, yet he open-mindedly picked up direct knowledge from the natives. The ravages of slow fevers appalled him. He caught bubonic plague, locally called the *mal de Siam* because it had been brought on a ship from the Orient, and was of the small minority that recovered. Describing the epidemic, he comments cheerfully: "The good side of this disease was that, when fatal, it carried off people very rapidly; six or seven days at most ended the affair."

His attitude in all situations is realistic, his humor unfailing. On a voyage through the neighboring islands his vessel was captured by Spaniards, and he was about to be put to death. The next moment his assailants were on their knees, for the Father had held before their eyes the cross worn by officers of the Holy Inquistion. "It did not belong to me," he says, "but to one of our brethren who had left it by accident among my effects."

If it were not for Père Labat, we should have a poor idea of the early years of the War of the Spanish Succession, as it affected the French Windward Islands. He chronicles how St. Christopher was overrun by the English in 1702, their final conquest of this island, though it was not the last time that fighting was to occur there. He portrays in detail the successful defense of Guadeloupe by Governor Auger, under whom he served as chief lieutenant without the title. He had mounted a cannon on a tower he had started to build near his church, and this proved so effective against warships pressing inshore that he was asked to fight a battery at the point of greatest peril in Basse-Terre.

The first assault of the English under Codrington with forty-five sail was repulsed. They landed troops up the coast and menaced the town so seriously by land and sea that the fort had to be abandoned. Labat retired with the bulk of the soldiery and helped Auger to keep the fires of resistance burning until help came from Martinique. The enemy was then attacked and driven out of Guadeloupe, which they had partially occupied for fifty-six days.

Labat draws a fascinating portrait of Auger, who had been born in St. Christopher and was the first Creole to become a Governor. The great Poincy had sent him to Malta to learn the *métier* of war among the knights there, and on his return he married into the noble family of D'Angennes Maintenon. His father-in-law was all-powerful in Martinique at the end of the century, which of course was the chief factor in getting him his appointment. But after the defense of Guadeloupe, he was promoted on his own merits to be Governor of Saint Domingue. A man of action, "he was slow at writing, and did not write any the better for that," remarks Labat, whose memoirs abound with thrusts of the sort. The Father is equally candid in gossiping that Auger was without the striking presence that befitted his deeds, "but his only son was the handsomest Creole that ever came out of the islands, and that is saying a lot."

The *Nouveau Voyage* could be quoted indefinitely. It is an example of the way in which the French spirit drew richly from a tropical background and created a cultural form acceptable to the inhabitants of all colors. Père Labat is still read in the French West Indies, and nowhere more than in Martinique where he lived longest.

CHAPTER IX

On the Gulf Coast

THE spread of the French to the coastal region of North America between the Mississippi River and Florida was an impulse that originated in their older settlements in Canada. Control of the continental prairie, above all of its superb waterways, had become a dream of the colonial lords of Quebec. But Louis XIV did not care to spend money on the enterprise as a whole. He was willing to back only the idea of a colony on the warm sea, and in this he was influenced by the mounting tide of profits from Martinique, Guadeloupe and Saint Domingue.

René Robert Cavelier, Sieur de la Salle, driven by genius that had an epic touch, came down from the Great Lakes and followed the Father of Waters in birchbark canoes until he emerged into the Gulf of Mexico in April, 1682. It was a rediscovery of the Mississippi, for after De Soto had died there more than a century before, the Spaniards had neglected and virtually forgotten it. La Salle went to France and persuaded the King to give him ships and supplies and appoint him Governor of the province where he planned to found a port. The disastrous finale was in no sense the fault of La Salle. He was ruined by the bungling of his associates and died at the hands of treacherous followers.

After the Peace of Ryswick, the King's interest in the Mississippi revived. Pontchartrain, Minister of Marine, had learned that the English were recruiting Huguenot exiles for the purpose of planting a colony at the mouth of the river. He and Louis decided that it was important for France to get

there first. The man entrusted with the task was Pierre le
Moyne, Sieur d'Iberville, and the one destined to carry it
out was his younger brother and aide Jean-Baptiste le Moyne,
Sieur de Bienville. They were Canadian born, both still in
their twenties, but already heroes of savage fighting against
the English in Hudson Bay. Visiting France together, they
were called to the attention of the Roi Soleil. The aging monarch appeared to be stimulated by their fresh buoyancy. His
gambles on men had not always been happy, but this time
he judged aright.

The Iberville expedition was assembled at Brest. It sailed
by way of the West Indies, stopping over in Saint Domingue
for a month. In January, 1699, it was cruising off the Gulf
Coast, guided by none other than Laurens de Graff, who had
taken his cue from Du Casse and quit buccaneering after
the Cartagena affair. A call was made at Pensacola, the
farthest point west garrisoned by the Spaniards of Florida.
The dispute over the sovereignty of the coast which threatened to develop from the haughty words of Don Andrés de la
Riola, the Spanish commander, became a comedy when it was
discovered that his men were mostly half-starved convicts
assigned from the galleys to this lonely post.

The French explored to the Mississippi and upstream to
beyond the site of Baton Rouge. It was then decided to build
a fort at Biloxi, where Iberville left most of his company and
his brother, Bienville, and himself returned to France for
re-enforcements. Pontchartrain, delighted with what he
heard, gave the Canadian ample support. But the written
instructions prepared by the Minister glowed with romantic
conceptions, striking a note which was to be the curse of
Louisiana for a quarter of a century. Gone was the rational
idea that it could become a sister colony of Saint Domingue,
that its source of wealth was agricultural. It was now seen as a
Golconda.

"The grand affair is the discovery of mines," wrote Pontchartrain. Travelers had told him that there were marvelous pearl beds in the Gulf, and Iberville was strictly enjoined to work them. Rural pursuits were not ignored. It was suggested that a unique local breed of wild cattle (probably the bison) could be domesticated for the sake of its wool! Also, that silk worms might be cultivated, as that would be a very suitable light occupation for the Indian women and children. What Iberville thought, he who had sloshed through the bayous and experienced the humid climate, has not been recorded.

In Biloxi six months later, he was disappointed that the settlement had only marked time. But Bienville had performed prodigies in the way of familiarizing himself with a huge territory, making friends with the Indians, and even turning back a shipload of English interlopers. This last had been an episode of vital historical import. Descending the Mississippi in a canoe, Bienville had come upon a vessel lying in midstream. He had asked to be taken aboard, where he immediately recognized the skipper as one Banks who had been captured by Iberville in the Hudson Bay fighting. Banks declared that he had brought the advance guard of a colonizing venture. The twenty-year-old youth calmly replied that France had already occupied the country. He was deputy for his brother as Governor, he said, and he had a large armed force near by which he would use to expel the strangers if they did not leave quietly. The bluff succeeded. The bend in the river where the ship swung around is still called English Turn.

Bienville simply had been born to take over the responsibilities of the peculiar problem in hand. His aptitudes were extraordinary. He could lead men three times his age and make an enemy regard him as a seasoned chief. His phenomenal ability to master native dialects in a few weeks enabled

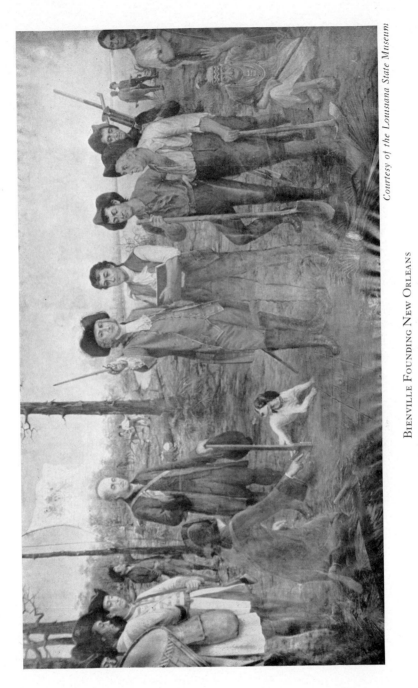

BIENVILLE FOUNDING NEW ORLEANS

From the Painting by Alexander Alaux in the Cabildo, New Orleans

him to baffle the aborigines by treating with them directly when they had supposed that he could be tricked by an interpreter. He was second only to La Salle in his intuitive comprehension of Indian psychology. Grace King, one of his biographers, says that he was "gentle and reserved in disposition, but he had a firm will and a courage that could not be quelled. . . . The Canadians were ever devoted to him and would follow him through any danger. The Indians of Louisiana learned to love and respect him. They called him 'Father.' "

Despite his admirable gifts, Iberville was not so well suited to the country. His temperament was northern. The climate did not agree with him. He wisely gave his brother more and more leeway, and when he again set sail for France in 1702 it was, unintentionally, a complete withdrawal from the picture. Assigned to temporary naval service in the West Indies, he operated against the English with considerable success and then succumbed to yellow fever in Havana.

Meanwhile, Bienville had built a fort at the head of Mobile Bay, and the town which sprang up there became the capital of the colony of Louisiana. He also established warehouses and a landing station for immigrants on Massacre Island, later called Dauphin Island, at the entrance of the bay. He was extremely conscious of the fact that the chief settlement should be on the Mississippi River, that a port to serve as outlet for the illimitable valley beyond was foreordained. But early attempts to find a spot safe from floods on the lower reaches had not been successful. A stockade built by Iberville had to be abandoned. Bienville made a new survey, and with unfailing judgment he chose the site of New Orleans. He was hampered by the indifference of his superiors in France, who withheld the equipment he needed and insisted that Mobile was town enough. The postponement became a matter of years.

The War of the Spanish Succession had repercussions in this distant theater. English pioneers in the Carolinas sent scouting parties to harry the French outposts. The dangerous practice of arming Indians as auxiliaries was followed by both sides. In this forest skirmishing along an undefined border, Bienville enjoyed an advantage because he was much more astute than his foe in enlisting Indians. There was an actual peril in too great intimacy with the savages. Shortage of European food and the failure of crops caused Bienville, several years in succession, to quarter parties of his young men with friendly tribes. He complained that they took native concubines, enjoyed the dancing and hunting so well that when the call to duty came they would desert to the woods.

Immigration from France was slow and not sufficiently varied. The records of the first ten years show a mere handful of artisans, a single physician and desperately few women. The arrival of twenty-three girls on one boat created a furore. It was to be a long time before that many prospective wives were seen again in the colony. We find Bienville writing about them sarcastically:

"The males in the colony begin, through habit, to be reconciled to maize as an article of nourishment; but the females, who are mostly Parisians, have for this kind of food a dogged aversion which has not yet been subdued."

In 1712, Louis XIV resorted to an outworn device. To be rid of the expense of maintaining during its infancy the imperial domain that La Salle and the Le Moynes had won for him, the King farmed it out as a commercial speculation to the Sieur Antoine de Crozat. Albert Phelps, the author of *Louisiana,* writes:

"The King granted to Crozat the exclusive right of trade

for fifteen years free of duty, throughout all the territory lying between the Illinois and the Gulf and extending from the English colonies westward to the Spanish colonies. Whatever mines might lie within these vague limits were granted in perpetuity, subject to forfeiture if abandoned. Whatever land might be reclaimed and cultivated and whatever manufactures might be established were also granted upon the same terms. Crozat was also given the exclusive right to trade in all hides and furs except beaver-skins—Canada being thus protected; and all other persons caught trading without the proprietor's orders were to be subject to confiscation. He was furthermore allowed the privilege of sending one ship annually to the Guinea coast for Negro slaves to cultivate his land or to be sold to the colonists.

"On his part, Crozat bound himself to send each year two shiploads of settlers, and after nine years was to bear all the expenses of the colony including the pay of officers and garrisons, but until that time the King agreed to contribute 50,000 livres a year. The laws, edicts and ordinances of France and the custom of Paris were to serve as the laws of Louisiana, and the executive function was entrusted to a council appointed by the King from Crozat's nomination. Two of Crozat's accredited agents were to represent his interests in this body."

Thus was outlined for the first time the vast estate eventually transferred to the United States as the Louisiana Purchase. The terms granted Crozat were typical of the economic short cuts in which the age believed, the mirages at which concessionnaires grasped. That those on the spot, those who had built as free Frenchmen in the King's name, had rights which should have been inviolable was a question which disturbed no consciences. Bienville himself, without whom there would have been no colony, was deposed as Governor and succeeded by La Mothe Cadillac, with a full set of new officials. He asked to be given a naval assignment, but Pontchartrain ordered him to remain.

A trickle of new settlers arrived. The influx of goods was

relatively much greater, for Crozat sent out chartered ships and filled his warehouses. Prosperity did not result. The monopolist had but one crude idea. He would set low prices for the products of the country, which at that time consisted mainly of furs, and force the consumption of his expensive merchandise. He expected to become immensely rich thereby. The people on the coast, however, were poor subjects for exploitation since they had no money, and the individualistic *coureurs des bois* refused to have anything to do with Crozat's agents. These hunters had gained their experience in Canada. They cut through the woods and sold their peltries to English traders in the Carolinas. The cheap manufactured articles got from the same illicit source they bartered with the Indians and did very well at it. The only authority they were willing to recognize was that of Bienville.

So the council, realistic for once, appointed Bienville to take command on the Mississippi. He was required to found a post among the Natchez people, with whom he had had good relations in the past. But he was met sullenly. Governor Cadillac had offended them by flouting their ceremonial forms in intercourse with strangers. They were taking revenge by ambushing white stragglers, robbing some and killing others. Though he had only thirty-five armed men with him, Bienville accepted the necessity of punishing the Natchez and carried out his plan with a cold—it has been called a treacherous—ingenuity which the red men were the first to praise, so Indian was the ruse.

Convincing them that he would not "smoke the pipe of peace" with any but their most prominent men and that the latter's interests demanded that they come to his camp, he made an opportunity to kidnap the Chief, whose title was "Great Sun," two of Sun's brothers and five other leaders of the tribe. His royal hostages had a semi-divine status, and by threatening to put them to death in a degrading manner

Bienville obtained the heads of the warriors responsible for the murdering of Frenchmen. He also compelled the braves to supply lumber, with which the French built Fort Rosalie on the river bluff, the spot chosen being the one that most fully dominated the Natchez villages. This triumph was, in a small way, a leaf taken from the book of Cortés in his dealings with Montezuma.

On reporting back to Mobile, Bienville found that he was again acting Governor of the colony, La Mothe Cadillac having been recalled. Five months later De l'Epinay arrived to supplant him, bringing fifty immigrants and three companies of soldiers. Although Bienville received at this time a decoration and the outright grant of Horn Island, one of the sandy chain running westward from Mobile Bay, he properly felt mistreated. Louisiana was being strangled by the restrictions on trade. A plantation could not be made profitable under those conditions, and he would have been satisfied with nothing less than the holding of office so that he could combat the follies of the regime. He thought seriously of returning to France as a private citizen.

But the strain was heaviest on the concessionnaire who had gambled large sums and failed to show a profit. In 1717, with two-thirds of his fifteen years still to go, Crozat petitioned to be freed from the bargain. The Crown resumed possession— briefly. Phantasmagoria was in the offing. For the ear of the Duc d'Orleans, regent for the infant Louis XV, had been reached by one of the wildest promoters in history, the Scotchman John Law.

CHAPTER X

The Mississippi Bubble

FRENCH finances were in a state of chaos when Louis XIV died in 1715. The resplendent monarch had wasted the country's wealth on extravagances such as the Palace of Versailles, on his personal vices, and in the waging of wars which toward the end of his reign had not turned out fortunately. He had left a public debt estimated at between two and a half billion and three billion livres, the livre being an old monetary unit of substantially the same value as the franc. His successor in power, the Regent Orleans, was a confirmed debauchee and a lazy administrator, but not devoid of intelligence. He tried to avert the menace of bankruptcy by arbitrarily scaling down the debt and issuing bonds to guarantee payment of the balance. The correct term for these government obligations was *titres de créance,* but they came to be known as *billets d'état* and were the forerunners of legal paper money. They fell at the beginning to a ruinous discount of seventy per cent, and if it had not been for John Law of Lauriston their complete deflation might have caused a revolt.

This amazing trickster, charlatan, gambler—call him what you will—was the son of an Edinburgh goldsmith. His father's business had been his introduction to finance, for in the seventeenth century the goldsmiths of a community were its moneylenders and to a large extent its bankers. John Law squandered his patrimony, killed a well-known man in a duel in London, and to escape being hanged fled to the Continent. He made his living at cards, but as the author of a couple of specious pamphlets on economics and money he impressed even his victims and was called to the attention of persons in high places.

Law suggested to Orleans the formation of a state bank. The idea was thought too radical, but the Scotchman was allowed to establish an ordinary bank with a capital stock of 6,000,000 livres, divided into shares of 5,000 livres each. Investors could make seventy-five per cent of the payments for their shares in the depreciated *billets d'état,* and the bank issued paper money which was to be redeemable in coin. It confined its operations to legitimate banking business and was a success. In less than a year its paper rose to a premium. Cheap money had been created, and there was a sudden if limited business boom. Orleans was so impressed that he made Law's bank the chief depository of government funds and accepted its notes for the payment of taxes.

At this juncture Crozat got permission to abandon his Louisiana concession. Law grasped at the opportunity to take his place, seeing in the mysterious but reputedly golden colony a basis for the gigantic speculation of his dreams. He talked Orleans into letting him form a company similar to those which had failed under Mazarin and Colbert in the West Indies. While controlling Louisiana upon practically the same terms as those granted to Crozat, Law promised that he would rid France of her entire outstanding debt.

The Company's shares of 100,000,000 livres would be purchasable only in *billets d'état.* Who could doubt that the holders of *billets* would rush to invest them? The Government would no longer have to worry about a horde of discontented citizens. Law's bank and Law's company would be the sole creditors. By exploiting Louisiana, particularly its mines and pearls, the wonder-worker guaranteed to produce tangible wealth in a flood that would enrich the kingdom, enable it to redeem the debt without turning a hair, and make everybody happy.

The corporation established in September, 1717, bore various grandiloquent names as its scope expanded, but is generally known as the Mississippi Company. It undertook to place 6,000 white settlers in Louisiana and 3,000 Negro slaves, and it obtained the right to give lands to colonists free of feudal obligation and exempt from taxation for twenty-five years. Law, of course, became chairman of the board of directors. He designed a coat-of-arms for the Company: a natural river couchant on a field of green and silver, leaning on a golden horn of plenty, the upper part of azure sown with golden fleur-de-lys, with a device also in gold, supported by two savages and a trefoil crown. It looked well on the prospectuses he issued at short intervals.

Law soon imposed his favorite scheme upon the Regent, the circulating of paper money in an unlimited quantity and unguaranteed. If he believed any of his theories of finance, it was this mad one. He seemed convinced—and he is not the only financier in history to have been so—that if a medium of exchange were made abundant, prosperity would result, merely because people would be stimulated into buying and selling. His bank was advanced to the status of a national institution and called the Royal Bank. It printed notes with a face value of three billion livres. The Government used these notes to pay its bills, and sheaves of them were handed to the Regent and his cronies to spend on their pleasures.

Meanwhile, the great gambler understood perfectly that he must make an impressive showing in Louisiana. The capital stock of the exploiting company had been sold with éclat; to meet the demand, additional shares had been issued, and no one complained that this would reduce the profits of the original subscribers. The horn of plenty portrayed on the coat-of-arms was held to be inexhaustible. Estates had been assigned to the chief investors. Law himself had taken three, a vast one at the junction of the Arkansas and Mississippi Rivers, a second at English Turn, and the last near Biloxi. But is was necessary that proprietors who figured in so lordly a fashion on the map should do something about settling the land. Partly to encourage them, and partly to whip all France into a mood of enthusiasm, Law sponsored an advertising campaign so florid, so persuasive and impudent, that any of those that have been waged in modern times could profitably have studied it for ideas.

An incredible number of pamphlets and broadsides for the literate, of prints to appeal to hoi-polloi, were distributed in every corner of the country. They were prepared by clever hirelings, but all bore the stamp of Law's hypnotic fancy. Louisiana was described as an earthly paradise where the crops reproduced tenfold, an Ophir rich in mines of gold, silver, copper and lead. A precious rock from which the Indians dug green stones of extreme brilliancy that resembled emeralds was declared to be plentiful there. The non-existent pearl fisheries were endlessly publicized. Brazenly, one pamphlet told of 10,000 Natchez women already at work in a factory weaving silk.

The prints outdid anything that could be said in words. They showed luxuriant landscapes in the midst of which Indians with classic figures knelt at the feet of condescending Europeans, offering golden nuggets, or fruits, or game. The physical charms of aboriginal maidens received full attention. Mass conversions to Christianity of the savages was the favored theme of pictures intended to edify the religious-minded.

It always has been hard to induce Frenchmen to leave their fatherland and become colonists. In this case, there were seigneurs with lands on the Mississippi to round up their dependants and more or less force them to go. There was also the contagion of Law's publicity. A ship left with a few men as early as two months after the company was founded, and the following May 300 emigrants sailed. Then the recruiting lagged. The promoter had recourse to his patron Orleans. Edicts by the Government authorized the transporting of convicts, vagrants, beggars, notorious libertines and infidels, the incorrigible sons of the well-to-do. A boatload of female prisoners was commandeered as future brides! These were mostly murderesses, prostitutes and thieves. Against its will, a human tide was set in motion toward the West.

As seen from Louisiana, the new regime was promising. No fool in many respects, Law had inquired who was the man with the best understanding of the region, the finest qualities of leadership. There was only one possible candidate, the Sieur de Bienville, who had promptly been appointed Governor-General for the Company. Furthermore, he had been given the permission long sought to build a port near the mouth of the Mississippi. Many of the restrictions on the freedom of trade were removed. These decisions heartened the old-timers.

Bienville made arrangements that Dauphin Island off Mobile Bay should be the clearing house for green colonists, little dreaming with what lack of common sense they would be dumped upon him. He then hastened to the Father of Waters, and at the crescent-shaped bend he knew to be the right spot he laid out a city and set fifty men to clearing the site in February, 1718. He called it New Orleans in honor of the Regent. Shortly afterward, Biloxi again became the seat of government, the change from Mobile having been engineered over the protests of Bienville. Yet he thought Mobile far from ideal. He was determined that New Orleans must be the capital of the province. He proposed this at once, but was blocked by a majority of the council of administration with which he had been saddled.

Only a few log cabins had been built on the swampy margin of the Mississippi when the first large group of colonists, the 300, reached Dauphin Island. Bienville sent orders that they should be distributed in three lots, the largest of which was sent to Fort Rosalie in the Natchez country, the second to the Yazoos, and sixty-eight arbitrarily assigned to New Orleans. The group last mentioned constituted the first citizens of the young metropolis. The names of heads of families have been preserved, and mentioned anonymously are a surgeon, a hairdresser, a mason and their assistants.

After that, the ships arrived in rapid succession. The Company was acquiring a fleet. Before the end, it had 165 transports, frigates and sloops of war. In those early days, the motley assemblage of passengers was simply put ashore at Dauphin Island and forgotten by the skippers, who turned about and went back to France for more. "Crowded, unsheltered and unfed, upon that barren sand-heap, the wretched emigrants sickened, grew discontented, starved and died," says Phelps. "Yet there they had to wait until Bienville with his few boats and small force of efficient men could parcel them out about the country. . . . Faster than he could dispose of this mass of confusion, the infatuated enthusiasm in France continued to unload upon him and Louisiana."

Le Page du Pratz, an intellectual of means who wrote the first history of Louisiana, came in a contingent of 800 in three vessels in August, 1718. His personal story is a salutary corrective to the note of disaster sounded by official reports and the letters written home by incompetent settlers. No colony could ever have succeeded if things had been as bad as the pessimists made out. A generation after the stormy beginnings, however—in Martinique, in Saint Domingue, in Quebec, in Louisiana—one finds rich estates, a proof that the pioneer fathers had solved their problems well. Le Page du Pratz was not unique, except as to his urbanity and literary gifts.

He had known Bienville in France, and he confesses drolly that Law's propaganda in the *Mercure,* a journal, had bedazzled him. He had read that New Orleans was already a flourishing city, surrounded by gardens. He sailed from Rochelle and debarked at Dauphin Island after a five months' voyage. Supposed to remain at the landing station a maximum of four days, he and his fellows were kept there four months, lodged in flimsy thatch huts. He draws a lamentable picture of the island and tells of finding on the beach the scattered bones of recent comers who had died of hardships and had not even been given burial.

At last he set sail in a small chartered boat, accompanied by some half-dozen servants and abundant baggage. He explored the coast, penetrating to New Orleans by way of Lake Pontchartrain and the Bayou St. John. On the shore of the last-named, he built a palmetto-covered house and laid out a farm. He planted peach stones, which "immediately began to sprout and by autumn had made trees four feet high with branches in proportion," a profuse result, to say the least. He was a bit disillusioned by New Orleans, which then had fewer than a hundred inhabitants, but he took an active part in its affairs, helping to construct a levee to hold back the Mississippi floods. He had bought an Indian slave girl to whom he became intimately attached, and also "several strong black fellows" to work his lands.

Hearing glowing accounts of the Natchez country up the river, he resolved to move there, a decision which charmed his Indian girl since it was her home territory. His first plantation was destroyed in the warfare that soon occurred between the French and the Natchez, but he escaped with his life and obtained more land, which he planted to indigo, tobacco, sugar cane and mulberries. "At his most prosperous time," writes Lyle Saxon in *Old Louisiana,* "Le Page du Pratz had a comfortable house, several hundred acres under cultivation and more than fifty slaves."

Such pioneers as he caused Bienville no difficulties. Law himself, as Georges Oudard points out, was eager "to have only fine people as colonists"; he sent out sturdy German and Alsatian peasants to cultivate his holdings, and the descendants of these still make good farmers in Louisiana. But the right sort of emigrants could not be recruited by the thousands. The Company resorted to hiring pressgang agents in Paris, who won the evil nickname of "the Mississippi bandits." They laid hands on anyone they could catch in the streets at night, including the sons and daughters of respectable tradesmen. If made worth their while, they would go to some trouble to kidnap persons whose enemies wanted to be rid of them. The victims were rushed aboard ship and sent to Dauphin Island.

The first five months of 1720 saw the climax, decline and fall of John Law's career. In January, his Mississippi Bubble had swollen, financially speaking, to unheard-of proportions. Speculators fought for the shares. After a dividend of forty per cent had been declared—and paid from the cash furnished by new subscribers—shares of 500 livres value rose to 18,000. They changed hands several times a day, and each time the gamblers paid a better price for them. The Rue Quincampoix, a short, narrow thoroughfare where the Mississippi Company had its offices, became a stock exchange. The cost of renting buildings there increased more than a hundredfold. As the month ended, the Regent appointed Law Controller-General of the whole finances of France.

In February, the Scotchman took charge of the mint. He absorbed the state-subsidized company which traded with the Orient, thus rounding out his system. That spring, "everything was concentrated in his hands. He seemed the real King of France, gorged with fictitious riches," says Oudard. Simultaneously, the reaction began.

Persons with some modicum of caution decided that it would now be prudent to realize on their gains. They threw their stock on the market. They demanded funds from the Royal Bank in specie. Law used his immense powers to force the Government not only to demonetize specie, but to proclaim that no individual could hold more than 500 livres in either gold or silver coin under penalty of confiscation. A frightful inflation of the paper money resulted. Through March and April, the prices of commodities fluctuated wildly. Public confidence in Law evaporated. There was a run on the bank. Men swarmed in the Rue Quincampoix, determined to get their funds even in the form of bushel baskets of paper. Scores lost their lives, trampled under the feet of their fellows or crushed by carriage wheels. During the course of a riot that spread through the city, an attempt was made to murder Law. Early in May, the bank suspended all payments.

Orleans tried to save his magician by appointing him to an office with high-sounding titles, which would in effect have made him the national receiver. But this was totally unpalatable to France. Law's every appearance in public was the signal for savage demonstrations. He was forced to flee the country, practically destitute. All that he possessed was confiscated. "Though subject to the errors of his time, he undoubtedly was a financial genius," states a well-known authority. Another, and the more usual, verdict is as follows: "He was a gambler, and a gambler only. He merely put into the pockets of some persons that which he had taken out of the pockets of others."

He must be credited, nevertheless, with having given Louisiana the impetus it needed to become a successful colony. When he took over in 1717, according to Oudard, there were only 400 permanent white inhabitants. Three years later, through his efforts, 7,500 persons had been sent out. A third of these are supposed either to have perished or gone back to France. The remaining 5,000, riffraff though most of them may have been, formed a respectably large community with interlocking interests. They built on the base the pioneers had founded, whereas if they had not come at the time they did, the pioneers might well have been vanquished by the problems of their vast, sprawling territory.

The bursting of the Mississippi Bubble by no means meant the dissolution of the Mississippi Company. The latter sent out agents who reported candidly on what was needed. It began the regular importation of Negro slaves. Unfortunately, it also sought to re-establish a monopoly of all imports and exports. In May, 1722, the Company authorized Bienville to remove the seat of government to New Orleans. It permitted him to heal an old religious quarrel by giving the Capuchins the exclusive right to conduct missions south of Natchez, while the Jesuits were allotted the central and upper region with headquarters among the Illinois people.

Louisiana's progress for the next twenty years was largely dependent on the genius of Bienville. Unjust complaints caused him to be summoned to France in 1725 for an inquiry. One of his last acts before sailing was to sign a *code noir* closely modeled on the one in force in the French West Indies. During his absence an inept successor allowed conditions to develop that culminated in a massacre by the Natchez Indians. The series of frontier wars that followed were so charged with venom that even Bienville could not stamp them out when he returned a few years later. He came as the first Governor under a new royal regime, for the Company had surrendered its grant. Apart from holding the red men in check, he concentrated on improving the administration, agriculture and commerce of the country. In 1743, wearied out, he relinquished the office.

The names of Du Casse of Saint Domingue and Bienville of Louisiana must be written side by side on the roll of builders of French colonial power in the warm lands of America. These were the two great men of their period. Equal in dynamism, Du Casse was the more brilliant military commander and Bienville the abler executive.

Chapter XI

Battledore and Shuttlecock

THE eighteenth century for the French in the West Indies, up to the outbreak of the Revolution in 1789, was marked by friendship with Spain, increasing rivalry with England, and the phenomenal prosperity of her sugar colonies. The broad historical pattern is simple, the details extremely complicated. Spain had ceased to be an enemy partly because of the success of Louis XIV in confirming a Bourbon, his grandson, as King in Madrid, and partly because of the decadence of Spanish military power. A few disputes between the two countries did occur, but they were quickly patched up. It was to the interest of France to support Spain, upon whom England warred seven times in the eighteenth century. The struggle for mastery of the Caribbean became primarily one between France and England. Few great naval battles were fought, but there was an almost incessant harrying of each other's possessions. Saint Domingue and Jamaica never changed hands, but lesser islands were batted about like shuttlecocks. Both sides were greedy for sugar land, and no speck of it was too small to snatch.

It would take a volume fully to discuss any one phase of this spectacular period. A running account covering all the phases would become arid, if rigidly condensed. The best approach is to give separate chapters to the headings of first importance, and to range over the century in each of these chapters. Let us begin with the competition for the Antillean chain between Puerto Rico and Trinidad.

The War of the Spanish Succession ended in 1713 with the signing of the Treaty of Utrecht. The French ceded their part of St. Christopher to England, but did not suffer any other territorial loss in the region. They had ceased to make effective use of St. Croix, which nominally reverted to the Knights of Malta. In 1733 it was sold to Denmark, already the owner of near-by St. Thomas and St. John. The case of Tobago was more curious. France had made good her claim in the preceding century over England, Holland and the Duchy of Courland. But she had never seriously exploited the place. It was too far south to be easily guarded by her Windward Islands fleet, and it was populated by hostile Caribs. Louis XIV, in a generous mood, restored it to the Duke of Courland, who sought to operate it through a company of London merchants. This made Tobago practically English, a status which France declined to acknowledge.

St. Lucia was disputed verbally throughout the reign of the Roi Soleil, with neither country anxious to come to grips with the Caribs there. In 1718, the Regent Orleans granted the island to the Marshal d'Estrées, who sent out an expedition. England filed an angry protest, and as a new struggle with her was not wanted the colonizing effort faltered. Four years later, George I calmly took a step identical with the one his government had resented. He granted St. Lucia to the Duke of Montague, who also dispatched a quota of settlers. One of those little wars, undeclared and indecisive, with which Caribbean history is dotted, now enlivened the drama. A force was sent from Martinique. After an appropriate amount of bloodshed, both nations agreed that they would evacuate the island and that their nationals would visit it only for the purpose of obtaining wood and water until some definite solution should be found.

In this period occurred the raids of Jacques Cassard, the most celebrated French corsair of the days of piracy which succeeded buccaneering. Merchants of Marseilles provided him with a fleet of eight large and thirty small vessels. He first appeared at Surinam, or Dutch Guiana, where he burned, plundered and carried off slaves. One of his deeds is said to have been the violating of a Jewish synagogue, where he considered it a huge joke to butcher a pig and sprinkle its blood over the walls and sacred ornaments. The people of the province bought him off for $250,000, paid in slaves, cattle, sugar, merchandise and jewelry.

Cassard passed on to St. Eustatius in the Lesser Antilles, which he seized and ransomed. He swung south to Curaçao and took that supposedly impregnable free port by means of a clever ruse. The Dutch felt he had conceded bargain rates when he let them ransom it unharmed for 600,000 *louis d'ors*.

He was compelled at last to return to Europe, virtually a prisoner guarded by a French fleet. A hostile squadron was encountered in the Atlantic, and although the French admiral declined combat Cassard broke from the line and fought alone, saying his duty to his King was above his duty to the admiral and that he would destroy the King's foes wherever he met them. He succeeded in capturing two small craft and taking them to Brest. Cassard is known as the "Hero of Nantes," his native town, where there is a statue to him today.

The next great conflict was the war between England and Spain, launched in 1739 by Sir Robert Walpole, under pressure from the English Parliament, over fairly frivolous charges that British sailors were being maltreated in the Caribbean. France's alliance with Spain involved her before long. She sent two squadrons. Her share of the fighting was naval and not very energetic. No help was given when Admiral Vernon reduced Porto Bello, or during the furious, unsuccessful attack on Cartagena by the same commander. But in Europe the war merged with that of the Austrian Succession. France, heavily engaged on several fronts, was victorious only at the

Battle of Fontenoy and in Savoy. She was glad to make the Peace of Aix-la-Chapelle in 1748.

A most interesting compromise on the Lesser Antilles was reached in the new treaty. It was solemnly covenanted that Dominica, St. Lucia, St. Vincent and Tobago should be left to the Caribs forever. These four were termed neutral islands. It was not a question of recognizing aboriginal governments; indeed, none existed. France and England simply promised that they would make no further attempts to colonize there. Humanitarians and ethnologists must regret that this just agreement was none too sincerely meant. The Caribs were worth saving, if only for their passionate attachment to liberty, and a breathing spell which would have tided them over into a more merciful age was the way to accomplish it.

Unfortunately, Dominica's situation between Martinique and Guadeloupe, from each of which it is distant about thirty miles, made it irresistibly tempting to the French. How could they ignore an island which had all the natural attractions of their two flourishing colonies, and which would seriously menace them if taken by an enemy? Planters began to infiltrate shortly after 1748, and in the next war this was used by the English as an excuse for throwing the neutrality pact overboard.

John G. Coulter, in *The Story of Modern France*, declares with admirable conciseness and truth:

"The Seven Years' War, 1756 to 1763, was as nearly a world war as could be managed in those days. France fought England in India, in America, on the sea, and in Germany. With Austria, Russia, and Saxony, she fought Frederick the Great. The winners were England and Frederick; the principal loser was France. The Seven Years' War revealed the weakness of her government and quickened the trend toward revolution."

It began informally in America two years before 1756. England had decided to cripple, if possible to destroy, the colonial empire of France, which at that juncture was larger than hers. The first attacks were on Fort Duquesne, now Pittsburgh, and were repulsed by the French. Then Louis XV's government went to the support of Maria-Theresa of Austria against Frederick the Great. Nation after nation became involved, and the Seven Years' War was on. Its repercussions in the West Indies are what concern us here.

France was not able to spare an effective fleet for those waters, which England swept with powerful squadrons. Guadeloupe was seized in 1759, in unusual circumstances. The Sieur, later the Marquis, de Beauharnais, whose son was to be the first husband of the Empress Josephine, was Governor of both Martinique and Guadeloupe, with his headquarters in the former island. His anxiety to engineer and then to attend the marriage of his mistress, who was Josephine's aunt, took his mind off the strengthening of the Guadeloupe defenses. The English appeared and won a fairly easy victory. This occasioned the recall of Beauharnais. His successor fortified Martinique, and it was not molested for the moment.

Instead, Dominica was occupied on the grounds that it was no longer neutral, but an unofficial French colony. This claim could be justified. It was followed, after a brief delay, by the conquering of St. Lucia, St. Vincent and Tobago, where the Caribs had been undisturbed since 1748. The English did not trouble to find an excuse for the new aggressions. Immediate strategic advantages and virgin tropical estates were the factors that counted.

The business of suppressing the French establishments in the Lesser Antilles was completed in 1762, when Martinique, Grenada and various islets were taken. Prominent in most of these actions was a young admiral, George Brydges Rodney, who twenty years afterward was to play a great and decisive role.

The English had a project for the overrunning of Saint Domingue, but did not proceed with it. They had already assured their triumph on the heights of Quebec and the plains of India. Peace was approaching. The future colonial set-up could be dictated. Yet the Treaty of Paris signed in 1763, while giving all of Canada, the whole Ohio valley and all of French Hindustan except five towns to England, made only minor readjustments in the Caribbean. Martinique and Guadeloupe were restored to France; she was awarded the "neutral" island of St. Lucia. Ironically, Guadeloupe was in a more prosperous state than when it had been lost. The Abbé Raynal says that the invaders had repaired all the damage caused by military operations, had imported agricultural tools and seedlings on a lavish scale, as if they had expected their tenure to be permanent.

England annexed Grenada, Dominica, St. Vincent and Tobago; she ignored opulent Saint Domingue. At the same time, she exchanged Cuba, which she had wrested from Spain, for Florida, where there had been no fighting. To console the Iberian monarchy, France turned over to it Louisiana and all the territory she had claimed west of the Mississippi.

The surprising West Indian settlement was due to the English sugar monopoly which desired new plantation land, but suddenly realized that it did not want the competition of established sugar colonies where foreign-born proprietors could hardly be dispossessed wholesale. If Saint Domingue, Martinique and Guadeloupe had been annexed, the sure result would have been to drive down the price of sugar on the London market. Dominica and the other little islands won, however, could be developed slowly.

The settlement was thought to be lasting. The creaking cordage of merchantmen in every port replaced the thunder of the guns. No one guessed that fifteen years later the American Revolution would set England and France at each other's throats again, and that the conflict in the Caribbean would flame to a fiercer intensity than had been the case in the Seven Years' War.

Sympathetic with the thirteen colonies from the start, France allowed their privateers to use her West Indian ports, especially those in Martinique and Guadeloupe. In 1778, the Treaty of Amity and Commerce was signed with the revolutionists, and France opened hostilities against her traditional foe, Albion.

Naval conditions were now radically different, and the change was to the advantage of France. She was not fighting a coalition in Europe and was able to send formidable units to the New World. England, also, was strong at sea, but in the North Atlantic the American privateers harried her sorely, and she was drifting into a separate war with Holland over the issue of contraband trade with the colonies. Nevertheless, she stationed two of her ablest commanders in the Caribbean, Admirals Rodney and Hood, while the French assigned to cope with them Admirals the Comtes d'Estaing, De Guichen and De Grasse.

The French ambition was to better old scores by making a clean sweep of the English possessions. They immediately struck at Dominica, landing troops from Martinique under General the Marquis de Bouillé, who captured the garrison after a brief resistance. A chronicler records that the expedition occupied the town of Roseau, the capital, "in most regular and solemn order, the drums beating a slow march, and the soldiers with small boughs and flowers in their hats."

St. Vincent was taken still more easily, and the French passed on to their old colony, Grenada. Some brisk fighting occurred there. A squadron under the Comte d'Estaing blockaded the island, and a landing force led by the Count Dillon, a gay Irish adventurer, stormed Hospital Hill. A naval effort by the English to reverse the verdict was beaten off. This closed the first phase of the offensive. Dominica, St. Vincent and Grenada were captured before Rodney arrived from England to take over his station with headquarters at Barbados. The French did not hold him lightly, and as their fleets maneuvered for position Rodney struck at St. Lucia, which he occupied as his advance base.

It is not the intention here to give an account of the naval war which culminated, under De Grasse and Rodney, in a grand test that fixed the lines of empire, as between France and England in the Caribbean, until today. The Battle of the Saintes will get its chapter. This one is a summary of the tossing back and forth of small island holdings, without which the reader would have but a vague idea of the background of colonial life before the Revolution and the Napoleonic Era. The planters were never certain which flag would be flying above them by the time the next crops were gathered, and consequently in which market they would have to compete. The wars cut down mercantile shipping, encouraged privateering and privacy, and grievously raised the prices of imports.

Rodney thought it of first importance to maneuver for the destruction of the French fleet. He refused to be drawn into patrolling activities that would have scattered his forces. This left the way fairly clear for the military operations of the Marquis de Bouillé. In 1781 and 1782, he mopped up all the remaining British colonies in the Lesser Antilles, except Barbados and Antigua. Tobago, Nevis and Montserrat offered no difficulties. Historic St. Christopher was another story.

Bouillé landed 8,000 men west of Basse-Terre, covered by a fleet commanded by De Grasse. The General drove the garrison into the fortress on Brimstone Hill, a remarkable isolated mass of volcanic rock and limestone 779 feet high, called the "Gibraltar of the West Indies.' This place was closely invested, while De Grasse lay in the roads. It is interesting to note that the islanders were sympathizers with the cause of the thirteen American colonies and, as one English historian puts it, showed "a real or tacit and understood neutrality from the first arrival of the enemy."

Two weeks later, Admiral Sir Samuel Hood arrived, cleverly tricked De Grasse into coming out, and anchored his ships at the exact spot the French had just quitted. It was but a tour de force. Hood was unable to raise the siege of Brimstone Hill, which surrendered in a month after a merciless bombardment. St. Christopher passed into the hands of the French for the last time.

When peace came in 1783, every conquest that had been made by either nation in the Caribbean was canceled, with the sole exception that France regained Tobago. And the next year, St. Bartholomew passed to Sweden in exchange for certain rights at the port of Gothenburg which that country conceded to France. Such was the instability that the eighteenth century offered to men whose more productive pursuits we shall now consider.

Chapter XII

Opulent Saint Domingue

In 1714, as the War of the Spanish Succession passed into history, Saint Domingue was created a separate colony with its capital at Léogane on the southern peninsula, a few miles west of Port-au-Prince. Until then it had been subject to the Governor-General of the French Antilles, who functioned from St. Pierre, Martinique. The change was long overdue. The old administration had been loose, and the former territory of the buccaneers had largely gone its way under individualistic chiefs. One cannot imagine such men as Du Casse paying much attention to Martinique. The exigencies of war, also, had thrown it upon its own resources for extended periods. Its varied crops, the presence of wild cattle and hogs in its back country, made it self-sustaining at a pinch, whereas the small islands were threatened by famine whenever communications with France were cut.

Saint Domingue, in 1714, was less than fifty per cent a sugar country. Tobacco, indigo and cotton were widely grown. The culture of cocoa had increased rapidly, and as there was a steady demand for this product it had come to be regarded as a mainstay of the colony. But the following year a blight killed practically all the cocoa trees. Even as many tobacco farmers had turned to cane during the revolt against the tax system under Pouancey, so practically all the cocoa planters now swung in the same direction. This occurred at just the moment when the unparalleled sugar bonanza of the eighteenth century was getting under way.

The loss of cocoa had been a blessing instead of the calamity it seemed. For there was far more money to be made per acre out of sugar. Coffee was introduced in 1726 and that, too, proved immediately successful. Saint Domingue's period of magnificence had begun, its opulent three-quarters of a century which ran, roughly, from 1715 to 1790. The Abbé Raynal, author of the *Histoire Philosophique des Deux Indies,* says, as of the year 1774 when his book was published, that no colony ever became rich so quickly. Assuredly, it came to be regarded as the most valuable tropical possession of its size on earth.

Along with the new Governor-General, there was appointed an Intendant. This was the common French practice both in Europe and overseas. The Intendant was a delegate, a sort of inspector and auditor combined, assigned to a province to see that the public services were properly conducted. He could, in the King's name, overrule the Governor on certain matters, mainly financial. Friction between the two high officials often occurred. No issue of the kind had previously disturbed Saint Domingue, but it was soon to appear in an aggravated form.

The first flush of prosperity drew to the colony a type of immigrant superior to the early settlers. This was normal and in every way desirable. Unexpectedly, however, Saint Domingue proved alluring to members of the French nobility, also, especially to younger sons, a class that had been wont to seek careers in purely military adventures. It was not a case of country squires like those who had flocked to Canada, or who had taken to the sea as privateers from the days of Francis I on. The *haute noblesse* was interested.

Pierre de Vaissière, a descendant of Saint Domingue planters, called attention to this movement in a valuable study published some thirty-five years ago. Other historians have scarcely realized that it took place. Vaissière lists the aristocratic names. He points out that fortune-hunting was not the sole motivation. Louis XIV, building on the work of Richelieu, had deprived the feudal lords of France of their share in the government, notably of their local powers, and had concentrated everything in the hands of the monarch. *"L'Etat c'est moi!"* These haughty, ambitious families sought a new outlet for their talents. Consciously or unconsciously, they chose Saint Domingue as a testing ground and constructed there a small political model of the vanished regime. They did not succeed so well in transplanting their esthetics.

The first symptoms appeared when noblemen serving in the garrison began to resign their commissions and devote themselves to managing estates. It had been the custom for officers to buy holdings and give part of their time to them. The Army stiffened its regulations, and when it came to choosing the aristocrats preferred the land, while the commoners pretty generally clung to the prestige of military rank. This was novel and significant. Then sons of the best houses in France came out as civilians and bought property. There never were more than a few score of them, but they wielded considerable influence. They were active in reforming the militia, a force which they dominated and in which they held nearly all the important commands.

Soon there were two distinct classes of planters: aristocrats and bourgeois. The line of demarcation between them was sharp. It had nothing to do with wealth. The bourgeois enjoyed the older standing in the colony, some of them being descendants of the original *forbans*. It made no difference. What developed was two factions, political as well as social, and in this division Vaissière sees the origin of the helplessness of the whites when they were faced by the great slave insurrection at the end of the century. He thinks that the upper class had the monopoly of ethics, courage and foresight, a judgment it is impossible to accept. The fact remains that this class was less guilty of absentee landlordism, that rooted in the soil it did seek to make a French provincial entity of Saint Domingue, whereas its opponents seemed to care only for amassing money and wasting it in Paris.

A struggle over the functions of their respective offices, between the Governor-General and the Intendant of Saint Domingue, became a serious factor in the 1720's. Its violence grew with each decade. The aristocrats supported the Governor-General and the bourgeois the Intendant. This was because of the differing powers of the two officials and the way in which they exercised them.

The Governor-General, over and above his daily executive duties, was the military commander-in-chief. He had regular troops under him. The militia, in which service was compulsory, was subject to his orders. He also had the right to mobilize in time of war all the inhabitants capable of bearing arms and to use them as he pleased, even to the length of employing them in foreign conquests. The Governor-General had arrogated to himself the right to control civil debts, which he delegated to the militia. This was on the theory that such action was necessary to preserve public order. On a simple complaint by the creditor, and sometimes without one, the debtor was seized by the ranking militia officer in his district, imprisoned and forced to pay without other formalities.

The Intendant supervised the expenditure of the revenue, and he ordinarily regulated its collection also. As has been said, he was the efficiency man of the administration, the King's watchdog, the supposed guardian against tyrannical excesses. On the score last named, he often interfered in judicial cases, both criminal and civil. He would open an emergency court, sit on the bench and dispose of some matter in which it was claimed that justice had been dilatory, or which he chose to rule had been mishandled.

It will be seen that the Governor-General and the Intendant clashed most gravely on their view of the judicial function, which actually they both usurped. As an extreme example, the Governor-General could have his militia compel the payment of a debt, and the Intendant could promptly declare that the money had been wrongfully extorted and order his bailiffs to see that it was reimbursed. This happened more than once.

The Governor-General accused the Intendant of playing to the mob and undermining authority. The Intendant charged that the Governor-General fostered militarism. They acrimoniously wrote their views to the Ministry in Paris, where, says the Abbé Raynal, "each had his protectors, influenced by pride or by interest, to maintain them in their posts. When they were in accord, or because their good or evil opinions chanced to be the same, or because one gained a decided ascendancy over the other, the condition of the colonists became still worse. Whatever might be the wrongs of these victims, their cries were never heard by the metropolis, which regarded the harmony of its delegates as the most decisive proof of a perfect administration."

The party supporting the Intendant early went into the lead, numerically and otherwise. It attracted not only the rich bourgeois planters, but the "small men"—lawyers, notaries, shopkeepers and artisans, for whose interests it ostensibly stood. The slur of "militarism" cast on its opponents was an effective one, for the spirit of Saint Domingue was primarily commercial.

As in all French colonies, the institution of the Superior Council had become important. It provided a simulacrum of popular representation. Saint Domingue had two Superior Councils, appointive, with semi-legislative attributes, one for the northern section and one for the western and southern. The complexion of the councils was bourgeois with the usual preponderance of lawyers in the membership, which placed them on the side of the Intendant. Gradually, his party fastened on the abolition of the militia as its chief objective, because this would abase the aristocratic officers of that force and would deprive the Governor-General of most of his real power.

The issue did not come to a head until 1760. It would be an error to assume that the everyday life of Saint Domingue, meanwhile, had been vastly affected by it. The colony was heaping up profits from sugar with a momentum that apparently nothing could halt, and that was what the average resident cared about. Let us see how he lived during this brief Golden Age, when "as rich as a West Indian planter" was a catch phrase in all the capitals of Europe.

Sugar estates were concentrated chiefly on the northern plain below Cap Français, the Artibonite region in the north-central part of the island, the Cul-de-Sac quarter behind Port-au-Prince and the plain of Léogane to the west of the latter. The two mountainous peninsulas did not lend themselves to this culture, though pockets of sugar cane occurred in the lower valleys of both of them and on narrow strips of coastland.

Sugar was extracted by primitive methods, the cane stalks being ground between rollers, with cattle, horses and mules providing the motive power, and the juice boiled in open kettles. As a result of wastage, the yield per ton of cane was much less than it is today. The sugar mills of all countries were run in the same way. But Saint Domingue had an advantage over the English islands, because its technique of cultivating the plants was superior. For one thing, it employed irrigation.

France easily absorbed the main product, which middle-men bought outright, some of it for sale to neighboring European lands. Despite the heavy export and import taxes, there was profit enough for everyone. The cane industry also produced molasses and rum, and these were barred on the theory that they would furnish a ruinous competition to the vineyardists of France. The chief use to which molasses was then put was the manufacture of beverages, distilled and un-distilled, and the prohibition was aimed at these. It was feared, too, that consumers might get to prefer good West India rum to brandy. Fortunately, there was a demand for the by-products in the British North American colonies, and the Saint Domingue planters did well from the trade, inter-rupted though it was by wars and spasms of protectionist legislation in London.

It is a commonplace that there could have been no sugar bonanza without Negro slavery. White men could not have done the necessary field labor in the tropics, under the con-ditions that then prevailed. The last point is cogent, but is usually ignored. White men can perform any kind of work in the tropics nowadays, because of the conquest of yellow fever, malaria and other malignant diseases. A certain num-ber of peasant immigrants always did become acclimatized and remain on the soil, especially in the Spanish colonies. The great mortality among white newcomers in the eight-eenth century, however, made it out of the question to culti-vate plantations with any but Africans. Since the latter were bondsmen, labor costs were held to a minimum. Hence the magnitude of the bonanza.

The salient fact in every branch of the life of Saint Do-mingue was the Negro. The numerical ascendancy of blacks over whites rose swiftly from the moment prosperity began, until at the last it was twelve to one. Some of the larger plantations had more than a thousand slaves each. Daho-means, Mandingoes and Senegalese were among the chief strains brought from Africa. All of these were intelligent races. The Dahomeans were, in addition, perhaps the most warlike of all blacks except the Zulus. Duller Angolans and

Eboes completed the tally. The majority worked in the
fields and sugar mills, but the quota selected for household
service was large, with the preference given to Mandingoes
and Senegalese.

Every member of a white household, down to the young
children, had at least one personal attendant. According to
the wealth of the family, it was not uncommon for the master,
mistress and elder sons to have from three to six each. The
commentators all remark on the inevitable modifying of the
white man's character by this incessant contact with the subject people. Few have troubled to draw the inference that it
also worked the other way around. If the planters were
coarsened, their house slaves improved the opportunity to absorb their way of thinking, their very mannerisms. The
illusion of being a black Frenchman which the modern
Haitian creates is doubtless due in part to this.

The Saint Domingue colonists were on more friendly
terms with their Negroes than was generally the case in the
English islands. Color prejudice of course existed, even color
phobia, but this was directed at the freed elements, especially
the mulattoes, who it was feared might develop political aspirations. By a curious quirk of Gallic logic, the condition of
slavery which the masters had themselves imposed was
thought to be forever degrading. Equality with the descendants of slaves seemed the intolerable possibility. The writer
cannot find that the French ever had a deep-rooted contempt
for Africans as such.

Miscegenation occurred in all the slave-holding territories,
but it was probably most widespread among the French. A
bachelor Saint Domingue planter chose an overlapping succession of concubines from the ranks of his bondswomen;
the latter were proud of the distinction and called one another *"matelotte,"* an amusing variation of the old buccaneer
term for a close comrade. A married planter usually was

more circumspect, confined himself to a single illicit relationship on the plantation, and perhaps maintained a free colored mistress in town. It stands to reason that there were exceptions, but a strictly moral man in that society was rare indeed. The offspring of unions with slaves commonly were manumitted, which served to build up the very class of jealous half-breeds the planters dreaded.*

It was not only the white man who fell under the subtle influence of the African, or part-African, charmer. His own women were affected in a different way. The obsequious, flattering attentions of their maids led them to depend upon these girls for companionship. The favorite was known as a *"cocote,"* and the relationship often took on an extravagant aspect. "Almost every young Creole female," writes Moreau de Saint-Méry, "has a young mulattress, or quadroon, and sometimes even a young Negress, whom she makes into her *cocote.* The latter is the confidante of all the thoughts of the mistress (and this confidence is sometimes reciprocal), confidante above all of her amours. The *cocote* is always with her, sleeps in the same room, eats and drinks with her—not at table or at formal meals, but at times when they devour Creole dainties, moments with which familiarity seems to mix a special salt, in private places and far from the observation of men."

The *femmes de couleur* who had obtained a hold upon

---

* An elaborate nomenclature was applied to the light-colored and dark-colored. The former regarded themselves as socially superior in exact relation to the amount of white blood in their veins. Here is a table of the ordinary classifications, omitting the products of crossing when both parents were partly colored:

	English	French	
Offspring of White and Black	Mulatto	Mulâtre	$\frac{1}{2}$ White
Offspring of White and Mulatto	Quadroon	Quarteron	$\frac{3}{4}$ White
Offspring of White and Quadroon	Octoroon	Métis, or Octavon	$\frac{7}{8}$ White
Offspring of White and Octoroon	Mustee	Mamelouque	$\frac{15}{16}$ White
Offspring of White and Mustee	Mustefino	Sang-Mélé	$\frac{31}{32}$ White
Offspring of Black and Mulatto	Sambo	Griffe	$\frac{1}{4}$ White
Offspring of Black and Sambo	Sambo	Sacatra	$\frac{1}{8}$ White
Offspring of Black and Sacatra	Sambo	Marabou	$\frac{1}{16}$ White

members of the ruling race came to be the paramount social factor in Saint Domingue. These women owed their power to white supremacy, which they consequently sought to preserve. The favored ones on the plantations spied on their fellow slaves and reported incipient plots. In the towns, the mistresses of rich men conducted salons where influential figures met. Their balls and other entertainments for their white admirers were easily the gayest events. They carried no weight, however, in the political feuds that disrupted the masters, and realizing the hopelessness of the situation from their viewpoint they swung on the day of blood to the side of their mothers. They have never received the historical study they deserve.

The homes of the well-to-do colonists, even the town houses of planters and merchants, were unpretentious until about the middle of the eighteenth century. Country homes were little more than barracks, the rooms being strung out in single file with verandas on both sides. The chief object was to have them as cool as possible. The wooden frames were flimsily constructed, and the abundant space left for windows was filled only with slatted blinds. Travelers wrote that it was almost equivalent to living outdoors.

When pretentious mansions began to be built, emphasis was placed on the exterior, the spaciousness of the rooms, the essential furniture. Everything was of tropical hardwoods, especially mahogany. Decoration and *objets d'art,* the niceties of luxury, the adjuncts of an intellectual life, were very seldom included. In a certain splendid house inventoried in 1787, there was practically no furniture but beds, tables, chairs, wardrobes and buffets. On other inventories, it is true, one discovers musical instruments, foils and the appurtenances of games, but rarely books.

Eating, drinking, dancing, gambling and the theater constituted the gay life to nineteen-twentieths of the colonists.

Fencing and horsemanship were usual masculine accomplishments. The women sometimes cultivated their voices. At least, neither sex was guilty of false pretensions. They were frank hedonists and they were extremely spendthrift.

Theaters flourished at Cap Français, Port-au-Prince, Léogane, Saint Marc and Aux Cayes. They announced that the plays they offered had the cachet of Parisian approval: *Le Légataire Universel, Cartouche, La Gageure Imprévue, Annette et Lubin, L'Ecole des Pères,* et cetera. In 1766 there were three troupes at Port-au-Prince, and during 1787 the leading playhouse of this town realized 340,000 livres in receipts against 280,000 in expenses. Yet a census the following year showed Port-au-Prince as having a population of 6,200, only 1,800 being white, 400 colored freemen, and the rest slaves. The planters of the surrounding territory flocked to the support of the theaters, as they did to those of Cap Français which had almost twice as large a population. They used their lobbies as centers of social intercourse and parades of fashion.

Other smart meeting places open to all whites were the public baths, "like those at Cap Français," says Vaissière, "where both men and women were freely admitted and where they could mingle if they wished."

Freemasonry was established in Saint Domingue in 1740. The first lodges had difficulties, because the women opposed them. They had been led to believe that the object of the institution was to enable men to hide from female society and eventually get rid of all women. One writer puts it quaintly that the lodges were boycotted "to a point where the members were not able to obtain the usual favors from their wives." It was also said that masons had vowed themselves to the service of the Devil. But the prejudice passed.

The most intellectual group, by all odds, was the famous

Cercle des Philadelphes, a club at Cap Français that was at the same time political, philosophical and literary, but mainly political. It professed to spread the teachings of the Italian humanist of the Renaissance, Francesco Filelfo. Actually, it was a radical organization which supported the party of the Intendant against that of the Governor-General.

In 1760, Jean-Etienne Bernard de Clugny arrived as Intendant. It was a remarkable appointment. Clugny, then only thirty-one years old, was born in Guadeloupe. He had made a glittering success as a civil servant in Paris, was looked upon by the Berryer Ministry as a young genius, financial and otherwise. His theories regarding the administration of colonies were known. That these were influenced by his own colonial birth is hardly to be doubted. He was sent out with tacit authority to bring matters to a head, and as if to aid his course the officer commanding the troops in Saint Domingue, the Vicomte de Belzunce, was shortly afterward made Governor-General.

Clugny waged a campaign against the aristocratic ascendancy in the militia, against the militia itself, such as had not yet been seen. He assuredly wished to break the power of the executive branch as it was then constituted, and to replace it with civilian rule in which the middle class would have the largest voice. He stood in a sense for democracy and was not uninfluenced by the principles of the Encyclopedists. His program implied a wide degree of self-government, and it appeared to some to carry a hint of eventual independence. Clugny, however, did not envisage local nationalism. He was anomalous as a representative of the absolutist regime of Louis XV, but he was ardently French. He wanted the colony to become a liberal-minded, loyal province, not a republic. If he stressed the responsibilities to be assumed by the middle class, it was partly because he sought to cure it of its growing tendency toward absentee landlordism. The Saint Domingue aristocrats shamed it in that respect, and so did the bourgeois of his native Guadeloupe.

Agitation stimulated by him in the two councils was a potent aid to Clugny. At last, in March, 1763, a decree revamping the administration was sent from Paris. The duties of all officials were precisely defined, with additional powers given to the Intendant. Compulsory military service in the colony ended. Elected syndics took over the police functions of the abolished militia, while defense was assured by regular French soldiers maintained by the King. At the same time, it was suggested that the royal revenue tax be raised from 2,500,000 livres to 4,000,000, to take care of additional expenses, and that some sort of public approval of the change should be registered.

Clugny brought about a joint session of the two councils, to which he ebulliently gave the name of National Assembly, thus launching an idea which bit in more deeply than he had intended. The body passed a resolution by a narrow margin of votes, endorsing everything. It continued to sit on its own initiative, and much radical oratory was heard.

But success did not attend the new state of affairs. The syndics lacked prestige; security vanished from the countryside where the militia no longer patrolled and soldiers seldom came. The roads fell into disrepair. Furthermore, a political crisis occurred in France. Berryer fell and was replaced by a stronger man, the Duc de Choiseul, who did not share his mistrust of the military and to whom Clugny's liberalism was distasteful.

Choiseul appointed the Comte d'Estaing Governor-General of Saint Domingue, clothed him with extraordinary powers, and bracketted with him as Intendant an unaggressive man named Magon. These two landed in April, 1764. Estaing packed Clugny home almost brutally and set to work to undo all that had been done. He little dreamed that twelve years later Clugny was to be Louis XVI's Controller-General of Finances, the successor of Turgot and the predecessor of Necker.

The militia was now restored under the thin disguise of swearing in men as "national troops," and the councils were enfeebled by a series of hostile decrees. No reduction of the special taxes accompanied these changes. There was violent disapproval. One councillor said that the King had tricked the colony out of 4,000,000 livres. Estaing weakly fell back on Clugny's idea of calling a National Assembly. Two such defied him in a single year. They aspired to control expenditures, went through the motions of legislating, and even challenged his authority. He dissolved them one after another. The last one reorganized itself, declined to receive the members named by Estaing and to exclude those he had dismissed. Choiseul advised him to be more tactful, then dubbed him a fool, recalled him and sent out the Prince de Rohan as Governor-General.

Rohan, a vigorous and ruthless chief, faced two incipient revolts of whites whom Vaissière says were "people of low birth, obscure individuals without distinction," and crushed them easily. He imitated Oliver Cromwell by personally breaking up the Port-au-Prince council and placing most of its members under arrest. Port-au-Prince had been the capital of the colony since 1750. Rohan was soon a dictator. The party that formerly had supported the Intendants was reduced to impotence. With this advantage gained by the reconstituted military hierarchy, it ruled Saint Domingue until the climactic year, 1789.

CHAPTER XIII

Josephine's Tropics

LIFE in the Windward Islands during the eighteenth century was a simpler affair than in Saint Domingue. We have seen that foreign wars touched these colonies more closely, to the extent that none of them escaped occupation by the English at one time or another. But their emotional attachment to France was profound, and their internal politics less heated. They did not experience the wild boom that drove their larger neighbor money mad. While chiefly dependent on sugar, they practiced diversification of crops. Estates tended to remain longer in the hands of the same families. This worked for social stability, and in Martinique at least a culture with some claim to elegance developed. Guiana, ordinarily called Cayenne, the most backward of all the French colonies, was a dependency of the Windward Islands and must be considered along with them.

The monopolistic trade policy to which French governments reverted, after brief interruptions, from the time of Colbert until the Revolution, was the main bogey of the small islands. They called it *"l'Exclusif,"* with a shade of meaning that made that term detestable. They needed to sell their surplus produce to the first comer, and to buy cheaper goods than those of France.

In 1717, there arrived in Martinique, MM. De la Varenne and Ricouard as Governor and Intendant, respectively, with more than usually severe instructions against free commerce. They happened to be two tactless men, and they made the mistake of applying the rules fully and of employing intemperate language to threaten the colonists with penalties for disobedience. About four months later, while they were on a tour of inspection, they were seized by an armed troop of planters and imprisoned "in the name of the colony." Colonel Dubuc of the militia, a leader of the movement, negotiated with the military garrison, which agreed to remain neutral. The officials were then placed on a boat and sent back to France, the government being assumed by acting administrators under the control of the Superior Council of Martinique. These made a point of strictly obeying the King's orders in the matter of commerce. In Paris, it was thought wise not to give too much importance to what had happened. The Governor of Grenada, M. De Feuquières, was transferred to the higher post at Martinique. He was received with full respect and held the office for longer than the average. Needless to say, he closed his eyes to certain infractions of the trading law.

This episode, the only one of its kind in the history of the French Windward Islands, is known as the *Gaoulé*, from a Carib word signifying a popular tumult. The name to remember in connection with it is that of Dubuc, whose son played a great and clever role later in the century. The father merely defended the practice of allowing, within reason, persons on foreign ships to act as smuggling agents for the planters. Many such agents could neither read nor write. They kept a bag for each planter they represented, putting money into it and taking it out according to the sales and purchases made. There was no other accounting. The planter accepted what was found in the bag at the end of a round voyage.

The year following the *Gaoulé*, the cocoa blight that had hit Saint Domingue in 1715 reached Martinique and Guadeloupe, destroying all the groves. The Ministry in France recommended that some absolutely new crop be attempted, in preference to planting more sugar cane. It had been given two coffee shrubs by the Dutch Government and had preserved them in a hothouse at the Jardin des Plantes, Paris. Offshoots of these were sent out, with the explanation that coffee flourished in damp valleys and at an elevation where cane could not be grown. The idea caught on. By 1723, coffee was widely established in Martinique and Guadeloupe, three years in advance of Saint Domingue and ten years before it was cultivated in the English islands. Nevertheless, this was not the earliest date of its appearance in a French colony. The Dutch had brought it from the Orient to Surinam. Plants crossed the border into Cayenne in 1716, and are believed to have yielded their first commercial crop in 1721.

Statistics covering economic growth and problems at regular intervals are not available. Illuminating flashes occur in the works of contemporary historians. Thus, Raynal explains the depressed state of Martinique on its return to France after the Seven Years' War and incidentally gives a clear impression of the normal plantation economy of the island. He writes:

"The land proprietors may be divided into four classes. The first owns 100 large sugar estates, exploited by 12,000 slaves. The second owns 150, exploited by 9,000 slaves. The third owns 36, exploited by 2,000 slaves. The fourth class, which goes in for the culture of coffee, cotton, cocoa and cassava may keep 12,000 slaves busy. Such other slaves of both sexes which the colony contains are employed in domestic service, in fishing, or navigation.

"The first class is entirely composed of rich men. Their agriculture has been carried as far as it can go, and their resources maintain them easily in the flourishing state they have reached. Even their special expenses for renewal of equipment are less considerable than those of less opulent

colonists, because the slaves who are born on their estates replace those which time and hard work destroy."

Raynal means by the above that a healthful, regular birth
rate could only be expected on well-staffed plantations, where
the Negro women of child-bearing age were allowed comparative leisure for the rearing of offspring. Miscarriages
and sheer sterility were common under less favorable conditions. The Abbé goes on:

"The second class, which we may call that of persons in
easy circumstances, has about half of the cultivators it needs
to attain to the wealth of the rich proprietors. If these planters had the means suddenly to buy the slaves they lack, they
would be hampered by a sad experience. There is nothing so
ill-advised as to place a large number of Negroes at one time
upon an estate. The maladies which the change of climate
and food brings upon these unfortunates—the difficulty of
breaking them to a work for which they have neither the
training nor the inclination—are too much for the colonist to
cope with in quantity. The most active proprietor is the one
who can increase his establishment of slaves by one-sixth each
year. Thus, the second class should acquire a total of 1,500
slaves a year, if the net returns of the business permitted it.
But it cannot count on credit, which the merchants of the
metropolis do not seem disposed to accord. Those who invest
their funds in the colony have too often seen them lie idle
or in danger, and have transferred them to Europe or Saint
Domingue.

"The third class, which is more or less indigent, cannot
emerge from its situation by any means open in the natural
order of business [on account of the war damages of 1762].
It will be a great deal if it succeeds in keeping itself alive.
Only the beneficent hand of the government can give it a life
useful to the State by lending it without interest the necessary
money to equip its plantations. . . .

"The fourth class, which grows crops less important than
sugar, does not need such serious aid to recover the state of

prosperity from which war, hurricanes and other evils caused it to fall. It would suffice for these two last-mentioned classes to acquire each year a total of 1,500 slaves to reach the level of prosperity which Nature permits to their industry."

The emphasis on new field hands, of which Raynal thought that at least 3,000 a year would have to be imported from Africa, was due to the fact that the English had plundered Martinique of large numbers of Negroes, apparently victimizing the small proprietors rather than the large ones. Replacements were not procured on the scale Raynal suggested. Yet it did not take long for the island to be accounted once more a rich sugar colony.

Many Creoles born in Martinique and Guadeloupe between the second and seventh decades of the century became French celebrities. It was as if a flowering of talent occurred in anticipation of 1789 and the *Epopee*. To name only the best known, there were Clugny, whose career in Saint Domingue has been sketched; the Revolutionary generals J. C. Dugommier and J. N. Gobert; Jean-Baptiste Dubuc, son of the hero of the *Gaoulé*, statesman, economist and famous pamphleteer; Thibault de Chanvallon, of whom we shall hear again in this chapter; the Marquis de Traversay, who died as a Russian admiral; the painter G. G. Lethière, whose *Mort de Virginie* hangs in the Louvre; the historian M. L. E. Moreau de Saint-Méry, a distant relative of the Empress Josephine;— and Josephine herself. Against this list, Saint Domingue has scarcely anyone to show, except the mulatto General Thomas Alexandre Dumas, who distinguished himself in the army of the Revolution and under Napoleon, and who was the father of Alexandre Dumas, the novelist.

Josephine is of perennial interest. She was born at Trois Ilets across the bay from Fort Royal (now Fort-de-France), Martinique, on June 23, 1763, the very year of depression which inspired the analysis just quoted from the Abbé Ray-

GENERAL THOMAS ALEXANDRE DUMAS
A native of Saint Domingue, the mulatto father
of Alexandre Dumas the novelist.

From an old print

nal's *Histoire Philosophique*. Directly descended from Adrienne, a sister of Pierre Belain d'Esnambuc, the founder of the colony, it would have been impossible to find an older and purer Creole type. But the family had gone down in the world. Her father was definitely of Raynal's "third class," a poor, shiftless planter who barely made ends meet and housed his family in an abandoned sugar refinery, crudely reconstructed as a home.

Her baptismal name was Marie-Josèphe-Rose Tascher de la Pagerie. As a child they called her Yeyette. The form "Josephine" was adopted in her maturity. There were two other sisters, both younger than she. Surprisingly little is known about how the family existed, who were its everyday friends, and how Josephine was actually brought up. Tascher de la Pagerie had received a small dowry with his wife, and this was a more important item than anything he was able to earn from his land. But the supreme fact in their destiny was the presence for a few years of the Sieur de Beauharnais as Governor of the colony.

Beauharnais was decorously married. His son, Alexandre, was born in Martinique in 1760, three years before Josephine. A sister of Tascher found the way to charm him, all the same, and he set her up in an establishment as his mistress. Doubtless influenced by her, he got Tascher a pension for services rendered in the militia fighting the English, and the financial problems of the family were eased a little. Then Beauharnais returned to France. It has been mentioned that he had found a husband for his mistress. The complacent couple, whose name was Renaudin, would ordinarily have been left behind by a retiring Governor. Beauharnais took them with him.

Josephine ran wild for the first ten years of her life, with Negro children for playmates. Her people were not in the rich plantation set which, as the writer has said elsewhere, "strove to re-create something of the vivacity and smart dressing of an aristocratic French countryside." Romancers have described her as romping with her future husband, little Alexandre de Beauharnais. This is an absurdity, for he had been removed to Paris, an infant, before she was born. From ten to fourteen, she was given a superficial education at a boarding school in Fort Royal. From fourteen to sixteen, she was Yeyette of the mouldering plantation, a belle of limited renown, with as good as no prospects of making an advantageous marriage. The careless amours with which the legend-makers have credited her at that early age are most improbable. The stories sprang from Napoleon's testy veto on public references to his Empress' childhood.

The circumstances of her marriage to Alexandre were curious enough to be rated a myth, had not modern research established them beyond question. Mme. Renaudin, Josephine's aunt, as a preliminary to her successful plan to end her days as the legal wife of Beauharnais, induced the latter to write Tascher de la Pagerie and ask for the hand of one of his daughters for Alexandre. The young man's wishes do not seem to have been consulted. The dazzling match was offered the poverty-stricken planter without reserves, free of the usual obligation of providing a dowry. It was merely suggested that the second daughter, Catherine-Desirée, then aged thirteen, might be the most suitable. But before the letter reached Martinique, Catherine-Desirée had died. Tascher wrote back, eagerly offering Yeyette instead, and she was accepted. He took her to France in the autumn of 1779. She was married to Alexandre de Beauharnais, to whom she bore two children and who, as if to get even, consistently mistreated her.

The career of Josephine in Europe does not concern this history. For obscure reasons, she once revisited Martinique. A statue to her stands in the public gardens of Fort-de-France, where the citizens take romantic pride in her memory, and where the casual tourist feels sure that she is the island's unique claim to glory. But having left it, she became quite disinterested in Martinique's fate. She was a woman of shallow intellect and a lust for luxury, caught up on a mighty wave at the summit of which only the personal mattered to her. From the standpoint of her origin, the most telling words uttered about Josephine were those of Napoleon when he first brought her to live at the Tuileries.

"There, little Creole!" he said. "You now have the chance to sleep in the bed of your masters."

Jean-Baptiste Dubuc and Thibault de Chanvallon were native sons of sterling worth. Their writings brought them to the attention of Choiseul, a Secretary of State with broad views and a special interest in rebuilding France's lost empire overseas. Dubuc had written pamphlets advocating what amounted to free trade with foreign countries. This heresy notwithstanding, Choiseul appointed him in 1764 his chief clerk for the colonies, delegating to him powers which made him the true administrator. Viewing matters from the inside, Dubuc came to the conclusion that the prevailing system could not be reversed brusquely without disrupting the commercial life of the nation. He decided to mitigate *"l'Exclusif,"* and to that end he prepared a series of ordinances and composed a brilliant memorandum, which Choiseul approved. Certain ports in the West Indies were opened to foreign ships. The untrammeled importation and exportation of certain goods was allowed.

"A colonist is nothing but a free planter on an enslaved soil. . . . The more colonies differ in their products from the country that owns them, the more perfect they are." Phrases of this sort now came from Dubuc's pen. His old admirers called him a traitor. But by means of his astute compromise, he breached protectionism so well that it was never fully restored. An authority says that it is "impossible to exaggerate the importance to the colonies" of his years in office.

Choiseul was not so fortunate in the use he made of Chanvallon, author of *Voyage à la Martinique,* an able survey of his native island. The loss of Canada to the English had made it hard to keep the Antilles supplied with goods they had been obtaining there, especially salted fish and lumber. Promptly after the calamitous treaty of 1763, the Minister began to look around for a substitute. An old resident of Guiana, M. de Préfontaines, suggested that that colony lay fallow awaiting development. Choiseul seized upon the idea and carried it much further than Préfontaines intended.

The dream of creating a tropical equivalent of Canada was taken seriously. Why, it was asked, should not the timber in equatorial forests be employed for building warehouses? Why should not the fish in warm waters be cured? Why should not rice take the place of wheat? None of these things were impossible. But they were impracticable for green Europeans. The cost of production would have been too great. It is necessary to hunt for suitable tropical timber in a riot of useless trees. Edible southern fish do not swim in huge shoals, like mackerel and cod.

Guiana, or rather the section of it surrounding Cayenne, was a backward, sleepy hierarchy of scarcely 500 whites and a few thousand slaves. The rest was wilderness. It had been governed since 1700 by the Orvilliers family, father, son and grandson. The latest Orvilliers protested against any sudden change. He was replaced by a new Governor, and Chanvallon was sent out as Intendant.

Despite the object lesson of Louisiana only forty-five years before, at the time of John Law, Choiseul proceeded to attempt high-pressure colonization. It was a State project and stock was not unloaded on the public. Otherwise, the follies and horrors of the Mississippi Bubble were repeated. Between 1763 and 1766, 10,996 settlers were dumped in the Kourou and Sinnamary districts, and 30,000,000 livres expended. The newcomers perished of fevers at an appalling rate. Somehow, the equipment they needed failed to materialize, or proved faulty. But as an example of the senseless way in which money was spent, a fine statue of Louis XV was shipped out and erected in the mushroom town of Kourou.

At the end of the three-year period, when Choiseul abandoned the enterprise, only 918 new colonists remained, and many of these straggled back to France. Chanvallon, who had been in administrative charge, was accused of errors which had been no fault of his, and imprisoned for dishonest practices of which his name was eventually cleared. He was then made Commissary-General of all French colonies, in which post he collaborated with Dubuc.

Two other minor efforts to boom Guiana as a source of raw materials failed. All this activity, however, did put a little new life into the colony. In 1788 the population stood at 1,307 whites, 480 freed persons and 10,478 slaves.

CHAPTER XIV

The Code Noir

THE truth about the treatment accorded slaves is very important to an understanding of the French colonial system, as compared with those of other European nations. By and large, the Spaniards imposed the mildest conditions of servitude, while the French were more humane than the English and Dutch. This assertion will surprise the American reader, especially as regards the Spaniards, whose cruelty in exterminating the Arawâks of the Greater Antilles is a notorious fact. But it was never intended by Ferdinand and Isabella, the Church and the Council of the Indies that the natives should be brutalized. Generous rules were often formulated, and at times strict orders to enforce them were sent to the Governors. The early settlers, from the highest officials down, consistently disobeyed. Mad for gold, they worked to death the Arawâks whom they succeeded in herding into the mines, and butchered those who resisted. On the continent, however, where labor was hardier and more abundant, they soon put in force the peonage system which was normal to their race in dealing with the conquered. When they introduced African slaves, they fitted them into their economy without undue harshness.

English and Dutch practices were based on wringing the utmost commercial advantage out of the slave. In theory, this was true of all peoples. But the northerners attached a peculiar sanctity to individual property rights. Each owner was a despot who made his bondsmen profitable in the way that

suited him. They were chattels. and at least until the rise of
the philanthropic movement toward the end of the eighteenth
century, the Government did not prevent his overworking
them and did little to restrain him from mutilating, or even
killing them. Extremes, of course, were rare. The system
remained a heartless one. Irksome forms of discipline, flogging and other punishments were freely applied. The important thing is that public opinion favored a policy of non-
interference.

Gallic ethics on this subject were superior. Primarily,
Frenchmen were never able to swallow the convenient doctrine that Negroes were a sub-human species. As far back as
1672, before regulations had been drawn, Governor-General
de Baas wrote from Martinique to Colbert:

"The slaves are forced to work twenty out of every twenty-
four hours. If, then, these miserable wretches do not have
beef to eat, how is it possible for them to endure so much
work by eating only potatoes, yams and cassava bread? If Irish
beef is not imported, it is certain that they will not be fed on
French beef. . . . I confess, Monseigneur, that I exhibit a
great deal of weakness in the matter of carrying out your orders, for slaves are human beings, and human beings should
not be reduced to a state which is worse than that of cattle."

Baas was challenging the folly, in the circumstances, of exclusive trade with France. Shortly afterward, the bars were
let down to Irish salt beef.

Half a century later, Le Page du Pratz wrote, in his
chronicles of Louisiana:

"As we know from experience that most men of low extrac-
tion, and without education, are given to thieving for their
necessities, it is not at all surprising to see Negroes thieve,
when they are in want of everything, as I have seen many
badly fed, badly clothed, and having nothing to lie upon but

the ground. I shall make but one reflection. If they are slaves, it is also true that they are men, and capable of becoming Christians. Besides, it is your intention to draw advantage from them. Is it not therefore reasonable to take all the care of them that you can?"

These excerpts, which could be matched from many sources, show that thoughtful, responsible Frenchmen had the interests of the Negro at heart. In 1685, between the times of Jean Charles de Baas and Le Page du Pratz, Louis XIV decreed the famous Code Noir, or Black Code, a charter for the protection of the slaves. Control of existing and future social relations between whites and blacks was also envisaged. It had sixty articles, meticulously phrased. The chief points covered were religious welfare, material welfare, punishment for offenses, the right to appeal to the courts in the event of maltreatment by masters, emancipation and miscegenation. The original code applied to the West Indies colonies. The version adopted for Louisiana in 1724 was substantially the same document. Important amendments by the Crown in 1736 and 1742 dealt with problems raised by the slave trade, the increasing number of half-breed children and the whole-sale manumitting of both mothers and offspring in such cases.

Let us consider the provisions of greatest significance. A group of articles required that all slaves be instructed and baptized in the Catholic faith, compelled to observe Sunday and feast days. They must, if Christians, receive the benefits of the Sacraments and be buried in consecrated ground. None but Catholic overseers could be placed in charge of Negroes. Priests were forbidden to perform the marriage ceremony for slaves without the consent of their masters, but the latter might not force a slave to marry against his will.

Another group set forth the kind of food and clothing to which slaves were entitled. Victuals must be furnished by the week and clothing once a year. Masters were forbidden to give slaves strong liquor in lieu of nourishment, or to evade providing food and other sustenance by having slaves farm for themselves one day a week. Old and sick slaves must be properly cared for; if abandoned, they were to be taken to the nearest hospital and there maintained at the expense of the master.

Apart from the obvious death penalty for murder, a slave was to be executed if he struck his master, mistress, husband of his mistress, or their children, wounding them or causing a flow of blood from the face. For the theft of horses and cattle, slaves were to be severely punished, "even with death, if the case merits it." But for stealing sheep, goats, pigs, poultry and vegetable foodstuffs, the penalty was not to exceed flogging and branding. Fugitives who had been gone a month or longer were to have their ears cropped and the fleur-de-lys stamped on one shoulder. For a second offense, the sinews at the back of a knee were to be severed and the brand applied to the other shoulder. A third offense was punishable with death. Freed Negroes who harbored fugitive slaves rendered themselves liable to a fine of thirty livres for each day each fugitive was with them. Other free persons incurred only ten livres a day for this misdemeanor.

Masters were prohibited from torturing or mutilating their slaves, "under any pretext," even that of obtaining evidence of heinous crime. They must not take the law into their own hands. All serious charges must be brought before a magistrate. The only punishment masters were allowed to inflict on their own judgment was a whipping with a light stick or piece of rope.

Slaves might appeal against their masters to the proper officials, if not adequately fed, clothed and housed, or if outraged physically. The courts were strictly enjoined to take action against cruel masters, without prejudice to the complainant—"ce que Nous voulons estre observé pour les crimes *et les traitemens barbares et inhumains des Maistres envers leurs Esclaves."*

The rules for emancipation were at first liberal. Any owner twenty-five years of age could release a bondsman by court action, or in his will. There were even some provisions for compulsory emancipation. Thus, if a slave were appointed by a master as tutor for his children, the slave was held by that fact to have been manumitted. Also, if a Negro man were freed and afterward married the woman slave who had lived in concubinage with him, she was thereby emancipated. Freed persons were regarded as naturalized and guaranteed "all the rights and privileges of those born free," but they were solemnly enjoined to be especially respectful to their former master and to the latter's widow and children.

In later years, attempts were made to discourage the practice of granting liberty to those of colored blood. The change of policy sprang from fear of the growing preponderance of blacks over whites, as well as a firm belief that miscegenation contained the seeds of political peril.

The original Code forbade whites to live in concubinage with slaves. A man who had offspring from such a union was to be fined 2,000 pounds of sugar. If the owner of the mother, he was to lose possession of the child, which was to be given to the nearest hospital as a slave and to be forever ineligible for emancipation. So severe a ruling was certain to be flouted. It became a dead letter from the start. When an occasional magistrate chose to make an issue of some case, the mother would coolly swear that she had been made pregnant by a roving sailor. Père Labat records humorously that a slave-woman questioned in court on a priest's complaint against her master most glibly and convincingly accused the priest of having been the father of her child. The judge thought it better to dismiss the case.

Strangely enough, the legal marriage of whites and Negroes

was not prohibited in the islands, though this was written into the Louisiana edition of the Code. Such marriages rarely or never took place, anywhere. Manumission of the mistress and her children came to be the practice of the West Indians. A new decree fixed a tax of three times her value as a slave, on every colored woman freed. This had an effect. Few were emancipated, except by testament, when the tax was sometimes collected from the heirs, but more often evaded. The percentage of free persons of mixed blood continued to rise, with the unfortunate result that the guarantee of equal rights and privileges was, in fact, suppressed.

The Code Noir rated slaves as furniture, but took benevolent cognizance of the human emotions involved. Thus, slaves might not be seized for their masters' debts unless the entire estate had been foreclosed. Families of slaves seized might not be broken up and sold separately. They were theoretically as fully protected from all forms of tyranny as were the indentured white servants who had come from France in the early days of colonization.

The question arises: Was the Code enforced? One can find many charges of cruelty to Negroes in the documents of the period. The answer would seem to be that the Code, intended to be a body of vital law, came to resemble a constitution by the authority of which serious cases could be decided. It really was unenforceable from day to day, since each plantation was a little kingdom, and the slave's privilege of appealing to powers beyond its frontiers was illusory. Sycophantish fellow-bondsmen could always be induced to give the lie to their kind. Public opinion in the colonies was strongly opposed to punishing a white man for any but a heinous offense against a slave. It will be noted that while the Code is positive in requiring that a master be prosecuted for killing a slave, it does not specify the death penalty for him in any circumstances.

But the colonists as a whole approved the Code and lived up to its provisions. This certainly was true in the small islands, in Guiana and Louisiana. The exceptions were chiefly encountered in Saint Domingue, where well-attested cases of torture appear in the archives, including some that were perpetrated by masters for no other reason save the amusement of their guests. The old buccaneer heritage was perhaps to blame. Men descended from the comrades of such sadists as l'Olonnois and Michel le Basque were apt to be scornful of the humane instincts. The entire record of the colony was one of violence, greed and crudity, in comparison with the other French settlements.

Even so, it is unbelievable that, as certain writers have implied, the majority of Saint Domingue planters and merchants were wantonly cruel to their slaves. The contrary must have been the case. The maltreatment of valuable human property was an economic folly, if nothing else, as Le Page du Pratz sagely pointed out. Saint Domingue could not have become the great sugar country that it was, had it been a common thing for Negroes to be burned to death, blinded, buried alive in ants' nests, or crippled by merciless floggings.

Transactions which necessarily came before the courts were handled, in all the colonies, strictly in conformity with the provisions of the Code. Among these may be cited the care given old and sick slaves who had been abandoned, and the selling of Negroes seized for their masters' debts.

The best way of measuring the relative humanity of the French rules is to compare them with those of their rivals. One quotation will suffice. It is from W. J. Gardner, the Jamaican historian:

"The free use of the whip was perfectly legal. The slave code [English] was cruel in the extreme; it gave the master almost unlimited power, and sanctioned some of the most horrid enormities ever tolerated by law. It was passed in

1696. . . . Striking a white person, having stolen goods in possession, and many other offences, were punishable either with death or any other punishment the judges might wish to inflict, dismemberment being particularly specified. And when, in 1748, an effort was made to abolish this latter punishment, petitions were presented against any alteration being made. . . .

"Legs were cut off, or one or both ears; noses were split or otherwise mutilated; branding on the forehead and cheeks was common, and cases are on record where two or more of these punishments were inflicted on the same person for the same offence. Flogging was often added. Three men at St. Ann's Bay had their ears and noses cut off, and received thirty-nine lashes every Sunday for three weeks. Another wretch was put to death by a mode of torture too horrible to relate or to read of without a shudder. Some one, evidently at a much later period, has tried to erase the record, but in vain."

Notoriously, the selling of members of slave families to different buyers was not prohibited by the English code.

CHAPTER XV

Louisiana under the French

AFTER the departure of Bienville in 1743, Pierre de Rigaud, the Marquis de Vaudreuil, became Governor of Louisiana. The population was somewhat smaller than it had been when the Mississippi Bubble burst. Not more than 5,000 white persons and half that number of Negro slaves were living in the vast province. But they were genuine residents and many successful plantations had been established, as well as minor industries, including sawmills. Wealth was being produced. In New Orleans, twenty-five men owned property ranging in value from 100,000 to 300,000 livres. The city had begun to flourish as a trading and shipping center. Its most considerable export was tobacco, of which 200,000 pounds was sent in a year to France.

Vaudreuil set up a miniature court and gave the colony a taste of formal elegance. His marquise had accompanied him, and though she appears to have been a censorious and grasping woman, she was qualified to be a hostess after the manner of Versailles. The period also saw the commencement of an intellectual life in New Orleans. Leblanc de Villeneuve, an officer of the Governor's entourage, was a poet of sorts. He was warmly encouraged by Vaudreuil, who gave him the entrée to his house at any hour of the day or evening, while men who came on political or business errands were often kept waiting for hours.

The administration was not, however, a strong or efficient one. Governor and Intendant pulled against each other, much as we have seen them doing in Saint Domingue, but for trivial motives. Charles Gayarré, Louisiana's most distinguished historian, collected the records, obtaining many documents in Paris from well-nigh forgotten archives. Phelps summarizes them as "chiefly a monotonous repetition of the petty quarrels of officials, contradictory and garbled accounts of petty happenings, and the meanest acts of mutual retaliation and interference. De Vaudreuil constantly complains that the Intendant kept the public stores for his own use and refused to surrender any for the bounties which the Indians claimed as the price of their loyalty. The Intendant, on the other hand, especially the last one during De Vaudreuil's rule, Michel de la Rouvillière, states emphatically that the Governor, in his attempts to rule *en grand seigneur,* had given the military such precedence over the civilians that soldiers might and did insult and bully the citizens with impunity; that he had surrounded himself with a petty court of flatterers and dependents who held his favor and prevented justice from being done; that these favorites were granted all the monopolies and privileges," and so forth, and so forth.

Grace King judges the decade of Vaudreuil's rule less harshly. "The new influx of French and Swiss officers," she writes, "fresh from the centers of fashion and politeness, more than overmatched, in the estimation of the society of the capital at least, the virile virtues of the first settlers. 'Who says officer, says everything,' was the growling comment of the old inhabitants. It is needless to say that the women of the city were the first and most enthusiastic converts to the higher standard of the newer and more fascinating gay world."

Near the end of the administration, a play in verse called *The Indian Father,* by Villeneuve, was acted in the Governor's mansion. The year before, a Choctaw had sneered at a Colapissa during a quarrel, to the effect that he and all his tribe were no better than the fawning and mean-spirited dogs of the French. The Colapissa shot the Choctaw, then took refuge in New Orleans. The relatives of the murdered man demanded that the fugitive be turned over to them, and as the Choctaws were the colony's first line of defense against the incursions of the English, Vaudreuil felt obliged to order his arrest. The man could not be found. Then the father of the Colapissa went to the Choctaws and offered his own life in expiation of his son's crime. He met death bravely at the hands of the rival chief. This was the subject of the first drama written and produced in Louisiana. It delighted the audience, and later it was performed successfully at a theater.

The Indian theme had symbolic meaning, which was perhaps not realized by the dilettante author. Louisiana was too dependent on native allies, and these were beginning to waver. With the promotion of the Marquis de Vaudreuil to the governor-generalship of Canada and the arrival in 1753 of his successor, Louis Billouard de Kerlérec, the problem became acute. The War of the Austrian Succession had roused few echoes in North America. But the disastrous Seven Years' War, with its curtain-raiser of Indian fighting on the Ohio, quickly made itself felt. The English fleet dominated the Atlantic and the Gulf of Mexico, and the privateers of that nation captured many convoys of supplies from France. The maritime trade of New Orleans was throttled.

Kerlérec put the approaches of the Mississippi and the coastal fortresses in a fair state of defense. No attack from that quarter materialized. But he was receiving no funds from Paris, and he was forced to suspend his payments to the savages, even the ceremonial and highly important yearly gifts. In these circumstances, the supposedly friendly Choctaws and the rest began to double-cross him. They bartered goods in the forest with the English, and helped instead of hindered the raids of the Chickasaws, who had always been hostile to the French. The story of this administration is one of seeking combines and desperately playing off the newest allies against the deserters.

The planters were plunged into want. A religious quarrel between Jesuits and Capuchins disrupted the colony at the precise moment when it would do the most harm. Kerlérec was fanatically blamed for allowing a Jewish merchant to bring much-needed goods to New Orleans, in violation of the ban on Jews. Yet it had been only a few weeks since he had been forced to report to Paris:

"The Choctaws and the Alibamons harass us daily to have supplies and merchandise. They threaten to go over to the English if we cannot relieve them, and in the meantime, during their frequent visits, they devour the little that remains of our provisions and exhaust our meager stock of merchandise. We have just ground to fear and to expect hostilities from them. Therefore, our situation is not tenable and the whole population is in a state of keen anxiety."

A vendetta between Governor and Intendant, which originated in the affair of the Jewish merchant, ended in the recall of Kerlérec. Unjust charges caused him to be imprisoned in the Bastille for several years. When released and largely exonerated, he was a broken man.

Louisiana did not have another regular French Governor. Philippe d'Abbadie was given the title of Director with vague powers, as the Seven Years' War closed and the news of colossal losses of territory in North America became known. On the face of it, Louisiana had been saved from the wreckage. But there had been devised between the Bourbon monarchs of Europe, notably France and Spain, the singular treaties of the Family Compact, in a last, desperate attempt to halt the triumphal march of England. This dynastic arrangement, which had not benefited the French people and had brought woe to the Spanish, provided for more than mutual aid. The burdens of defeat were to be shared. Toward the end of the war, the English had seized Cuba. They gave up this magnificent island at the peace, taking in exchange Florida, which was not so valuable, but which the Spaniards prized for reasons of strategy and sentiment.

This was where the Family Compact figured in a deal that at first was kept secret. England had expressed dissatisfaction with the offer of Florida, unless that province could be extended to the Mississippi. So Choiseul agreed to let England have the part of Louisiana east of the river, excepting the city of New Orleans. Then, to indemnify Spain for the loss of Florida, the rest of Louisiana was yielded to her, for occupation at some later date. The plan was drawn up well in advance of the Treaty of Paris. Title was transferred to the Spanish plenipotentiaries on the day of the signing of the peace pact. But the first New Orleans heard of it was the order to evacuate all posts on the east bank, in favor of the English. The Spanish phase of the cession did not transpire until 1764.

It was bad enough to see the redcoats take over Mobile, Baton Rouge and Natchez, while foreign ships sailed freely on the Mississippi. The only help given Abbadie from France was a sum of money large enough to pay off the bonuses due the Indians for two years. Failing this, there would have been a massacre of the French. But the expensive friendship of the savages had not been purchased for long. They became insolent, a grotesque effect having been produced upon them by the English custom of firing frequent salutes on the river, as well as sunset guns. The Indians believed that these noisy discharges were for the purpose of celebrating victory and uttering defiance. As the French did not rush to silence them, or even make an effort to duplicate the uproar, they were rated as cowardly, a people who admitted their defeat.

Shortly after he received notice that Louisiana now belonged to Spain and that it would be his duty to surrender it on demand, Abbadie died. Foul play was suspected, but never proved. The ranking military officer, Commandant Philippe Aubry, took over the administration, and the indifferent Choiseul did not trouble to supersede him.

The year 1765 was marked by important events, the overture to one of the most dramatic periods of uncertainty that a colony ever knew. Distress over the imminent loss of French citizenship was unanimous. A party which hoped to reverse the decision came into existence, and as a first move sent young Jean Milhet to Paris to plead with the King and his advisers. Milhet went straight to the most imposing figure connected with the fortunes of Louisiana. This was none other than the Sieur de Bienville, then eighty-six, feeble and living in the strictest retirement. The youth gave the old chief an account of the loyalist movement, explained that it was led by Chauvin de Lafrénière, the Public Prosecutor, a son of one of Bienville's Canadian followers; that the two De Noyans, nephews of the founder and ex-Governor, were ardent adherents. Deeply affected, Bienville agreed to do his utmost to arrange an audience with Louis XV.

But it proved impossible to reach the ear of the Bien Aimé, himself aging now and sunk in debauchery. The favorites at Versailles were a new lot, and utterly indifferent to America. La Pompadour had died the year before. The best that could be had was a formal interview granted by the Prime Minister, Choiseul. Bienville took the word away from Milhet. Tears ran down his cheeks as he implored Choiseul to influence the King against giving up Louisiana. Then the colonial delegate filed his petition, made a brief speech.

The Minister was profoundly disinterested. His wildcat scheme for exploiting Guiana was under way, and such enthusiasm as his cold heart could muster spent itself there. He said that the cession to Spain was irrevocable. Bienville argued that the French monarchy had the upper hand and could reopen the question with Madrid. Choiseul shrugged. Advice to that effect could not come from him, he declared, since he had himself advocated relinquishing Louisiana. He thought it good business to palm off the financial burden of a province that had always been an expense to the Crown.

No further argument was possible. Bienville withdrew, the last political gesture of his life accomplished. Milhet sent a report to New Orleans, the receipt of which found the situation unchanged. Nothing had been heard from the Spaniards. The hope had dawned that they might never take the trouble to come.

But there had been a development, seemingly of no great moment at the time, which was to give Louisiana some of the virility of Quebec as a French country, no matter who its future rulers might be. Between January 1 and May 13, 1765, there arrived about 650 Acadian exiles, who took up land at Attakapas and Opelousas, west of the city. They were the forerunners of some 2,500, who came in the next few years and built up a sturdy peasantry. Their descendants are colloquially known as Cajuns.

The story of the expulsion of these people from Nova Scotia, after the English had conquered it from the French, is one of the poignant epics of American history. Longfellow's poem *Evangeline* is based on it. The French name for their Canadian maritime province had been Acadie. The inhabitants showed extreme distaste for English rule, and in 1755 their settlements were ruthlessly broken up, their farms confiscated. First sent to New England and other near-by British possessions, they maintained a stubborn passive resistance. Gayarré perorates on the subject as follows:

"How could they forget their wrongs and labor on English ground! How could they plough the soil that England owned, unless it were with the hope of sowing the Dragon's teeth,

destined to spring up in hostile array and to shed the blood
that vengeance claimed! During ten years the Acadians
thought of nothing else than finding the means of seeking
some genial clime, where they could be gathered under the
flag of France, and kept their eyes steadily fixed on the French
West Indies and particularly on Louisiana. Luckily for them,
they proved . . . *an intolerable burden to the English colonies,* and after ten years of suffering and vain longings, many
of them were permitted, encouraged and assisted to execute
their deeply cherished design of moving to the French colonies."

A few went to Guiana and stayed there. Some who had
scattered to even more distant places decided eventually to
make Louisiana their home. A strange destiny drew them
there just as the beloved flag was leaving. But it mattered
little. The parishes where they settled became lastingly
French.

Lafrénière's party was supported by the very first Acadians
to land. This was typical of them. Their able-bodied males
trained as a militia regiment, which placed itself under the
command of Jean-Baptiste de Noyan, a former cavalry captain, the one of Bienville's nephews who remained active in
the French loyalist movement.

Early the next year, word was at last received that a Spanish
Governor was on his way. Antonio de Ulloa landed in March,
1766, accompanied by only ninety men. His official standing
was high, yet not of the sort that might have been expected
to recommend him for the post. Ulloa was a savant, a most
distinguished astronomer and naturalist, whose naval career
had been used to serve the ends of science. He announced
that he would postpone taking possession of the country
until the arrival of all the soldiers he expected. Refusing to
recognize the Superior Council, he dealt only with Aubry,
who informed him that the people of Louisiana were "a set of
reprobates, infected with the rebellious spirit of republi-

canism." This leaked out, and a cry of indignation was raised by the colonists. No more Spaniards came. The French troops refused to obey Ulloa, and an unpopular compromise was arranged between the two chiefs. Aubry remained the nominal acting head of the administration, but governed according to the dictates of Ulloa. The opposition seethed.

As winter approached, the enigmatic Spaniard went down to the mouth of the Mississippi, where he lived for months in a shack, making scientific observations. He was thought to be demented. The populace could scarcely believe it when, in March, 1767, a ship from Peru brought one of the loveliest young heiresses of that viceroyalty, who became Ulloa's bride, the service being privately performed in the shack. There was then an attempt at establishing a social regime in an executive mansion, but New Orleans refused to warm to the couple.

Jean Milhet did not get back from Paris until the end of 1767. His prolonged absence had been interpreted by some as meaning that he still had hopes that his mission would be successful. The idea of passing to violent measures was doubtless reached after he had fully informed Lafrénière of the Court's attitude.

On January 20, 1768, Aubry wrote to his Government:

"I am still waiting for the arrival of the Spanish troops, without whom it is absolutely impossible that Ulloa should take possession of the colony. In the meantime, affairs are conducted as much as possible as if it had been effected."

He was a sturdy soldier, not clever enough to perceive what was going on under his nose. The better part of 1768 passed in apparent quiet. But the group headed by Chauvin de Lafrénière met frequently at the town house of one of their number, or at the suburban home of Mme. Pradel, mistress of the Intendant-Commissary Foucault. The important subordinates were J. B. de Noyan; Joseph Milhet, Jean's elder brother, a rich merchant; Pierre Marquis, a Swiss army officer; Joseph Villeré, commander of an out-of-town military district; Pierre Caresse, Pierre Poupet and Joseph Petit, merchants. Only the personality of Lafrénière need be considered in this brief survey.

Though of plebeian origin, he had so fine a presence that he had been nicknamed "Louis Quatorze." He was immensely ambitious, a man of strong passions, a domineering temper and luxurious tastes. Gayarré says that in all honesty he was temperamentally the aristocrat one moment, the democrat the next. This is an amalgam that—given Lafrénière's platform magnetism and burning eloquence—always succeeds with the crowd.

In October, he called a mass meeting which was attended by most of the influential persons of New Orleans and the nearby parishes. Five hundred signed a petition to the Superior Council, calling for the immediate expulsion of Ulloa and the restoration of the French regime. The next day, volunteers poured into the city, Noyan leading the Acadians and Villeré the descendants of John Law's German and Alsatian colonists. Marquis was appointed military chief. Aubry had only 110 men at his disposal, and he did not try to oppose the manifestation. The next day, the twenty-eighth, the Council met and listened to a fiery address by Lafrénière. Some of his words were memorable:

"In proportion to the extent both of commerce and population is the solidity of thrones; the two are fed by liberty and competition, which are the nursing mothers of the State, of which the spirit of monopoly is the tyrant and step-mother. Without liberty there are but few virtues. Despotism breeds pusillanimity and deepens the abyss of vice."

The Council then took unanimous favorable action on the petition. Ulloa was notified that he must leave on short notice. Escorted aboard a Spanish boat in the river, he departed calmly for Havana, where he wrote a long and dispassionate report on the Louisiana "rebellion," including the statement that it "would not have occurred if there had been twelve fewer persons in the colony."

Lafrénière's party, which had public opinion solidly behind it at the moment, sent three delegates to France to ask that the *fait accompli* be accepted. A great silence swallowed them. Nor was it possible to get the least inkling of how the Spanish Government felt.

In the spring of 1769—seven years, be it noted, in advance of the Declaration of Independence at Philadelphia—the leaders debated a momentous idea. Why should they not expel Aubry and his garrison, and form a republic? Marquis, the Swiss, suggested that it might be modeled on that of his native land. Lafrénière would be chief of state, with the title of Protector. Louisiana would become a refuge, where "the oppressed and the needy among all the nations of the earth could find a home." On reflection, the majority concluded that monarchial France, England and Spain would never permit it, and they put the dream away from them.

But, as Gayarré says, they "bequeathed to their posterity the right of claiming for Louisiana the merit of having been the first European colony that entertained the design of proclaiming her independence."

Their marking of time cost them much of their popularity. Lafrénière knew it. A few weeks longer, and it was too late to do anything. General Alexander O'Reilly, bearing a commission as the new Spanish Governor and backed by an overwhelming force, cast anchor at the mouth of the Mississippi. Aubry hurried to pay his respects. He was followed by Lafrénière, Marquis and Joseph Milhet, who went as spokesmen for their party, promising there would be no resistance since France had failed to support their first attempt. The three were suavely detained by O'Reilly to dinner.

The General was an Irish soldier of fortune, who after serving in the French and Austrian armies had met with brilliant success under Charles III of Spain. He had just been appointed inspector-general of the King's Caribbean colonies when word of Ulloa's misadventure came, and he was given sweeping authority to pacify Louisiana and to govern it temporarily. He was a strong man, yet soft-spoken, with a gift for being liked. Clemency as well as justice would guide him in dealing with the situation, he said, and the impression grew that no one was going to be punished severely.

O'Reilly took firm hold of the government. He conducted an investigation in a deceptively amiable manner, then seized the outstanding French loyalists. Twelve men were tried, the precise number mentioned by Ulloa, and all found guilty. Six were sentenced to be hanged, of whom the best known were Lafrénière, Noyan and Marquis. Six received prison terms.

No white man willing to act as hangman could be found, and it was thought improper to employ a Negro. So O'Reilly ordered out a platoon of grenadiers to shoot the condemned men. They died bravely. "The cry of liberty has been heard!" shouted Lafrénière as he fell.

After that, O'Reilly did inaugurate a moderate regime, keeping many of the French laws and not tampering with racial customs. The colony settled down to forty years odd of Spanish domination.

Two significant points about the tragic loyalist episode should be realized. It was motivated by a democratic, yet pro-French impulse, and it occurred at the same time as the culminating struggle of the Intendant's party against the Governor-General's party in Saint Domingue. Both these movements were influenced by the teachings of the Encyclopedists. Far from wanting to cut loose from the old country, the liberals of Louisiana and Saint Domingue desired to be in a stronger position to share as Frenchmen in whatever popular revolution might eventuate.

CHAPTER XVI

The Battle of the Saintes

FRANCE and England fought many naval engagements in the Caribbean, but few of battle proportions and only one that was of major historical import. The War of the American Revolution saw England beaten in the New World for the first time by sea and land. Northward, she was thrown back to the wastes of Canada, while Spain reconquered Florida. Southward, she still had Jamaica and a powerful West Indian fleet, but she lost in quick succession nearly all her smaller island holdings. If that fleet could be vanquished and Jamaica seized, her rout would be complete. France would take her place in control of the Caribbean, for by then such marine force as Spain possessed had become an appurtenance of the French Navy. There seldom has been a juncture when so much could be decided by a single battle. It is beside the point to argue, as some have done, that England would have regained everything in the Napoleonic Wars. Each climactic event must be credited with its face value. We do not know to what extent French dominance of the West Indies would have altered the course of the Napoleonic Wars.

The chance presented in 1782 was one for which France had been waiting from the date of her earliest rivalry with England in those waters. Afloat, the Anglo-Saxon, a born seafarer, had always had an advantage over the Gaul whose genius shone in land fighting. The personal had reflected itself in the general situation. France had never quite had the upper hand, even for a short period. At last it looked as if this could be reversed. The Battle of the Saintes, therefore,

deserves the most careful study, along with the strategy that
led up to it.

Sympathy with the American colonies was not the only
consideration that caused France to fight her ancient enemy
once more. She sought revenge for the crushing, humiliating
peace terms which had been imposed on her after the recent
Seven Years' War. But a successful revolution did not seem
very promising, and for two or three years France confined
herself to giving aid to Washington surreptitiously. After
the capture of Burgoyne and his army at Saratoga in 1777, the
case looked more hopeful, and the following year France
openly entered the war. Spain soon followed her under the
terms of the Family Compact.

It has been told in Chapter Eleven how the French gained
the ascendancy in the Lesser Antilles. We shall now trace the
activities of François Joseph Paul, Comte de Grasse, as the
best means of understanding the finale which was staged under
his command. He came to the West Indies at the age of fifty-
seven, as commodore of a small squadron to join the Comte
d'Estaing, then in charge of all naval operations there. De
Grasse was in the fight off Grenada which prevented the
British from retaking that island. He shared in an abortive
attack on Savannah.

Estaing was replaced by the Comte de Guichen. This admiral fought an indecisive engagement with Rodney off
Martinique. De Grasse, leading the van, distinguished himself by rescuing two ships from superior numbers. But the
French plan for a descent on Barbados was thwarted, and the
fleet retired to Guadeloupe for repairs. De Guichen performed little else. He escorted one convoy with troops into
Havana, then sailed for Europe with almost the entire Franco-
Spanish naval force, including De Grasse's squadron.

In the spring of 1781, twenty ships-of-the-line were ordered
to the Caribbean, and on the King's insistence De Grasse,

whose health was poor, went out with them as the new commander of the station. He found Admiral Samuel Hood blockading Fort Royal, Martinique, and forced him to be gone. De Grasse covered the seizure of Tobago, then went north to the Chesapeake on the greatest operation of his career.

The voyage was made at the request of Washington and Rochambeau, who had written to him describing their military problem and asking his help in attacking the English either at New York or at Yorktown. Rochambeau sent private word that he favored the southerly coup, and this preference De Grasse accepted. He arrived at the end of August with twenty-eight ships-of-the-line and cast anchor just within Hampton Roads.

Hood, meanwhile, had rushed from the West Indies to New York, under the mistaken impression that the action would be there. He joined Admiral Thomas Graves, a far less gifted officer, who had seniority over him and took command. The English fleet, consisting of nineteen ships-of-the-line, repaired to the Chesapeake. Though outnumbered, it squared off and fought when De Grasse came out. The fighting was relatively tame, only one ship, an Englishman, being destroyed. But the French won, and as Graves beat his retreat Cornwallis at Yorktown was left with no choice but to surrender. It is well to recall what historians have written about De Grasse's victory.

"It is doubtful whether any more decisive battle was ever fought on land or sea," says G. A. G. Callender, a Britisher. "Not since the Armada certainly had English vessels participated in a struggle that bore in its train consequences so momentous and world-embracing. It was not the Declaration of Independence that called the United States into being. It was not the French alliance or Burgoyne's defeat at Saratoga. It was the Battle of Chesapeake Bay that decided the main issue of the war." And Reich declares: "The battle off Cape Henry had ultimate effects infinitely more important than those of Waterloo. . . . De Grasse's action entailed upon the British the final loss of the thirteen colonies in America."

Foreseeing, or at the least believing, that the game in the north would offer no further difficulty, De Grasse inevitably passed to the campaign which, if successful, would have rounded out the French objectives and fixed his standing as one of the great admirals of history. The time had come to drive the English from the Caribbean. His plan was to assemble an overwhelming force, conquer Jamaica by a *coup-de-main*, turn and destroy the combined fleets that would gravitate to the spot.

De Grasse's first act after he got back to the West Indies was to participate in the capture of St. Christopher, which gave him an unbroken chain of bases from Martinique north. Lying securely at Fort Royal, he accumulated re-enforcements from France until he had thirty-five ships-of-the-line, as well as freighters and 6,000 soldiers. At Cap Français another 6,000 fighting men were waiting, and a Spanish fleet expected there was to consist of thirteen warships carrying 9,000 troops. The Admiral proposed to go first to the Saint Domingue rendezvous, then descend on Jamaica by way of the Windward Passage between Hispaniola and Cuba. He definitely did not want a preliminary naval battle in the Lesser Antilles.

The English position at first seemed weak. Rodney had been forced to go to England for an operation, and Hood on his return from the North American coast could rally only twenty-two sail. But in February, 1782, Rodney was on the scene again after crossing the Atlantic in five weeks, a speed which he declared to be "scarcely credible." The squadron he brought raised the English total to thirty-six ships-of-the-line, or one more than the French. He enjoyed another advantage which is rarely mentioned save in technical treatises. Accompanying him as chief-of-staff on gunnery was Sir Charles Douglas, an innovator who made six vital improvements in the handling of large pieces of ordnance aboardship. These revolutionized the delivery of a broadside, made it possible to fire the guns twice in three minutes, an efficiency until then unheard of. Experts feel that, barring accidents, victory was assured to the fleet that first used Douglas's reforms, used them that is to say before they were generally known and could be copied.

Rodney took his station at Gros Ilet Bay, St. Lucia, twenty miles from the southern tip of Martinique. He was resolved to compel a battle right there, for if De Grasse evaded the issue it might not be possible to overtake him before he reached Jamaica, which was defended by only four ships and 500 soldiers. To make sure that he would not slip away, Rodney stationed frigates strung out in a line to within sight of Martinique, and every day he climbed the hill on Pigeon Island to watch for himself through the telescope. He was sixty-three, and a martyr to gout.

Late in March, De Grasse received a rich convoy of supply ships from France. He held a grand ball which he invited the English officers to attend under a flag of truce. Few accepted, but the commanders exchanged gifts, choice French liqueurs and sweetmeats against English ale and cheeses. Civilities of the kind on the eve of battle were common in the elegant eighteenth century.

The secret of De Grasse's sailing orders was well kept, though rumors flew and the enemy was in a continuous tremor of excitement. At dawn on the morning of April 8, the fleet came out of Fort Royal harbor. It was a magnificent spectacle: thirty-five of the finest warcraft afloat, led by the chief Admiral's flagship, the *Ville de Paris,* a three-decker of 2,300 tons and 110 guns; and ranging to starboard, a convoy of 150 cargo ships, some of them loaded with ammunition and foodstuffs for the expedition, the rest merchantmen on their way to Saint Domingue. Second in command of the fleet was the Marquis de Vaudreuil, grandson of the former Governor of Louisiana, while the third ranking officer was Louis Antoine de Bougainville, celebrated as an explorer, the man for whom the bougainvillea vine was named. The soldiery had been embarked in the battleships, so there were no transports to hamper maneuvers. With a spanking breeze behind, the armada streamed north.

Rodney was almost immediately advised, but it took him until noon to be out, Hood's squadron in the van. By two-thirty in the afternoon, the respective lookouts could see one another from their crow's nests. De Grasse swept along the west coast of Dominica, easily holding his lead until night-fall. In the morning, however, Hood was uncomfortably near and coming on so fast that a brush was imperative. De Grasse decided to order his convoy into Guadeloupe, and to see that it got there safely he was forced to detach two fighting ships, his smallest. This reduced his strength to thirty-three.

The French were then off the group of islets called the Saintes, thirteen miles from Dominica and ten from Guade-loupe. To prevent pursuit of the convoy, it was necessary for De Grasse to engage Hood. He sent Vaudreuil's squadron of fifteen ships to the attack, which had scarcely been begun when extremely favorable conditions developed. The Eng-lish van had outsailed its main body, and Rodney was be-calmed under the lee of Dominica. If De Grasse had hastened to the scene with all his remaining vessels, he must have de-stroyed Hood, or crippled him and driven him in flight to-ward the Atlantic. The subsequent defeat of Rodney him-self would then have been probable.

Vaudreuil, however, was left to fight a conventional de-laying action. He sailed past Hood's craft to windward, cannonading at extreme range and doing some damage, especially to the rigging. No English ship was so hurt as to be forced to retire, but one Frenchman received injuries that made it necessary to send her to Guadeloupe. Callender puts it picturesquely that Rodney, meanwhile, "strained every nerve to pull and push his ships into the firing line. He dropped his boats and towed them. He set sails to entangle the breeze. Little by little he worked his will, and De Grasse then thought the time had come to discontinue the action. Such was the battle of the ninth of April."

During the next two days the fleets maneuvered, dissatisfied with their positions. Rodney was eager for a decision. De Grasse still wanted to shake off his pursuers, but he had bad luck with the great ship-of-the-line *Zélé*. She lost a mast, collided with a consort and rendered her *hors de combat,* then lagged far behind. To save the *Zélé* from capture, De Grasse changed his course and lost ground. Another collision occurred, this time with his flagship, the *Ville de Paris*. Her bowsprit and foremast gone, the *Zélé* was useless. The Admiral had a frigate take her in tow and head for Guadeloupe. Only thirty effective fighters were left him against the British thirty-six. Nor were his troubles with the *Zélé* ended. At dawn on April twelfth, he saw her within easy reach of four enemy vessels. If he had been willing to sacrifice her, it is likely that he could have escaped beyond the Saintes that day, for the wind was in his favor. Instead he ordered a right-about-face, interposed his van, and knowing well that that meant a general conflict he ordered battle signals flung out all along his line.

The two fleets moved parallel to each other on contrary courses, each ship firing, but not as yet throwing her full weight of metal. These common tactics were known in the lingo of the day as hauling one fleet across another. Battles often consisted of nothing else. When the adversaries got clear, they either swung around and repeated, or they continued on their way, each claiming victory. This was a sterner occasion.

De Grasse in his *Ville de Paris* occupied the exact center of his line, and Rodney in the *Formidable* the English middle. It took about an hour and a half for the two commanders to arrive opposite each other. They exchanged shots at point-blank distance, a few dozen yards, and passed on. The ships astern of De Grasse were in some disorder, caused by a veering wind. The *Glorieux* and the *Diadème,* last of the Admiral's division and preceding the rear led by Vaudreuil, had fallen out of position. There was an abnormal gap between them. As the *Formidable* came up, the *Glorieux* engaged her hotly, supposing that in a minute she would be succeeded by a new antagonist. It was ten o'clock of a hot, cloudless day. The water in the Saintes Passage was a most brilliant blue, darkening to purple on the Caribbean side.

Rodney at this point unleashed his celebrated stroke of "breaking the line," a maneuver that had not been employed for a hundred years and was now so admirably executed by him that his fame is forever associated with it. The accounts differ. There seems little doubt that it was not premeditated, that in consultation with Sir Charles Douglas he seized the opportunity that arose. But it is certain that, without warning, he swung the *Formidable* to starboard between the *Glorieux* and the *Diadème,* pouring simultaneous broadsides into both of them. The improved gunnery of Douglas then paid tremendous dividends. The *Diadème* was sunk by the first broadside, the *Glorieux* sent reeling into the fire of one of the English Admiral's following ships.

Most of Rodney's division had automatically turned when he did, and they went down the broad path that had been **blazed. Hood** to the rear was quick to imitate. He burst through a short distance south of De Grasse's *Ville de Paris,* punishing the *César* and *Hector* with broadsides as he came. Only the English van, under Sir Francis Samuel Drake, a descendant of Queen Elizabeth's privateer, did not take part in this phase of the battle. It had sailed clear beyond, but was now signaled to go about and return.

The French fleet had been broken up into three disjointed sections, no longer competent to act together. The center became a chaos of scattered ships. The day already was lost. Vaudreuil, commanding the rear, maintained some sort of order and kept the way open for the escape of survivors. Bougainville wasted no time in leading the van to safety; any other course on his part would have been a useless gesture.

A *mêlée* of terror and grandeur raged, with the *Ville de Paris* as the chief objective. Rodney was intensely eager to subdue her himself, but although he fought the *Formidable* in circles around her he was unable to close in. The first French ship to strike her flag was the battered *Glorieux*. She had made a magnificent fight of it, losing four-fifths of her men. Her captain fell, and his body was thrown to the sharks, which ominously swarmed that day. The ranking lieutenant nailed the fleur-de-lys standard to the stump of a mast and fiercely urged his men on. Mere strips of the cloth remained to be torn away in token of surrender when resistance was no longer possible.

The *César*, also, battled to the last gasp, which for her was a geyser of flames leaping up from her hold, where stored liquors had become ignited and spread to the gunpowder casks. She burned to the water's edge and went down, many of the survivors being snatched from the wreckage by sharks. The *Hector* proved tenacious, as did the *Ardent,* a prize taken from the English a few years before. They both surrendered shortly after five o'clock, and that these mauled craft could have lasted the seven hours since the line was pierced at ten in the morning illustrates the remarkable staying power of wooden walls. A modern ironclad similarly overwhelmed would not have survived twenty minutes.

At the heart of it all, the *Ville de Paris* endured the supreme punishment. Ship after ship bore down on her, blasted her with round-shot and sheered off. De Grasse had informed his officers that he would not quit in any circumstances. His courage was superb, but he moved as one in a dream. He was not a well man. It is curious that both the chiefs should have been ill that fateful twelfth of April. Rodney suffered so from his gout that he spent much of the time on the bridge in an armchair.

The *Ville de Paris* was raked until not a spar remained on her, and she drifted helpless, her rudder gone. More men had been killed on her than in the entire British fleet. Only three were left unwounded on the upper deck, and strangely enough one of these was De Grasse. Then Hood came in his flagship to within pistol shot, took the fire of the lone gun the French could operate and retorted with a last and crushing broadside. Callender says colorfully that De Grasse, "compelled by a stronger power to do that which he had vowed he would not do . . . somehow found his way to the halyard and lowered the flag of France with his own brave hands."

This occurred precisely at sunset. De Grasse was escorted to the *Formidable* and into Rodney's presence. He was shown every courtesy. The carping Hood sneered later that in his joy over this capture Rodney accepted the victory as complete, when he should have pursued "under easy sail, so as never to have lost sight of the enemy in the night, which would clearly and most undoubtedly have enabled him to have taken almost every ship the next day."

Vaudreuil got away with his command intact. He picked up five more fugitives en route and reached Cap Français with nineteen ships-of-the-line, a respectable fleet. Bougain-

THE RAVINE AUX COULEUVRES
Defeat of Toussaint l'Ouverture by Leclerc's forces.

From the engraving by Karl Girardet

ville fled 600 miles southwest to the safety of Dutch Curaçao. Only seven main units had been destroyed or captured by Rodney, but two of those that had been damaged before the battle also were lost. The *Ville de Paris* and the other prizes which still floated never reached England. They were towed first to Jamaica and patched up. During the Atlantic passage they all foundered.

It was Rodney's intention to proceed against Vaudreuil. Ironically, he found orders at Jamaica to "strike his flag and come home." They had been sent before the news of the Saintes was known in London. Nevertheless, he thought it incumbent on him to obey. There was no further naval action in the Caribbean before the end of the war. It turned out that none was needed. The French were unable to assemble another grand fleet. When the treaty of peace was signed the following January, England gained terms to which she could not have aspired without Rodney's victory. In the West Indies she ceded only Tobago.

Louis XVI's statesmen probably did not accept it as a final decision regarding the hegemony of the Antilles. The answer has been given by the Muse Clio. France was never again in a position to challenge England in that sphere.

Chapter XVII

The French Revolution

THOUSANDS of books have been written on the French Revolution, and in few of these do we find more than a paragraph or two recounting contemporaneous events in the French West Indies. On the other hand, there is a fairly large bibliography of the slave revolts which culminated in the independence of Haiti, histories overshadowed by the colossal change in France, but showing little comprehension of its true effect upon the colonies. It amounts to this: In the story of the Revolution, the colonies have been given a footnote when they rated at least a chapter. They were swung by the same tide, produced their quota of heroes and scoundrels; they experienced massacres, saw the rise and fall of desperate, misguided factions. Separation from France was not the objective. It occurred only in Saint Domingue and under a later regime, that of Napoleon, who sought to destroy the popular liberty that had been won. An attempt will be made here to correct the warped perspective which has been characteristic of this matter.

The Revolution did not come suddenly. It had been prepared by the enlightenment spread by the Encyclopedists; by the opinions of Voltaire and Rousseau, the man who believed that liberty is a human achievement, and the man who believed that it is a natural right. The immediate cause of violent measures was the financial chaos of the realm, with its accompaniments of gross extravagance in high places, unemployment, crushing taxation and famine conditions among the poor.

In 1787, the Société des Amis des Noirs was founded in Paris by Brissot, Sieyès and Condorcet, all three to be eminent on the moderate side in the Revolution. The membership of this organization grew with extraordinary rapidity. Lafayette, Mirabeau and the then unknown Robespierre joined it. Louis XVI commented amiably that he was an abolitionist himself at heart. The Amis des Noirs was an example of the philanthropical drift among well-meaning persons toward the end of the eighteenth century. It stood for just treatment of the blacks in the French colonies, and looked toward suppression of the slave trade and early emancipation. Almost at once circumstances enabled it to champion the Negro as an equal, and this it did with much more aggressiveness than its creators had intended. So much so that it became a common error to suppose that the Amis des Noirs was formed after the Revolution, instead of before it.

The little colonies had no understanding of what was happening in France. Saint Domingue, politically alert, with its Cercle des Philadelphes and the remnants of the Intendant's party, seemed to sense that great things were in the air. The acts of the States General in 1789 were followed with keen interest, which the six or seven weeks' delay in receiving the news by sailing ship merely intensified. That body voted itself a National Assembly, a term which had memories for the liberals of the colony. It was ordered by Louis XVI to disperse, and refused to the thunder of the voice of Mirabeau:

"We are here by the will of the people, and we will leave only at the point of the bayonet."

The vacillating King let the tribunes stay, and soon Paris was bringing a weight of public opinion, passionately republican in sentiment, to bear on them. Camille Desmoulins shouted the call to arms and the Bastille was stormed on July fourteenth. *"Liberté, Egalité, Fraternité!"* became the watchword. The Marquis de Lafayette, his glittering service in the cause of American independence but a few years behind him, was made chief of the national guards and personally devised for them the tricolor cockade. By August fourth, the National Assembly had adopted decrees which swept away the privileges of feudalism. Again the King acquiesced. The next reform was to be a written constitution and its preface, "The Declaration of the Rights of Man and of the Citizen."

For the rest of that year and through 1790, the Revolution in France followed the comparatively slow course with which students of history are familiar. But the colonies reacted in bewildered and violent fashion. The plantation owners chiefly feared the confiscation of their property. Those of Saint Domingue rallied behind the aristocrats and military leaders of the party that had been dominant since 1764, and they were joined by most of the "small whites" who had material holdings of any sort. This faction preached, at the beginning, unquestioning loyalty to the King. The landless professional men and the artisan class came out against him. The garrisons of regular soldiers grew disaffected and refused to obey their officers. People did not really know where they stood. All authority declined.

Saint Domingue's Governor-General and Intendant of the old regime struggled helplessly to maintain order; they were glad at last to go. The men sent in their places found themselves equally powerless. The troops on which they depended had become quite lawless. The militia was controlled by the Royalists, as it will be most convenient to call the rich planters and merchants, and to the latter the new officials were creatures of the upstarts of Paris.

Meanwhile, important moves had been made. The Royalists decided that they ought to be represented in the French National Assembly. They chose deputies by a process that had no legal justification and sent them to claim seats. Almost at the same time, the Comité Colonial, an organization of

Saint Domingue proprietors living in France, many of whom had never been in the colony, came to a similar conclusion and brought pressure to bear. But the Société de Correspondance des Colons Français, commonly called the Club Massiac, sprang up in opposition. The last-named was guided by cautious liberals of the type of Moreau de Saint-Méry, the famous writer of Martinique birth, and Duval-Sanadon. The colonial Royalists and the Comité won. The National Assembly agreed to admit ten deputies from overseas, six of whom were credited to Saint Domingue.

Vaissière thinks that the whites committed an error when they agitated for these seats. Instead, they should have maintained special agents in Paris to lobby for non-interference with the colonies. The deputies were lost in the mass of the Assembly and their ideas were voted down. "From then on, Saint Domingue's fate was to have laws imposed on it." That, however, is the view of an extreme conservative.

The National Assembly was all too timid about extending liberty to slave-holding territory. In October, 1789, a delegation of free mulattoes from Saint Domingue, headed by Vincent Ogé, who had been residing in France, appeared before it and demanded equal political rights, including the franchise and eligibility to public office. Moreau de Saint-Méry remarked, "If you apply the Declaration of the Rights of Man in this business, well—there will be no more colonies!" A furious debate resulted in the Assembly conceding the franchise only to "all persons" twenty-five years of age, owners of real estate or taxpayers. This gave the vote to a few thousand mulattoes. Also, though not on the same occasion, the legislative body proclaimed that the colonies were no longer possessions, but "integral parts of the French empire." The setting up of Colonial Assemblies to handle all local matters was authorized.

The effect upon the whites in Saint Domingue was electric.

It unified them on the one question of keeping mulattoes from even the most remote participation in government. The propertied believed that otherwise the supremacy of the planter class could not be maintained. They felt that they must remove colonial affairs from consideration of the French National Assembly. But they could not agree on the best way to attain their end. So they broke into two groups. The true Royalists looked to army officers for leadership and decided to support the Governor-General as a symbol of authority. The second group took the name of the Patriots and swept to its support the discontented lower class that had previously been impassioned for the Revolution. In this strange climax there vanished forever the issues between aristocrats and bourgeois described in Chapter twelve.

Elections for the new Colonial Assembly were held in the spring of 1790. The Patriots easily obtained a majority. When the body convened, it elected as its president a fire-eating nobleman, Bacon de la Chevalerie. Disdaining the term "Colonial" as being beneath its dignity, it declared itself the General Assembly of the country. It adopted the motto, "The King, the Law, Union is Our Strength," without mention of France, and voted a constitution which was tantamount to an act of independence. The King was the sole bond with the past retained. Thenceforth, laws passed in the colony were to be at once applicable; they could be quashed only if the King vetoed them. Laws originating in France were not to run, unless accepted by the colony. The entire structure was an anticipation of the self-governing Dominions established by Britain in the following century. The Assembly required of the Governor-General and his troops a special oath of fidelity. This was refused, the Governor-General was declared deposed and the troops were ordered disbanded.

This action had the drawback of being insincere. The

Patriots confidently looked for the eventual triumph of the Bourbons. When that occurred they wanted Saint Domingue to be once more a colony, not an autonomous state. The temporary severance they desired was a severance from the France of the Revolution. If they had proclaimed their country a nation, jettisoned the King along with all other European impedimenta and called on the people to follow an American flag, they might have received general support. But it was not in them to do so. They feared they would be unable to keep control for their race within the new framework. Nor, it must be admitted, would it have been in character for transplanted Frenchmen of any caste to adopt the course that has at times appeared so logical to Anglo-Saxons and Spaniards. Even Lafrénière in Louisiana, twenty-five years before, had shrunk from it.

The gathering at Saint Marc proved unable to put its constitution into effect. The Royalists marched against it with regular troops. Its membership began to disintegrate. Finally, on August eighth a rump of eighty-five members, the most radical, voluntarily sailed for France to appeal to the National Assembly.

In Paris this was called the insurrection of the whites. The National Assembly scornfully refused to sanction any of the acts of its colonial imitator. But it did nothing to punish the authors of the Saint Marc constitution, and later it allowed many of these persons to go back to Saint Domingue.

With some variations, the march of events in the other West Indian colonies had been parallel. Opposing the distracted regular authorities, extremist groups struggled for power. The worst of these leaned on disorderly elements: the unemployed populace of the towns, merchant sailors and discharged soldiers. The plantation owners clung to what was left of the royal prestige and did their utmost to orientate the new Colonial Assembly against the Revolution. Armed clashes were avoided in Guadeloupe, but in Martinque a civil war broke out.

The Martinique conflict turned into one between town and country, that is to say between Saint Pierre and the rest of the island which had always hated Saint Pierre as being the creditor community. In imitation of the large commercial cities of France, the capital had gone heavily democratic. Legislators and agriculturists, great and small, decided to resist it. Blockaded by land and sea, it was a besieged place throughout the autumn of 1790. There was talk of destroying it utterly. It might well have been burned if volunteers from Guadeloupe, led by J. C. Dugommier, had not come to the aid of the "Pierrotine citizenry," to employ a term then current and which rings fancifully in modern ears.

Dugommier's intervention was accompanied by further bloodshed. Yet it had the fortunate result of establishing an even balance between the factions and disgusting them both with strife. The rancor that ate so deeply into the social life of Saint Domingue did not exist here. A truce was patched up. Men waited with various emotions to see whether the parliament in France would go so far as to emancipate the slaves. The ideals of the Revolution assuredly pointed to this. But powerful reactionary forces were at work in Paris to counteract the propaganda of the Amis des Noirs, and so far even the scandalous importation of living cargoes from Africa had not been outlawed.

In the autumn of 1790, Ogé came from France to Saint Domingue. The whites treated him like a pariah, even those who had declared themselves on the democratic side. The decree of the National Assembly giving the vote to free mulattoes (the word is used here to signify all gradations of mixed-bloods) had been venomously denounced. Ogé was warned that if he tried to take any part in an election he would be killed. He fled to a mountainous district in the northeast near the Spanish border, then rashly uttered a call to arms. There had been no preparation worth speaking about. Ogé simply appealed to the emancipated of his color to rebel and take over the country. He offered the services of himself and his lieutenant, Chavannes, as chiefs.

That as many as 300 volunteers responded is astonishing. Ogé started to lead them in the direction of Cap Français. A strong column of regulars and militia met the little band, fought a sharp engagement and scattered it. Ogé and Chavannes escaped into Spanish Hispaniola, where they were arrested and turned over to the French authorities under an extradition agreement then in force.

The imprisonment, trial and execution of these two men constitutes a lamentable chapter in the drama of sadism that was now on the verge of its swift unfolding. They were taken to Cap Français, where all the elements most hostile to them were concentrated. Not least was the rabble of "poor-white" adventurers of this largest city in Saint Domingue. Vaissière says that the rogues and criminals of the Cap needed close police supervision even in ordinary times, and that with the Revolution they became a serious peril. They professed a ferocious Jacobinism to cover their lust for cruelty and plunder. He adds that their brutality to the Negroes and mulattoes, whom in theory they should have hailed as comrades, did much to aggravate the race question.

Ogé and Chavannes were victimized at a court-martial unnecessarily prolonged, during the course of which they were exposed to the insults of the vengeful. Their place of confinement was by intent carelessly guarded. Ruffians surged about it day and night, threatening to drag them out and tear them to pieces. Inevitably, they were found guilty and sentenced to death. It was specified that they must be publicly broken on the rack and wheel.

The savage penalty was exacted on March 12, 1791. Parties

of planters, including many of their women, drove in from the countryside to witness it. But nine-tenths of the audience was made up of the Cap Français mob, which howled gleefully over the tortures applied with medieval skill and callousness. The exhibition was supposed to be for the purpose of striking terror into the colored people. Few Negroes and mulattoes stood there to watch.

Large numbers, a majority it is said, of Ogé's followers had been apprehended after his defeat. About twenty of them were sentenced to be hanged, the rest given prison terms. The executions were strung out over a period of weeks, the gibbets being erected in various parts of Cap Français and the bodies left dangling for several days.

As is often the case with the leaders of forlorn hopes, Vincent Ogé became a martyr in the minds of his people. His death accomplished some good, though not so much as it might have done if the white colonists had been capable of a modicum of tolerance regarding the political rights of the mulattoes. In France it occasioned great horror. The Amis des Noirs made the most of it. Sympathizers produced a tableau of Ogé's end upon the stage. Almost immediately, the legislators responded with the following enactment:

"The National Assembly decrees that it will never deliberate on the political status of colored persons not born of a free father and mother, without the spontaneous previous consent of the colonies; that the Colonial Assemblies now in existence shall continue; but that persons of color, born of a free father and mother, shall be admitted into all future parochial and other Assemblies, if they have the other requisite qualifications."

The number of mulattoes who could benefit under the above compromise was small, for most members of their caste had been born of slave mothers. Nevertheless, the color line had been broken, and if the colonists had had the sense to take advantage of this in circumstances for which they could disclaim responsibility, they might have prevented the rebellion of the slaves. A three-cornered alliance, to consist of the officials appointed from France, the mulattoes and the white Creoles of all factions, was clearly indicated as the course of reason. It was adopted in two possessions off the east coast of Africa—Bourbon (now Réunion) and Ile de France (now Mauritius)—and as a result those islands escaped the horrors of a race conflict.

But the whites of Saint Domingue fiercely resented the action of the National Assembly, called it a violation of the powers conceded to the Colonial Assembly, and declared that they would resist it to the death. Blanchelande, the third Governor-General since 1789, took their side. He wrote the Ministry that he absolutely refused to enforce the decree. After describing the state of public opinion, he added:

"Three powerful motives combine to excite the present feeling: offended pride, fear for the colony's safety, and indignation at a broken promise. Seigneur, do not force me to repeat the threats which are upon every tongue; threats each more violent than the one before. The most loyal hearts are estranged, and a frightful civil war or the loss of the colony to France may well follow."

Blanchelande was not overstating the case. A few months earlier he had been driven from Port-au-Prince by Patriot agitation and forced to take refuge in Cap Français. Now he found himself the hero of both Patriots and Royalists. It was unfortunate. His vacillating nature prevented him from being a good influence. He did nothing to save the mulattoes from wanton persecution, and sporadic revolts of these people soon broke out in different parts of the country. Then the slaves began to stir, and neither Blanchelande nor the

Creole leaders had a plan ready for dealing with that problem.

Fears of a black revolution had been often expressed, but the general belief appears to have been that it would not occur, because the Negroes lacked arms and were strictly guarded. Saint Domingue, during the two years since the fall of the Bastille, had lived in a frenzied dream remote from the great reality. Whites and mulattoes alike imagined that they were the sole competitors for power. They thought that the message of liberty abroad in the world could not penetrate effectively to submerged and illiterate bondsmen. The subservience of the handful of freed blacks helped, no doubt, to delude them. It should also be remembered that the rich mulattoes were themselves slaveowners. Yet the population statistics of the year 1789 were ominous: Whites, 40,000; Free people of mixed blood, 25,000; Negro slaves, 480,000.

If the above figures are incorrect, the error lies in an underestimate of the third classification. Proprietors were given to falsifying their reports, in order to escape the detested poll tax on slaves. Some authorities hold that there were over half a million Negro slaves in Saint Domingue, a good eight to one over whites and mulattoes combined.

CHAPTER XVIII

The Black Revolution

WE COME now to the most somber, in many ways the most important, event in the history of the West Indian islands since
the Spanish conquest. The black revolution is one of the rare
examples of a completely successful servile uprising. It was
inevitable, but it need not have occurred at the time it did, or
need ever have taken the extreme form to which it was stimulated by the impolitic conduct of the whites. The first of-
fender was the National Assembly of France, which declared
in uncompromising terms for liberty and the rights of man,
yet refused to free the slaves. A gradual emancipation would
have sufficed. The Assembly, as we have seen, hesitated to extend the privileges of citizenship even to colored men already
freed, and it at last brought forth a grudging compromise
which penalized those whose mothers were in bondage.
Second, the master class was intransigent on the whole race
question to the point of mania, yet did not maintain a united
front. White colonists argued and fought about the kind of
government they wanted, while putting mulattoes to the
torture for demanding a voice and proclaiming that blacks
were beneath consideration.

Common soldiers landing at the ports of Saint Domingue,
simple fellows who believed that the National Assembly was
as revolutionary as the Revolution, gave the fraternal embrace
to Negroes whom they met and told them they were free men.
Before long, these soldiers had been "educated" and were
found supporting either the Governor-General or the Patriot

faction. However, they and others introduced radical pamphlets into the island. Some reached the hands of literate slaves, who read them to groups of their fellows.

It was within the capacity of the most submerged of mortals to draw a lesson from this combination of facts. The Negroes understood that the chains of Frenchmen in France had been broken and a better order established, but that Frenchmen in Saint Domingue would have none of it for those whose skins were not white. Plainly the colonists belonged to the old order. So if the Negroes were to take liberty by force, they would be allies of the new France.

There had been slave revolts in the past, crude outbursts of violence, or attempts at mass poisoning of the whites. The motivation had been vengeance, and the chances of success limited. At last an idea was abroad. Unhappily, the tens of thousands who responded to it were savages who harbored grotesque superstitions and whose methods of warfare were completely barbaric. As always, due to the low fertility of slaves, more than half the able-bodied black males in Saint Domingue were African-born.

The early phase of the insurrection was plotted at meetings of the voodoo cult, the gory ritual of which served to enflame the hesitators. Historians friendly to the Negro used to deny this, but modern research work has shown it to be true. Voodoo, which still persists, is not a mere hocus-pocus of sorcery. It is a primitive religion transplanted, chiefly by Dahomean blacks, to the New World. The worship of the snake, the offering of human and animal sacrifices, the pulsing drums, the orgiastic dancing: these are only the outward manifestations. A hierarchy of gods commands the devotion of the faithful, and the voodoo *papaloi* and *mamaloi,* priest and priestess, exert great authority.

Boukman, a *papaloi,* and his accomplice Jeannot organized a conspiracy among the plantation hands of the northern plain of Saint Domingue in the summer of 1791. The program was simplicity itself. On a given night, the slaves would rise simultaneously and massacre their masters, man, woman and child. They would put the torch to everything, growing crops as well as houses. Then they would assemble under Boukman and march to the conquest of Cap Français, where the town Negroes were expected to co-operate.

Rumors of the business leaked out, but the planters and military officers refused to take it seriously. Their minds were fixed on mulatto rebellion as the only possible variety. Even a premature coup on August eleventh, at Limbé, a short distance west of the Cap, was treated as a labor mutiny, though white lives had been lost. Defense works had been begun on the outskirts of the city during the Ogé revolt. This was fortunate. They could be strengthened quickly.

The night of August twenty-second, Boukman presided at a voodoo ceremony in the woods, at which the blood of a sacrificed pig was drunk. No one will ever know exactly what vows were made. Other voodoo meetings occurred near by. It was the hurricane season and a storm raged that night, with lightning and thunder, and torrential rain. As the weather cleared around midnight, hundreds of slaves ran over the Turpin plantation and butchered all the whites they found, accompanying the slaughter with the iniquities of torture, mutilation and rape. They spread to adjoining estates, where the tumult was already under way. A few of the planters fought tenaciously, but most were caught in their beds and their resistance was on the whole futile. Dawn found the massacre and burning of property unabated. The Negroes took especial joy in smashing sugar factories, machinery and tools, regarding them as symbols of bondage and taking no thought that they could be used for their own profit in the event of victory. They yelled deliriously as the flames devoured everything.

Cap Français had been warned by wind-borne cinders and a sky of lurid copper. Occasional fugitives arrived with disjointed reports. The next day a party of militia went out into the plain a short distance, but was driven back by a huge mob of Negroes. Regulars followed, with equally poor success. The appalled inhabitants of the Cap were thrown into desperate confusion. The blacks either had been unable to get arms, or had not dared to rise. The mulattoes felt that this slave explosion was no affair of theirs. The whites saw no way of taking the aggressive. Anticipating an assault on the city, however, the soldiery kept vigilant watch in their entrenchments.

At the end of a week, the better part of the northern plain, the richest section of Saint Domingue, was a wilderness of ashes strewn with the decaying corpses of men and beasts. Then Boukman and Jeannot led their hordes against Cap Français. They were routed at the fortifications, with the loss of hundreds in dead and prisoners. Boukman was killed, his head cut off and raised on a pole within the city. All of the captives who appeared to have acted as instigators and many who had not were broken on the wheel.

The rebels fell back into the plain, where they continued their work of carnage and blind destruction. Joined by the slaves in the surrounding hill country, they ravaged the coffee plantations with the same fury they had shown toward the sugar estates. Their dominance reached eastward to the Spanish border. Jeannot was insanely cruel even to his own people. They put him to death and elected Jean-François and Biassou as their new leaders. These men soon found themselves in a tense struggle with mounted bands of whites, who had organized in the parishes adjoining the devastated region. Their overwhelming numbers enabled the blacks to keep the upper hand, mainly by guerrilla tactics. When they did engage in a pitched battle, they followed the old African pattern to the letter. The anonymous author of the *Désastres de Saint-Domingue* writes:

"Their enterprises have about them something truly terrifying by the very manner of execution. . . . They first advance with a frightful clamor, preceded by a great number of women and children singing and yelling in chorus. When they have arrived just out of gunshot of the whites, the most profound silence suddenly falls, and the Negroes now dispose themselves in such a manner that they appear six times as numerous as they are in reality. The man of faint heart, already daunted by the apparent multitude of his enemies, is still further shaken by their noiseless posturings and grimaces. All this time the ominous silence continues; the only sounds coming from the voodoo priests, who now begin to dance and sing with the contortions of demoniacs, to assure the success of the coming fight. . . . The attack takes place with cries and howlings which, nevertheless, should not shake the courageous man."

Bryan Edwards, the eminent British West Indian historian, came early to the Cap from Jamaica, bringing relief supplies voted by the Government of that island. He wrote of "cruelties unexampled in the annals of mankind; human blood poured forth in torrents, the earth blackened with ashes, the air tainted with pestilence." According to his computation, "within two months after the revolt began, upward of two thousand whites had been massacred, one hundred and eighty sugar plantations and about nine hundred coffee, cotton and indigo settlements had been destroyed; and twelve hundred families reduced from opulence to abject destitution." He believed that more than ten thousand insurgents had died by the sword or famine, the latter caused by their own folly in destroying foodstuffs.

Chaotic conditions developed thereafter in all parts of Saint Domingue, with loyalties so mixed that it is well-nigh impossible to disentangle them. But the central, lasting fact was the success of the Negro slaves in maintaining what they had won and slowly extending the frontiers of their control until that distant day when they engulfed the whole colony.

The events of the northern plain inspired the mulattoes to break out in revolution at several points. Assuredly they did not do this in the cause of human liberty, but for the purpose of taking the political rights which the National Assembly had granted them and which the whites on the spot were nullifying by hook or by crook. They had concluded that they could become the dominant caste, and it is not to be denied that it was their intention in that case to trample on the whites and perpetuate slavery.

An extraordinary alliance was formed. The mulattoes of Port-au-Prince, where they had seized full power, and the Royalists of the plantations inland from the capital agreed to co-operate. The vote and eligibility to office was conceded to free mixed-bloods by the terms of the famous pact which took its name from the township of La Croix des Bouquets. It is often quoted as proof of sweet reasonableness on the part of the best whites. These Royalists, however, were insincere. Their leader, Hanus de Jumecourt, received a letter from his commandant at Saint Marc, in which it was stated:

"You have three classes of brigands to fight. First, white brigands [the Patriots], who are the most to be feared. Leave them to be destroyed by the mulattoes, if you do not care to destroy them yourself. Next, with the aid of the mulattoes, you will reduce the rebel Negroes. After that, you will gradually restore the old laws, and by that time you will be able to suppress the troublesome element among the mulattoes themselves."

The double-dealing of the other party was equally flagrant, and the concordat of the Croix des Bouquets did not long endure. Its aftermath was consistent mulatto opposition to the whites, then a reluctant turning toward the blacks—too late to be convincing.

Some of the strangest anomalies were as follows:

The slaves in the parishes at the extremity of the southern peninsula, the district called the Grande Anse, remained unaffected for years by either the French Revolution or the black uprising in the north. This made it possible for the planters to arm their people, use them to expel or kill the mulattoes and long maintain independence of the rest of the country.

The wild Negroes of the western central mountains, descendants of runaway slaves and new recruits of the same type, were known as *marrons,* or in English maroons. Their counterparts had played an important role in Jamaica, and in imitation of the compromise that had been reached there the colonial Government of Saint Domingue had recognized the tribal existence of the maroons by a formal convention, in the year 1784. The wild men had always declared themselves the most steadfast advocates of freedom. Yet they would have nothing to do with the Revolution. They aided the conservative whites, and after these had passed they got behind every new force that promised to check the mob democracy in which they dreaded that their individualism would be swamped.

Weirdest fantasy of all, many of the revolting slaves at the outset regarded themselves as the stanch vassals and champions of the King of France. They mixed up this idea with that of their personal emancipation, which they imagined he had ordered and that the colonists were selfishly withholding. They confused him with the Amis des Noirs. The voodoo priests had perhaps found it the easiest form in which to present to the ignorant a cause worth fighting for. It was reenforced by the perpetually smoldering lust for vengeance on the taskmaster. One of their leaders, and by no means the least intelligent, said later, "Since the beginning of the world we have obeyed the will of a king."

But childish notions of the sort did not impair the potent, deep fermentation of the black revolution, and were in time abandoned. Real chieftains emerged, of whom the greatest was Toussaint l'Ouverture. His immediate predecessors were the already-mentioned Jean-François and Biassou. The former merits some notice.

We know little about the antecedents of Jean-François, except that he was a Negro slave, one of the original plotters of the revolt and on friendly terms with Boukman, the *papaloi*. When Boukman and Jeannot were killed, it was logical that Jean-François should be raised to leadership. He domineered over his partner, Biassou. Everything indicates that Jean-François was a shrewd fighting man, but self-seeking and absurdly vain. On the strength of succeeding to the honors of the butchery on the northern plain, he took the title of Grand Admiral of France. It will be seen that this was not quite so grotesque as it appeared to be, for he may have had a premonition of the finale toward which he was heading.

The National Assembly sent three commissioners to Saint Domingue in November, 1791, to investigate and to use special executive powers with the object of restoring order. The position of Jean-François was stronger than it had been at any time since the massacre. Yet, in a letter signed by himself and Biassou, he offered the commissioners peace, in return for certain privileges for himself "and several hundred chiefs whom the writer will name." That was the measure of Jean-François.

Naturally, the commissioners were eager to accept. But the colonists protested bitterly at terms, much more rewards, being granted and "a premium put upon subsequent rebellions," as one planter expressed it. The black rank-and-file was equally indignant. Jean-François perceived that he had made a mistake. He befuddled his people into crediting him with having tried a clever ruse which he had hoped to turn to their advantage. He then fought with redoubled vigor. As his lines extended to the eastern border, he found the Spaniards willing to help with arms and food. They were influenced by religious horror at the French Revolution, as well as their ancient resentment at the colony planted in their territory by the buccaneers. Jean-François could scarcely believe his good fortune. He fraternized with the Spaniards, accepted an officer's commission from them, and behaved generally as if they could count on him to bring about the reannexation of Saint Domingue.

It is a question what would have become of the black revolution if this opportunist had been its supreme guide for long. But the man of destiny was on his way, indeed had risen in the service of Jean-François. Superficially, a bizarre savior. An ugly little Negro with a prognathous jaw, in his late forties. An island-born slave of Guinea ancestry, who had been stableboy, coachman and finally steward of the livestock on the Bréda plantation in the north. He was Toussaint l'Ouverture, the odd surname having been originally a sobriquet, it is said, given him by fellow bondsmen because of a gap in his teeth.

Toussaint took no part in the first uprising. He had been well treated, had learned to read and write, had been allowed the use of whatever books the house contained. For this he was grateful. He protected his master's wife, Mme. Bayou de Libertas, and her family during the early weeks of terror. His influence over the other Negroes already was large, on account of his knowledge of herbs. They called him "The Physician." There is no reason to suppose that Toussaint indulged any fanatical hatred of the whites. His reflective mind condemned their system, that was all. He had a sense of nationalism for his people, but believed that Saint Domingue should remain attached to France as a self-governing black commonwealth.

In the late autumn he decided to enlist. He gave Mme. de Libertas full warning, helped her to pack her most treasured belongings and sent her to Cap Français, escorted by his brother Paul. The insignificant-looking fellow then joined the band commanded by Jean-François, who made him its doctor with vague authority as an officer.

The genius of Toussaint was quickly apparent. He introduced discipline and superior tactics in the field, and under his urging something resembling diplomacy was practiced by the rough chiefs in dealing with friends and foes. Where he had learned his technique is an unanswerable mystery. He was one of those born leaders of men who require no formal training. He was soon at the head of his own troop. Throughout 1792 he bided his time and perfected the best-drilled, best-armed force on the Negro side.

It is impossible, in the small space available, to record the progress of this revolution except by drastically summarizing many of the outstanding events. Now that the inception has been told in some detail, it becomes necessary to be much more terse.

The first set of commissioners sent by the National Assembly having proved ineffective, they were recalled and three new ones appointed in 1792. They arrived the middle of September, and almost simultaneously the National Assembly was replaced in France by the National Convention, a far more radical body. The commissioners, Sonthonax, Polverel and Ailhaud, were all Jacobins, fired by the extremist spirit that was to gain the ascendancy in the Convention. Of the three, the baleful Sonthonax had the strongest will and consistently overrode the somewhat milder Polverel. Ailhaud, a weakling, dropped out of the picture before long.

Establishing himself at Cap Français as a dictator backed up by the 6,000 soldiers that had accompanied the commission, Sonthonax dissolved the Colonial Assembly and replaced it with a temporary advisory council composed of six whites, five mulattoes and one free Negro. He shipped Blanchelande to France under charges of maladministration and suspected treason to the Revolution. It was the archcommissioner's plan to smash everything resembling royalism, humble the planter class and set up a Government composed of proletarian elements. He was not friendly at first to the revolting slaves.

Léger Félicité Sonthonax—such was his ironic name—merely succeeded in intensifying the civil strife. The favoritism he showed to mulattoes ended the least trace of cooperation between them and the white Creoles. For a season, the latter kept the upper hand in the field. But this crisis marks the rise of the very able mulatto leader, André Rigaud, and his scarcely inferior lieutenant, Alexandre Pétion. Rigaud later received the mission of conquering the tenacious planters of the Grande Anse in the south. He was bloodily repulsed, but entrenched himself at the town of Aux Cayes, which became the center of the only area of genuine mulatto supremacy. It should be clearly understood that during the period of the second commission the black revolution did not extend beyond the northern plain and the mountains that enclosed it to the east and south.

In January, 1793, Louis XVI was beheaded, and the world knew France to be democracy incarnate, the sworn enemy of kings. War followed almost immediately with England, Spain and Holland. This placed Saint Domingue in peril of foreign conquest, an eventuality which the white colonists hailed as preferable to any of the other threats hanging over them. Such matters moved slowly, however, in the eighteenth century. Sonthonax was prepared to resort to any measure that would give him control and at the same time make the colony too hot a chestnut for outsiders to wish to touch. He began to think of the blacks as allies.

The arrival at Cap Français in May of General Galbaud as the new Governor-General temporarily disconcerted the arch-commissioner. Galbaud was a steady soldier, and he had of all things married a local heiress through whom he was the proprietor of a coffee estate. This won him the confidence of many of the whites. It was an astonishing appointment for the Convention to make.

Sonthonax met the difficulty by calling a mulatto detachment of militia to the Cap in June, then, with Polverel upholding him, he abruptly examined Galbaud's credentials and pronounced them to be invalid. He forced the General aboard a ship with sailing orders for France. A squadron of war vessels lay in the harbor. Part of the crews and the troops they carried were furious at the incident. Aware they would have considerable support in the city, they mutinied, swept their officers along with them and offered Galbaud to follow him in a coup to re-establish his authority. He landed at dawn on the twentieth with over 2,000 men, and for twenty-four hours a sanguinary struggle raged, involving every man old enough to bear arms. The whites rallied to the General and the colored came out against him.

Beaten back to the fortified lines at the entrance of the plain, Sonthonax reached a fearful decision. He sent word to the blacks massed just beyond, offering them a free passage to loot and destroy Cap Français. Possibly 20,000 revolutionists poured in, killed and plundered, and at last set fire to the city. It burned to the ground. Galbaud retired to the ships in good order, and was able to save large numbers of refugees. He fled to Chesapeake Bay, where he and his company were kindly received, the first batch of Saint Domingue *emigrés* to land in the United States. Others followed, the majority finding their way to Louisiana. A white leader of irregulars named Borel, whose success had earned him the name of the "Land Corsair," escaped with many of his partisans to Jamaica.

The ruin of Cap Français is commonly regarded as the death blow to white prestige in Saint Domingue. Sonthonax proceeded in August, on his own responsibility, to proclaim the unqualified emancipation of the slaves and their admission to full citizenship. This act was ratified by the Convention, and the colored delegates the arch-commissioner had caused to be elected were seated in that body. But he deluded himself if he thought that history had cast him for the role of arbiter. Foreign adversaries had still to be reckoned with. Above all, the sweeping tide of the black revolution was ready to overflow its previous bounds. There was gratitude among the slaves for emancipation, but indifference to the claim of Sonthonax that he was the author of it. Toussaint l'Ouverture proposed to shape the destiny of the country in his own way.

War had no sooner been declared between France and England than the whites of the Grande Anse opened parleys with the Governor of Jamaica, looking to intervention. The project was submitted to the British Prime Minister, Pitt, who gave his approval. Formal articles were drawn up, which the southern planter, the Baron de Montalambert, ambitiously signed in the name of "the inhabitants of Saint Domingue." In September, 1793, three months after the Cap Français disaster and one month after emancipation, an English squadron entered the harbor of Jérémie, stronghold of Montalambert, and landed 900 troops. They were warmly received. The entire Grande Anse declared itself subject to the King of England "until the general peace." The combined forces moved against Rigaud at Aux Cayes.

A few days later, a single British warship appeared off the

Môle Saint Nicolas, at the tip of the northern peninsula. This place was garrisoned by an Irish battalion and a militia unit. The Irish had become disgusted with French republicanism as manifested in the colony. Their commander promptly surrendered the fortress, and the English occupied the peninsula as far east as Port-de-Paix, where General Laveaux, the acting Governor-General, checked them.

A third expedition landed in the western province, received the submission of Saint Marc and laid siege to Port-au-Prince. Re-enforcements continued to arrive from Jamaica. During the winter months, large stretches of low-lying territory near the coast were conquered from Sonthonax and the Patriots with ease, since the white Royalists never failed to give assistance and at some points the mulattoes co-operated. Even the wild maroons helped. The feeling was that the English, whatever else they did, would restore the institution of slavery.

Meanwhile, the Spaniards had attacked up and down the eastern border, but particularly in the north, where they had the formidable aid of the black revolutionists. Jean-François was chief of these auxiliaries, with the rank of General in the Spanish Army. Toussaint had gone along with him, had been given the command of a band of 600, and after winning some striking victories obtained his own army of 4,000 picked men. Most of these were his personal followers, trained by him while he was subordinate to Jean-François.

Toussaint was the spearhead in the assault on the French. He raised the Spanish flag over the eastern interior and the north, attaining the western gulf at Gonaives. Why did he do this, when the Spaniards were slaveholders and France had promised freedom? He was a master of constructive duplicity, and it was soon evident that he knew exactly what he was about.

In the spring of 1794, the English held the extremities of

both the northern and southern peninsulas, and the better part of the western province; they had reduced Port-au-Prince. Toussaint was unchallenged in the regions mentioned above. The French had only Port-de-Paix under Laveaux, and the southern section under Rigaud.

Then Toussaint entered into secret negotiations with Laveaux. He agreed to change sides, in return for recognition as "first of the blacks," and the French made him a General. His own people were delighted. The Spaniards, demoralized, offered poor resistance, and in a few weeks he had driven them from Saint Domingue, incidentally discrediting Jean-François, who had thrown in his lot with them. About this time, Sonthonax and Polverel were recalled to France by the Convention.

The next move was against the English. It occured in early summer, Toussaint calculating that at that season yellow fever was due to appear among them as his ally. So it fell out. But expelling the English was to be a long and weary business. They were only checked that year, and four years later they still had footholds.

In September, 1795, matters were greatly simplified for Toussaint by the conclusion of peace between France and Spain. The latter ceded her part of Hispaniola to the Republic, though retaining possession until called upon by Paris to evacuate. The French intended to set it up as a separate colony. That same year, Laveaux was made full Governor-General of Saint Domingue. One of his first acts was to appoint Toussaint his chief aide with the title of Lieutenant-Governor.

White Creole resistance was at its last gasp. As the English were thrust out of one position after another and took to their ships, the influential planters and merchants went with them. Laveaux was the only prominent white official left in the country. Toussaint had become the real ruler, save in

Rigaud's territory. Talented Negro lieutenants had developed in his service, the best known being Jean Jacques Dessalines and Henry Christophe, a native of Saint Christopher.

The year 1796 was noteworthy for the arrival of a third board of commissioners, representing the Directoire, the new governing body in France. The persistent Sonthonax was chairman, but the existing situation proved too much for him. He tried to play off Toussaint and Rigaud against each other, and ended by backing the mulatto. Toussaint got rid of Sonthonax by having him elected one of Saint Domingue's deputies in the French legislature. He used soldiers to accelerate his sailing. Laveaux, too, was given a toga and was bowed from the scene, somewhat more courteously. With their departure, Toussaint became commander-in-chief.

The last English garrison was driven out in 1798. Toussaint turned his attention to Rigaud, who had been playing the despot in the south and had re-established slavery there, in fact if not in name. The civil war that followed was one of diabolical savagery. Seconded by Dessalines, Toussaint smashed Pétion and he smashed Rigaud, forcing them to flee to France by way of the Danish island of St. Thomas. Dessalines was left to clean up. He did it thoroughly, massacring mulattoes, regardless of age or sex, with all the ferocity that had previously been directed at whites. His chief shook his head when he heard the details. "I told him to prune the tree, not to uproot it!" he remarked.

Toussaint then overran Spanish Hispaniola. Among those he drove before him was Jean-François, who died years afterward in Spain a pensioner with the rank of Captain-General, which was not so different from being Grand Admiral of France. When Toussaint entered the ancient city of Santo Domingo on January 28, 1801, he was undisputed lord of the entire island. He proclaimed a constitution later that year, by the terms of which he assumed the office of Governor-

General for life with the power to name his successor. The status of a French protectorate was claimed, rather than that of a colony.

The black revolution had won. But the authority to whom its constitution went for approval was no inchoate Convention or temporizing Directoire. It went to the First Consul Bonaparte.

CHAPTER XIX

Leclerc's Debacle

TOUSSAINT L'OUVERTURE has been almost deified by his admirers. Among detesters of slavery, fanatical democrats and race-conscious Negroes, there have been apologists for his every act and even for the awful deeds committed with his tacit approval by such lieutenants as Dessalines. On the other hand, Toussaint has been given only a grudging recognition by those who could not bear the thought of the triumph of the black revolution. None has denied his military gifts, but he has been called treacherous, conceited and harsh. The truth lies between the viewpoints to be found in *The French Revolution in San Domingo,* by T. Lothrop Stoddard, and *The Black Jacobins,* by Cyril L. R. James. Stoddard is an uncompromising champion of white supremacy, and James a Negro radical. The bitter effusions of French contemporaries of the *Ancien Régime* need not be considered seriously, nor the sentimental, dated panegyrics of abolitionists like Wendell Phillips.

To do him plain justice, Toussaint was an extraordinary man. The writer has described him elsewhere as having had "truly noble moral qualities and the most statesmanlike brain that has as yet been produced by the Negro race in America." Being human, he made mistakes, and he was not devoid of guile. But the good far outweighed the bad in him.

In advance of his conquest of Spanish Hispaniola, Toussaint had launched a plan of economic rehabilitation. Many large estates had been confiscated, because their original

210

owners had resisted the revolution, and given to Negro leaders. Others lay abandoned, and to the amazement of the world Toussaint invited those planters who had not been proscribed to return. He not only guaranteed them protection, but promised a steady supply of labor. Many accepted, and although in the end this proved a tragic decision for them, the fault cannot be laid at the door of Toussaint. He met the labor problem by adopting an ordinance against vagabondage, which required unemployed Negroes to report to the plantations where they had formerly been slaves, to work a fixed number of hours per day on a crop-sharing basis. It was temporary serfdom, but chaotic social conditions and the danger of famine justified it.

After Santo Domingo City had been occupied, the agricultural program was enlarged and merchants aided, with excellent results. Shipping, especially from the United States, began once more to crowd the ports of the country. Toussaint showed marked and increasing favor to the repatriated whites. The firebrands of the insurrection objected to this. He paid no attention to them. For, as Stoddard says shrewdly enough, he needed to enlist experience and intelligence, and he also knew that the whites "would be thoroughly trustworthy, both through lack of sympathy with the Negroes and from fear of their vengeance should he be overthrown. Again, he realized that nothing would so raise his prestige among the blacks as the sight of their former masters in his service. Lastly, in case of war with France, the whites would be most valuable hostages."

The political structure rested upon the army, which was about 20,000 strong, all picked and seasoned veterans. Toussaint divided the island into three districts. The north, with headquarters at Cap Français, was placed at first under the command of his nephew Moise, seconded by General Maurepas. Moise grew rebellious, assailed the policy of the Government, allowed whites to be murdered. Toussaint had him shot out of hand, and gave the post to Christophe. The west and south, unified from now on as the south, obeyed the orders of the fierce and efficient Dessalines. Spanish Hispaniola was commanded by General Clervaux, a mixed-blood, with Paul l'Ouverture, Toussaint's brother, as chief lieutenant and civil Governor. The seat of the central administration was Port-au-Prince.

For more than a century afterward, the people of that blood-stained island would never again have so good a chance—despite independence, despite the benevolence of the United States—to become a prosperous, orderly, self-governing Negro community. They needed the right leader to transmute the turbulence of warriors into creative citizenship, the right dictator, if you will, and they had him in Toussaint. Probably the whites of the Spanish part would have thrown off black rule anyway, but that is beside the point. We have in mind the unalterably Africanized section.

The smooth road forward was not to be. Would even the most sympathetic French regime have left Toussaint undisturbed for long? That, too, is doubtful. With Napoleon in power, there could be but one answer.

The First Consul had been paying close attention to the colonies, and notably to Saint Domingue. The principle of assimilating them with France as overseas departments had been rejected by him. The constitution which he fathered in 1800 provided that they should be governed by laws suitable to their special problems, and on this score Toussaint's constitution of 1801 was a flat defiance. Already, Napoleon had started to organize an expedition for Saint Domingue, but the English war had prevented him from sending it. The Peace of Amiens freed his hands. He at once pushed ahead with his characteristic vigor, thoroughness and lucidity in planning a campaign. Nothing resembling it had been aimed at the colony since Boukman's massacre. The English invasion had been half-hearted in comparison.

Napoleon detailed to the mission 20,000 of his best troops, men who had fought under him in the Alps and Italy. He gave the command to his brother-in-law, General Charles Victor Emanuel Leclerc, the husband of Pauline Bonaparte. Generals Boudet, Kerverseau, Humbert and Donatien Rochambeau were the principal lieutenants. Officers familiar with the island held staff appointments and these, significantly, included the former mulatto chiefs Rigaud and Pétion.

But the most impressive feature was the set of truly Napoleonic orders issued to Leclerc. The procedure was mapped out for him. There were to be three periods. He was required to occupy the coast towns and ready his columns there in from fifteen to twenty days. The second movement must consist of rapid, converging blows from several points to shatter organized resistance. Then mobile flying columns must rout the fugitive Negro bands out of the forests and mountains. Subsequent policy was to be as wily as it was ruthless. After declaring that he would not restore chattel slavery, Napoleon instructed Leclerc:

"Your conduct will vary with the three periods mentioned above. In the first period you will disarm only the rebel blacks. In the third you will disarm all. In the first period you will not be exacting; you will treat with Toussaint, you will promise him everything he asks—so that you may get possession of the principal points and establish yourself in the country. As soon as you have done this, you will become exacting. . . .

"All Toussaint's chief agents, white or colored, should in the first period be indiscriminately loaded with attentions and confirmed in their posts; in the last period all should be sent to France—with their rank, if they have behaved well during the second period; prisoners, if they have acted ill. All blacks in office should during the first period be flattered, well treated, but undermined in authority and power. . . .

"If the first period lasts fifteen days, all is well; if longer, you will have been fooled.

"Toussaint shall not be held to have submitted until he shall have come to Cap Français or Port-au-Prince in the midst of the French Army, to swear fidelity to the Republic. On that very day, without scandal or injury but with honor and consideration, he must be put on board a frigate and sent to France. . . .

"A few thousand Negroes wandering in the mountains should not prevent you from regarding the second period as ended and from promptly beginning the third. Then has come the moment to assure the colony to France forever. And, on that same day, at every point in the country, you will arrest all suspects in office whatever their color, and at the same moment embark all the black generals no matter what their conduct, patriotism, or past services—giving them, however, their rank and assuring them of good treatment in France. . . .

"You will allow no temporizing with the principles of these instructions; and any person talking about the rights of those blacks, who have shed so much white blood, shall under some pretext or other be sent to France, whatever his rank or services."

There was not one valid military reason why Leclerc should fail. He arrived off Cape Samaná in Spanish Hispaniola on January 29, 1802, with 12,000 of his splendidly equipped force. Without waiting for the rest, he split the expedition into four parties, which within a week had attained their objectives. Rochambeau seized Fort Dauphin (now Fort Liberté), the most easterly point on the north coast of Saint Domingue. Sweeping around the island to Port-au-Prince, Boudet's squadron terrorized the capital into submission, almost without striking a blow. Kerverseau was defied by Paul l'Ouverture at Santo Domingo City, Clerveaux being then in the interior. But the Spanish inhabitants rose

GENERAL LECLERC
Napoleon's brother-in-law, who failed disastrously
to reconquer Saint Domingue.

en masse for the French, and both the colored leaders were obliged to surrender.

Leclerc himself had more trouble at Cap Français, before which he appeared with 5,000 troops and peremptorily summoned Christophe to capitulate. In their exchange of notes, the future black King had the rhetorical advantage: "If you put in force your threats of hostility, I shall make the resistance which becomes a general officer. Should the chance of war be yours, you shall not enter Cap Français till it be reduced to ashes. . . . You are not my chief; I know you not and can make no accounting to you, therefore, till you are recognized by Governor-General Toussaint. For the loss of your esteem, General, I assure you that I do not desire to earn it at the price you set upon it."

Both meant what they said. Leclerc struck with all his might. Christophe put the torch to the lately rebuilt city and retreated to the mountains. The French managed to save fewer than a hundred houses. But there the Captain-General, as Leclerc was titled, established his headquarters. He sent Humbert down the coast to eject Maurepas from Port-de-Paix, a task which was accomplished quickly, though with greater losses than had been suffered at any other point. In the south, a black General deserted to the French with his entire force. Thus strengthened, Boudet sent Dessalines reeling into the interior from Léogane.

Toussaint did not even contemplate submission at this time, though subtle pressure was brought to bear on him. His two young sons, Placide and Isaac, had been sent to France for their education. At Napoleon's suggestion, they accompanied the expedition. They were now dispatched with a tutor to their father's temporary capital in the wilds, where they gave him a conciliatory letter from the First Consul advising him to aid Leclerc. The Negro chief impassively demanded time to weigh his decision, which he really used to rally supporters. He evaded a subsequent urgent invitation to go to Cap Français for a conference.

Meanwhile, the second division of the army of conquest landed from France, and Leclerc had 9,000 troops personally available, the rest being with his sub-commanders. He decided that Toussaint was irreconcilable, and that he was stalling. So on February seventeenth, a bare three weeks after he had sighted Saint Domingue, he proclaimed Toussaint, Christophe and Dessalines to be outlaws, and all their armed followers guilty of rebellion. He ordered simultaneous attacks by Rochambeau, Humbert and Boudet. He led his own army across the northern plain, pointing it directly at the Ravine aux Couleuvres, Toussaint's main position. Spanish Hispaniola was no longer in question. The last straggling Negro bands there had laid down their arms.

In the north, the campaign went according to plan, and with remarkable speed. Rochambeau drove through the eastern mountains and cut off Toussaint from the old Spanish border. Leclerc stormed the foothills, and in two days was at Plaisance, halfway across the range. The gorges, tangled with dense tropical vegetation, the forested peaks and the sudden deluges of rain were novel obstacles to the European soldiery. But they surged ahead, and on the fifth day they smashed into the Ravine aux Couleuvres. Here was fought the engagement that came closest to being a pitched battle. Toussaint himself stood on the defensive with at least 6,000 men. The discipline and superior weapons of the French caused his defeat with losses of about a thousand, but he retired to the south in comparatively good order.

It had been intended that Boudet, marching north, should isolate and capture him. This did not occur. Boudet had run into difficulties with Dessalines, who fought him tenaciously, burned Saint Marc in his face and immobilized him for two days longer than Toussaint needed to escape into the moun-

tains of the center beyond the Artibonite valley. Boudet fell
back on Port-au-Prince.

Operating on the northern peninsula, Humbert assailed
Maurepas outside Port-de-Paix and was heavily repulsed. Re-
enforcements came up, however. Maurepas was surrounded
in the hills. When the black commander learned that Toussaint had been beaten at Couleuvres, he not only capitulated
but took his 2,000 soldiers into the French service.

Leclerc's situation was, on the whole, extremely favorable.
He had proved himself a brilliant general. He was living up
to Napoleon's schedule, and notwithstanding the partial success of Dessalines in outmaneuvering Boudet the confidence
of the Negroes in their ability to win had been broken by the
Captain-General's triumphs. One thing, from the military
point of view, remained to be done. The Crête-à-Pierrot, at
the entrance to the Artibonite valley, must be reduced. It
was an immensely strong fortress, and without it to protect
their chief source of food supply in the valley, Toussaint,
Dessalines and Christophe would become wandering guer-
rillas.

The investment of the Crête-à-Pierrot was completed early
in March. Its garrison consisted of 1,200 resolute blacks,
who were helped by almost nightly raids on the French by
picked veterans of Dessalines' army. Leclerc massed some
10,000 troops for the job. He ordered four frontal assaults,
which failed against the terrible ramparts with losses of 1,500.
Then he brought up artillery and pounded the place merci-
lessly. At the end of a three days' bombardment with new
and larger guns, the defense could endure the punishment
no longer. The survivors cut their way through the French
lines on the night of March twenty-fourth, leaving half their
number dead on the way. Leclerc's total casualties had been
2,000. He returned to Cap Français, assigning General Lacroix to overrun the Artibonite.

Desultory fighting in all parts of the country went on, but the first phase of the war was ended. In April, despite his fine words at the beginning, Christophe offered to submit if pardoned and made a French general, as Maurepas had been. This was conceded. He came over with 1,200 men. On May first, both Toussaint and Dessalines capitulated. They went down to the Cap to take the oath of allegiance. It was observed that the crowd saluted them as heroes, and that in their different ways they maintained an air of assurance.

The bloody Dessalines asked for and was given a command. Toussaint retired to his estate at Ennery.

Now this was all very well, as far as it went. It made Leclerc seem an absolute victor. But in granting pardons and employing black generals after he had entered the third period forecast by Napoleon, he was disobeying orders. Why did he do so? There is reason to believe that he looked upon the concessions as temporary, and that he intended to withdraw them as soon as he got re-enforcements from France. He had lost 5,000 men in his brief but sanguinary campaign. In April, there were 5,000 others in hospital suffering from wounds, malaria and enteric diseases. It was not the moment to be high-handed, no matter what Napoleon wanted.

The moment would never come. Yellow fever, which had often been the deciding factor in Caribbean enterprises, was about to give the most fearful of all recorded manifestations of its power. We have scientific treatises on this malady. Its conquest in Havana in the year 1901 is an American epic. But the historical part that it has played is yet to be written. It rode, a veritable Horseman of the Apocalypse, between Leclerc and his victory.

With the coming of the May rains that precede the tropical summer, the fever appeared throughout Saint Domingue with unexampled virulence. Newly arrived whites were peculiarly subject to it, the acclimatized and Creoles much less so, and Negroes hardly at all. The French troops and sailors of the fleet were stricken by the hundreds each day. Few recovered. In a month 3,000 men were dead, and this ruinous quota increased month after month. The army, already weakened by casualties, was simply paralyzed, and the re-enforcements from France helped not a whit. For the latecomers—Poles, Germans and Netherlanders, for the most part—immediately contracted the fever and died faster than the French, Leclerc became dependent on the dubious loyalty of his black soldiers.

Those who disparage Toussaint l'Ouverture maintain that his act of submission was wholly false, that he never ceased to plot a renewal of the war and his own return to power. Others say that the epidemic decided him to break faith with Leclerc. A third group would have it that at Ennery he was innocence personified, a saddened, fallen leader in seclusion from the world. His captured correspondence has been quoted against him. In passing judgment the middle course, as usual, would appear to be the soundest. Toussaint probably believed on May first that the black cause was irretrievably lost. He would have been less than human if the fabulous intervention of Yellow Jack had not revived his hopes by June first. Rumors to that effect certainly were abroad. Leclerc concluded that he must eliminate him, a course which it is only fair to recall had been enjoined in Napoleon's original instructions.

The ruse employed to trap Toussaint, however, was base enough. General Brunet wrote him a letter from Gonaives the first week in June, inviting him to come to that town and confer on "important matters which it is impossible to explain by letter." When the great old Negro arrived, he was seized and sent to France. Napoleon imprisoned him in the fortress of Joux near the Swiss border, where he died the following year from the effects of the cold.

A general uprising in protest at Toussaint's arrest had been feared, but the populace marked time. Leclerc then ordered a general disarming of the blacks, to be carried out by Dessalines, Christophe and their fellows. Some were lukewarm at this task. Dessalines performed it with his habitual savagery. It might have been successful if July had not brought another development calamitous to the French. Napoleon wrote the Captain-General authorizing him to restore slavery whenever he saw fit. Leclerc had the good sense not to attempt it, and even to warn his brother-in-law that it was impracticable. But the gossip leaked out, and presently it was learned that human bondage had actually been re-established in Guadeloupe.

Now the black revolution flamed once more. It possessed the common people like a fanaticism, to quote Leclerc's own word for it. "These men may be killed, but will not surrender. They laugh at death—and it is the same with the women. I begged you, Citizen Consul, to do nothing to make these people fear for their liberty till the moment when I should be prepared. . . . The moral force I had here acquired is destroyed." In the same letter, Leclerc pleaded for money and large drafts of fresh troops from France. He predicted a catastrophe unless they were furnished.

The Negro generals continued to serve France for a few weeks longer. They tried to suppress the revolt of their own people. Suddenly they began to see the situation in a new light. The mortality from yellow fever had soared to an appalling figure. One regiment which had landed from Europe 1,395 strong had only 190 men left alive, and of these 107 were in hospital. Another regiment had landed 1,000 strong and now numbered 150, of whom 133 were in hospital. Never had the blacks had such an ally.

Led by Dessalines and Christophe, the chiefs deserted Leclerc and resumed their leadership of the masses. Even the

JEAN JACQUES DESSALINES
Negro General and first ruler of independent Haiti.
He proclaimed himself Emperor.

mulattoes, Rigaud and Pétion, went with them. By the middle of November, the military state of the French was desperate. They held only some half-dozen important coast towns. Leclerc was dead of yellow fever. The command had devolved upon Rochambeau.

That cataclysmic year is famous in the history of Saint Domingue for other events than the plague and the swiftly changing fortunes of war. The lovely, frivolous Pauline, *née* Bonaparte, had accompanied her husband. She set up a court amid the ruins of Cap Français, which for intrigue and sexual abandon was a small edition of Mme. Tallien's salon under the Directoire. The amatory escapades of Pauline herself were flagrant. They involved some of the highest officers, including General Humbert. The wives of many planters gleefully went wild with her. This sort of thing was obnoxious to Napoleon, who did not quite forgive his sister, when she returned a widow, for the revels she had staged with death as the chorus to the tune of 160 military funerals a day. Leclerc, while he lasted, had cared less. He had been a distracted man, an almost continuous sufferer from malaria before Yellow Jack destroyed him.

The efforts of Rochambeau to retrieve the party need not be told in detail. He won some successes and was slowly building up a force of men immune to the fever, because they had had it and recovered. The resumption of war with England, however, made the case hopeless. The English blockaded the island, cutting off supplies, and afterward gave direct aid to the revolutionists. The latter took the coast towns, one by one, until Rochambeau was confined to Cap Français. On November 10, 1803, he sailed out of that harbor and surrendered the remnants of his force to a waiting English admiral.

Saint Domingue declared its independence under the Arawâk name of Haiti. It acknowledged Dessalines as its supreme lord for life. He called himself Governor-General at the start, but soon assumed the title of Emperor Jacques I in admitted imitation of Napoleon. His main policy was extirpation of the last of the whites, which he accomplished in a series of massacres supervised by himself. His excesses disgusted the majority of his countrymen, and in less than three years he was assassinated.

"Accursed be the French name! We declare eternal hatred for France!" he had written in a proclamation.

Yet when culture, law and letters flowered among the elite of Haiti, the form they took was completely and devotedly French. This is an outstanding phenomenon of the story of the West Indies. It has been remarked by every intelligent visitor to the black republic for more than a hundred years.

Chapter XX

The Brigands' War

In A previous chapter, we saw how the factions in Martinique and Guadeloupe composed their differences and settled down to a form of autonomy, early in the Revolution. Their Colonial Assemblies were the centers of power, and it was not long before these became heartily Royalist. The propertied classes regarded the throne as the only symbol to which it was worth while to cling, and the poor whites accepted the fiction that the King still reigned and that France was being reformed with his approval. Slave insurrections occurred here and there, but they were on a small scale and were easily repressed. Indeed, the stability, the conservatism of the two ancient island colonies became a catchword of envy among the tormented planters and merchants of Saint Domingue.

St. Lucia, Tobago and Guiana, the sparsely settled minor possessions of France in the region, were affected in substantially the same manner as Martinique. The waves from the great upheaval that rocked them were feebler, that was all. They, too, awaited developments, and their mood was one of readiness to hail anything within reason that came out of France.

The war with England that followed the execution of Louis XVI brought widespread changes, some within the logic of the circumstances and others unpredictable. The English had regretted giving up the little sugar islands after the Seven Years' War. They had fumed over their impotency to recapture them at the time of the American Revolution. Rodney and other admirals had emphasized the great strategic value of the harbor of Fort Royal, Martinique. Westminster had resolved to take advantage of French naval weakness and sweep up all the odds and ends.

The first move was made against Tobago, which had no means of defense and where many of the inhabitants were English, survivors of previous occupations. The place submitted after a short struggle. A force of 800 was then landed in Martinique. It received the support of several hundred Royalist planters, horror-stricken at the death of Louis XVI and persuaded that the National Convention would quickly send out a Sonthonax. But the attempted collaboration with the English was wretchedly planned. Regular troops and militia dispersed the expedition, which re-embarked, taking many of the Royalists with it at their own request. The effect was to revive party strife in Martinique. Royalists were viewed as traitors by the majority. A republican regime dominated by mulattoes was set up. The slaves grew restless, and all the horrors of Saint Domingue seemed about to be reproduced.

But the English came back in February, 1794, and this time with a powerful force under General Sir Charles Grey and Admiral Sir John Jervis. They landed at a number of points and overwhelmed resistance. Martinique remained in their hands until the Peace of Amiens.

St. Lucia was taken with even greater ease than Tobago had been. Guadeloupe was invaded and the towns of Basse-Terre and Pointe-à-Pitre reduced by April twenty-first. The French Governor capitulated, surrendering the island and all its dependencies to Major-General Dundas, with the canny proviso that he and his officers be allowed to go to the United States.

"Happy, if the scene had shut at this period, and no envious cloud overcast the close of a campaign, the opening and progress of which had shone with so bright a lustre!" exclaims

Bryan Edwards. He is one of the most candid of British historians and makes no apologies for the bungling that led to the astonishing sequel.

Early in June, a small French fleet carrying 1,500 soldiers ran the Atlantic blockade and arrived off Pointe-à-Pitre. Jervis and Grey had departed with their ships to inspect St. Kitts, as the English called St. Christopher. So the French seized the anchorage, put their troops ashore and captured Fort Fleur d'Epée. This dominated the town. The English invaders, who, as in Martinique, had been joined by local Royalists, retired to Basse-Terre. Men were rushed from other islands to their support, but Jervis exhibited a strange helplessness in employing his fleet to cope with the situation.

The French commander was none other than a commissioner appointed by the Convention to "regulate affairs" in the Windward Islands, and he had sailed without realizing that the English held Guadeloupe. He was Victor Hugues, destined to be the animator of the obscure but ghastly contest known in the Lesser Antilles as the Brigands' War. He followed his coup at Pointe-à-Pitre by declaring the slaves emancipated and raising armed levies of Negroes. He did everything he could to belittle the authority of the white colonists, a comparatively mild beginning, had they guessed it.

Though born in Marseilles, Hugues was reputed to have colored blood. He had been a merchant-captain and later had been in business in Saint Domingue, where the first uprising had ruined him. Proceeding to France, he had become an extreme Jacobin, the intimate of Robespierre, through whom he had obtained the mission to the Windward Islands while serving as public prosecutor at Rochefort. He was the type of whom the adherents of the "Mountain" spoke admiringly as an *enragé*.

When the English and their Royalist auxiliaries came marching back from Basse-Terre in a few weeks, Hugues was ready for them. He repulsed them bloodily from Pointe-à-Pitre, isolated them at Berville and forced their surrender. The English received fair terms, but the condition they demanded for the Royalists, that they should be treated as British subjects, was declared inadmissible. Eight hundred and sixty-five Creoles fell into the hands of Hugues, who relentlessly put them to death the next morning on the Morne Savon. This is the account given by Bryan Edwards:

"The Republicans erected a guillotine, with which they struck off the heads of fifty of them in the short space of an hour. This mode of proceeding, however, proving too tedious for their impatient revenge, the remainder of these unhappy men were fettered to each other and placed on the brink of one of the trenches which they had so gallantly defended. The Republicans then drew up some of their undisciplined recruits in front, who firing an irregular volley at their miserable victims killed some and wounded others, leaving many, in all probability, untouched. The weight, however, of the former dragged the rest into the ditch, where the living, the wounded and the dead shared the same grave, the soil being instantly thrown in upon them."

The large number of men killed makes it likely that more than one trench was used, and that the massacre was staged in relays.

Hugues drove the English from the few forts they still held, and Guadeloupe was his. He turned his attention to local matters. His proclamation of freedom had not taken full effect. Many planters had defiantly continued the old system by coercing the slaves, or bluffing them into supposing that false rumors had been fed to them. The retort of Victor Hugues, the terrorist, was barbarously direct. He called on the Negro population to make good its own liberty and to avenge itself on its masters. Going further than Sonthonax had ever dared, except on the occasion of the burning of

Cap Français, he invited a general carnage and sent out his colored troops to stimulate it. He got what he asked. The upper-class whites and slaveholding mulattoes were decimated with all the accompaniments of fell cruelty. The government set up was a pure Jacobin dictatorship.

But this did not satisfy the ambitions of Hugues. Audaciously, under the noses of the English at Martinique, he led a raid the next year to St. Lucia, St. Vincent and Grenada. In all three he incited slave rebellions similar to the one in Guadeloupe. He armed the blacks and urged them on to butcher the white officials, military officers, planters and merchants, whether English or French. They rushed joyously to the work. In St. Vincent and Grenada the Caribs joined him. The Governor of Grenada, Ninian Home, was slain with forty-seven others in a single ambush. Hugues gained full control of the three islands, this being the phase of his operations which is properly described as the Brigands' War. He held them until 1796, when a British expedition retook them and drove him back to Guadeloupe. During the second fight in St. Vincent, the Caribs let themselves be virtually exterminated for the conception of liberty the French had brought them.

The English were chary of disturbing Hugues in Guadeloupe. He became less of a danger, anyway; for with the rise of a moderate French Government he showed himself to be an opportunist by modifying his conduct. He compelled the Negroes to resume field labor, under regulations similar to those adopted by Toussaint l'Ouverture in Saint Domingue. The later years of Hugues' regime is remembered for two things: the frightful eruption of the Soufrière volcano accompanied by earthquakes, in 1797, which destroyed large sections of fertile land; and the commissioning of privateers against the United States during France's quasi-war with her recent ally toward the end of the century.

Guiana, in the meantime, had been having a milder experience, but a fantastic one. Jeannet Oudin, nephew of Danton, was sent there as Governor in 1794. As soon as he landed in Cayenne, he issued an emancipation decree. The following year, he requisitioned for the plantations all former slaves under penalty of counter-revolution. Such civil disturbances as occurred were of no great import.

Coincidental with the rule of Oudin, it was the "dry guillotine" that began to give Guiana the sinister reputation which has since clung to it. Chosen as a place of exile for political offenders and dangerous criminals, the first batch it received were members of the repudiated "Mountain," including two former members of the Committee of Public Safety, Collot-d'Herbois and Billaud-Varennes. The first succumbed to the climate almost immediately, but Billaud-Varennes accommodated himself very well. He lived in Guiana until 1815, fleeing to Haiti to die because he feared the restored Bourbons. Few of the deportees were as fortunate as he.

In 1795 came those of Fructidor, as well as hundreds of refractory priests. Of 321 that arrived on one boat, 163 died in a few months. One of the last batches, 600 strong, was dumped on the banks of the Sinnamary River without shelter or food, and two-thirds of them perished. Then the Consulate supervened, which meant for Guiana, as for the other colonies, the restoration of slavery. The man of all men placed in charge of it at Cayenne as Governor in 1799 was Victor Hugues. He kept the word he had given to show his celebrated zeal in executing no matter what orders he received from the Government. The First Consul attached much importance to Guiana, where he was well served by Hugues. Commerce and accessions of slaves from Africa rose rapidly.

Napoleon's choice for the Guadeloupe assignment was

General Antoine Richepanse, who went vigorously to work. He met with unexpectedly bitter opposition by the Negroes, who must have known that in that small island their cause was hopeless. A great many committed suicide rather than return to bondage. Four hundred former slaves locked themselves up in a fort, and when they became convinced that they would not be exempted from the abhorred decree they touched off the gunpowder magazine. All were killed. They may be said to have had their revenge. For although slavery was re-enforced in 1802 the moral effect on Saint Domingue was, as has been noted, calamitous to the French there.

This is as suitable a point as any at which to interject a last word about Moreau de Saint-Méry, the gifted writer and statesman of West Indian birth. His defense of the planter class had caused him to lose his influence with the revolutionaries, and he had fled to the United States. In Philadelphia he founded a publishing house which put out an English edition of his famous history of Saint Domingue. Napoleon recalled him in 1801 and made him Resident at Parma, Italy. Saint-Méry took possession of the duchy in the name of France the following year and governed it ably as Administrator-General. Disgraced in 1806, he faced the Emperor boldly. "Sire, I do not ask you to reward my probity; I ask only that it be tolerated," he said. "Do not fear, this malady is not contagious; flowers on the tomb are its only recognition." He was pensioned at the Bourbon restoration.

The difficulties of maintaining American colonies when England controlled the sea, and particularly the loss of Saint Domingue, decided Napoleon to sell Louisiana to the United States. He had got back Martinique and other small islands at the Peace of Amiens, but he was well aware that that peace was only a truce.

Louisiana had been reacquired from Spain by the secret Treaty of San Ildefonso in 1800. At the same time that he sent Leclerc to Saint Domingue and Richepanse to Guadeloupe, the First Consul planned an expeditionary force to Louisiana under General Victor, for which he set aside 3,000,-000 francs. He knew that the French on the Mississippi would welcome a return to their old allegiance. Whom, then, did he think that Victor might have to fight? The answer is furnished by Thomas Jefferson, who said early in 1803:

"If there is on this earth a place where the possessor is our natural enemy, it is New Orleans. By taking this port France has committed an act of hostility. She forces us to ally ourselves with the English fleet and nation."

Suddenly Napoleon countermanded the Victor expedition. He negotiated the sale instead, agreeing to take 60,000,000 francs, which has been estimated to be the equivalent of four cents an acre. On April 11, 1803, he said to his ministers:

"I am aware of the value of Louisiana. I give it up with extreme reluctance. To insist on keeping it [in the face of English and American opposition] would be folly. If I were to set my price at what this vast territory is worth to the United States, there would be no limit to the indemnity. I shall be moderate because of my obligation to sell."

On May twelve, as England renewed the war with France, Napoleon commented:

"This accession [of Louisiana by the United States] affirms for always the power of the United States. Thus I have given England a maritime rival who, sooner or later, will humble her pride. . . . Henceforth the United States is numbered among the first-rate powers. Exclusive influence over the affairs of America has been lost by England without hope of regaining it."

Formal transfer was effected toward the end of the year.

Pioneers surged westward into the primeval hinterland of the Purchase and carved a dozen commonwealths from it. But the real Louisiana on the Gulf yielded slowly to American influences and has kept to this day a broad streak of the Latin temperament.

England did not grab promptly at the French Lesser Antilles on the resumption of war. The greatest of her naval leaders, Horatio Nelson, then at the height of his glory, cared more about destroying the allied French and Spanish fleets. The main French squadron under Admiral Pierre de Villeneuve lay at Toulon during the early weeks of 1805, with Nelson hovering close by to pounce on it if it emerged. Napoleon had ordered his navy to draw all English warships away from the shores of Europe before giving battle, the strategy being to clear the Channel for his projected invasion from Boulogne. The blockaded Villeneuve cleverly contrived to serve this strategy. He took advantage of a day in March when Nelson had been tempted over to Sardinia by a false alarm, slipped out and got through the Straits of Gibraltar unharmed. Then he steered for the West Indies, making no effort to hide his intentions. Nelson, obliged to follow, had poor luck with the weather and his crossing was much the longer.

Villeneuve arrived at Martinique on May fourteenth. He found traffic in and out of Fort-de-France (formerly Fort Royal) being hampered by one of those spectacular feats in which English sailors of the day delighted. A shaft of rock rising some two hundred feet from the Caribbean, just off the southwest coast, had been fortified and named *H. M. S. Diamond Rock*. A full man-of-war's crew had been told off to it and the appropriate guns installed in caves in the sides. This stationary "battleship" was more irritating than a swarm of cruisers. Attempts to board it had all been repelled. Villeneuve decided to lay siege, caught the Rock at a moment when food and ammunition were low, and in two weeks had starved it into surrender.

He had barely completed the task when Nelson was reported at Barbados. Villeneuve sent spies to spread the word that he had gone south to Trinidad, whereas he actually started north to raid the British Leeward Islands. Nelson's marvelous instinct urged him to proceed straight to Martinique, and if he had done so it is almost certain that he would have come up with Villeneuve at the very place where Rodney had destroyed De Grasse. There would have been a second Battle of the Saintes. But the Trinidad story had so authentic a ring that he felt he could not ignore it.

Failing to discover the Frenchman at Port-of-Spain, he hastened back to learn that Villeneuve had disappeared after landing a large consignment of troops at Guadeloupe. Rumor now said that he had gone to capture Jamaica. But Horatio Nelson was not to be misled a second time. The soldiers put ashore in a French colony convinced him that no attack on Jamaica could be under way. He divined that Villeneuve had returned to Europe, and he pursued him there without delay. The finale was the Battle of Trafalgar on October 21, 1805, which made England undisputed mistress of the seas.

Villeneuve's maneuvers are significant in the history of the West Indies as the last show of naval power made in those waters by the French. They did not constitute a challenge, because the plan successfully carried out was to confuse Nelson while evading a fight in American waters.

The seizure of all the French Caribbean colonies for the last time by England, in the period between Trafalgar and Waterloo, offers few points of interest. In Guiana it was a joint occupation by English and Portuguese troops. At the general peace, Martinique, Guadeloupe and Guiana were restored to France, and they and some tiny islets have constituted the stake of that country in tropical America up till the war that is now convulsing the world.

CHAPTER XXI

France and the Spanish Colonies

THE France of liberal eighteenth-century thought, of the great Revolution and the Napoleonic Era, shone as a fierce white light to the Spanish colonies of the New World. They were thereby stimulated to throw off European bondage and emerge, after a series of sanguinary wars, as free republics. France was not the only exterior force that impelled them in that direction, but she was by far the most powerful one. Two contradictory aspects merged to create a whole. The Spanish-American intellectuals fervidly admired the achievements of France in the cause of liberty and glorified her leaders, up to and including Napoleon. They resolved to imitate them. Yet when Napoleon overthrew the Iberian monarchy, substituted his own brother as King of Spain and sent agents to regulate the American possessions, that was the final impulse needed to launch insurrections from Mexico to Buenos Aires.

F. García Calderón, the Peruvian historian, writes:

"From France, as emissaries of the ideal, came the doctrines of the Revolution. In the *Encyclopedia* we find the intellectual origin of the South American upheavals. The patricians in the archaic colonial cities smiled upon Voltaire; they adopted the essential ideals of Rousseau, the social contract, the sovereignty of the people, and the optimism which conceded supreme rights to the human spirit untainted by culture. Bolívar had read the *Contrat Social* in a volume that had formed part of the library of Napoleon; by will, he left this book to an intimate friend. The great, sounding promises—democracy, sovereignty, human rights, equality, liberalism—stirred the patriotic tribunes like fragments of a new gospel. The masonic lodges worked in silence against the power of Spain and Portugal. . . . Not only did French thought predominate, but the Revolution, the Terror, the Jacobin madness, the eloquence of the Girondins, the dictatorship of the First Consul, and the Empire, even, all exercised an immense influence upon the rising democracies of America."

The above are generalities. For the purposes of the present history, it is important to know how the influences accumulated, the lessons drawn from them by a personality such as that of Bolívar the Liberator, and how they affected the course of events in the regions adjoining the Caribbean Sea. A study of the subject has been made by another Peruvian, Victor Andrés Belaúnde, to whose profound work the author takes this opportunity of acknowledging a debt of gratitude.

Apart from the *Encyclopedia,* the most widely read foreign books were those of Jean Jacques Rousseau and the Abbé G. T. Raynal, and the one that obtained the widest distribution was the *Histoire Philosophique des Deux Indes* by Raynal. Citations from it have been given in previous chapters. It was a survey of European colonies in various parts of the known world. Nowadays, it is rightly considered superficial. It did not have the merit of being wholly based on personal knowledge, for the Abbé used contributed material to cover places he had not visited. But the viewpoint was extremely liberal. Whenever English methods seemed superior to French ones, they were showered with praise. The colonial policy of Spain and her treatment of the Creoles were severely condemned. Creole capacity for self-government was exalted as a manifest truth.

Inevitably, the book was hailed in America, where it made its appeal to the political-minded. It was called "the true sum of the Revolution" (though published in 1774), and the Chilean, Rojas, proclaimed Raynal a "divine genius."

The subtle and artistically effective romanticism of Rousseau, propounded in several masterpieces, had a deeper and longer influence. The Genevan reached poets, altruists, the noblest intellects among the patriots, and along with them that vast company of the literate to whom feeling is more potent than thought. Rodríguez, the tutor of Simón Bolívar, saw in his pupil the aristocratic child of nature extolled by Rousseau, whom Rodríguez idolized. Many of the early theories of the Liberator can be traced to this source, and his literary style to the end was often Rousseauistic. Belaúnde points out that although Rousseau felt that the worst tyranny ought to be suffered before there was a resort to violence, although he maintained that a republic could exist only in a small territory, the *Contrat Social* was "the basic theory of the Revolution [Spanish-American], inspiring the writers and the leaders of the movement." The brilliant young Francisco Xavier Espejo, of Quito, expressed the new tendencies in a pedagogic system based on *Emile* and died in prison for his ideas.

Montesquieu, author of the *Esprit des Lois,* also swayed the best minds. Because of his depth and realism, Belaúnde thinks that he was more frequently quoted at second-hand than read. Bolívar, however, knew him thoroughly and in one of his most notable utterances, the Angostura speech, he utilized the principles of Montesquieu.

It must not be thought for a moment that any of the French books mentioned had free entry to the Spanish colonies. All were most strictly prohibited. But they were smuggled in, a practice that became more and more widespread as the eighteenth century drew to a close. Enlightened members of the clergy and certain powerful Creoles, whose houses enjoyed partial immunity from the searches of the Holy Inquisition, hid the books cunningly and brought them out for trusted friends behind locked doors. In Venezuela, it is said, the favorite place for concealing the works of Rousseau and Raynal was in the hollowed beams of the roofs.

The Peruvian friar, Diego Cisneros, took wholesale advantage of his authorized trade in missals, breviaries and other pious literature. He imported under that guise great quantities of liberal books, which he made available to a group of young men in Lima. A periodical in which the teachings of French, English and Italian thinkers were cautiously disseminated, was one of the results.

So long as the texts of fundamental works could be had only in foreign languages, the public they affected was small and the authorities did not worry inordinately. But translations began to appear. The writings of the Encyclopedists and the *Contrat Social* were rendered into Spanish and scattered over the empire. How many editions were printed locally it is impossible to say; some were from Spain. Official alarm grew, and new energy was brought to the enforcement of the benighted laws. We come to the period when individual leaders acted with the virtual certainty that they would be detected.

The title of Precursor has been given to two men, of whom the best known to American readers is General Francisco de Miranda, of Venezuela; his agitational and military program clearly forecast the work of Bolívar. The other was Antonio Nariño, a talented intellectual, whose library in Bogotá was a celebrated gathering place of liberals. Contemporaries tell of his enthusiasm for the French Revolution and the excitement with which he and his group read the first accounts of the National Assembly, as well as the smuggled text of the Declaration of the Rights of Man. Nariño decided on the spot to translate and publish the Declaration. This he proceeded to do in 1794, with dynamic consequences.

He was arrested, of course, and his library confiscated.

Placed on trial, he most ably seized the chance to explain, in his defense, his political ideas under the signature of his lawyer. He was then in favor of self-government under the Spanish flag. His main pleas were for equality between Europeans and colonials, religious toleration and a reform of the commercial system.

Nariño was treated with astonishing gentleness. Though found guilty, he was merely deported. Belaúnde says:

"He decides for absolute independence and consecrates his life to the revolution. Sent to the Peninsula, he makes a jest of Spanish justice and travels through France and England. In England he makes suggestions to Pitt, but rejects the idea of annexation to the British Empire, 'because this would be selling his country to another nation.' He returns to his country to spread the revolutionary ideas in a series of romantic journeys. Surprised by the Spanish authorities, he is obliged to enter into an agreement with them to forego his seditious enterprises."

It went much harder with certain enthusiasts who had been inspired by this civilian Precursor, and by the *Derechos del Hombre* (Rights of Man). In Venezuela, in 1797, Captain Manuel Gual and José María España started a conspiracy to eject the Spanish rulers and set up a republic. They had prepared a "plan of ordinances," which the historian Gil Fortoul remarks was saturated with the ideas of the French Revolution. It guaranteed, among other things, racial equality, the only distinction to be based upon merit and virtue; freedom of commerce, and the abolition of slavery. The movement was ferreted out before it could get launched, the Audiencia of Caracas ascribing it to "the sending to La Guayra of 800 French prisoners taken in Santo Domingo who contaminated the people of the colony with the revolutionary maxims, and the admission of French immigrants who abandoned Trinidad when this island passed under English control."

España and several companions were put to death barbarously, their corpses hanged in chains in Caracas. Gual escaped and, like Nariño, figured in the grand upheaval afterward.

A small revolt that occurred among Negroes and persons of mixed blood in western Venezuela proved that even the most ignorant could be touched by the new doctrines. The rebels proclaimed the Republic, the abolition of slavery, and the "law of the Frenchman." They were bludgeoned into submission.

As we approach the years of actual liberation, increasing importance attaches to the mental processes of three leaders in the zone under review. Chronologically, these are Miranda, Father Miguel Hidalgo of Mexico, and Bolívar himself. But as Miranda and Bolívar are closely linked, let us first dispose of Hidalgo.

He was the parish priest of the village of Dolores, a Creole and consequently not marked for promotion in the Church. Of a quick intelligence, tolerant, skeptical, he filled his home with books condemned by the authorities and gathered friends around him to read and discuss them. The house came to be known as "Little France." Hidalgo carried his unconventionality into his personal life. He had two illegitimate daughters living with him. As early as 1800, he was questioned and sternly reprimanded by the Inquisition. He admitted that he studied the Bible critically. He showed small respect for the Pope, but professed loyalty to the King of Spain without condoning the evils of the monarchy's colonial policy.

This was the man who would utter the famous "Cry of Dolores," prematurely, and die for it, but not before he had marshaled tens of thousands of Indians in Mexico's original tragic revolution. No more thorough disciple of the *Encyclopedia* is to be found among the pioneers of Spanish-American freedom.

Miranda had the distinction, rare in a Creole, of having

won high military honors under several flags and acquiring a cosmopolitan culture. This gave him prestige among the elite. To some extent, it was a disadvantage with the populace of Venezuela, because it made him seem a foreigner. He had gone to Spain as a young man and entered the army. In 1781, he was a captain in a regiment sent to aid Bernardo de Gálvez, the Spanish Governor of Louisiana, in the reconquest of Florida from the English. Miranda's first conception of liberty for his own people came to him on that campaign, in which he distinguished himself and rose to be a colonel.

He transferred his services to the struggling North American colonies. Then he returned to Europe and traveled widely. Shortly after the outbreak of the French Revolution, he joined the army of the Republic with the rank of brigadier-general and commanded in several battles. He got into disfavor with the Jacobin extremists, of whom he disapproved, and was imprisoned. On his release he settled in London, where for a decade he intrigued vainly for help from the Governments of England, France and the United States in his plots to overthrow the colonial regime of Spain.

What were his ideas? He was a devoted student of Montesquieu, to whose principles he clung to the last. A true child of the eighteenth century, he absorbed the theories of most of the radical philosophers, but the excesses he had witnessed in Paris caused him, as Belaúnde points out, to depart entirely from Jacobin doctrines, "leaning rather toward the old English conception of moderate and organic liberalism."

It was as the Precursor in action that Miranda proved most valuable to his cause. He went to the United States in 1805, and although snubbed by Jefferson and Madison he got the assistance of private persons in fitting out a filibustering expedition against Venezuela. Early the next year, he sailed in an armed ship with 200 volunteers and seized the port of Coro. The people were not ready for so drastic a coup and they failed to support him. He was lucky to escape with minor losses.

The adventure at Coro, however, furnished a dazzling object lesson of what could be done, of what there was yet to do. When Miranda got back to London his voice as an oracle had been strengthened. He was a hero to the finest of his countrymen, including the young genius for whose triumphal career it had been his destiny to prepare.

Simón Bolívar, greatest of Spanish Americans, was born in Caracas, the son of a rich and aristocratic family. He finished his education in Spain. References have been made throughout this chapter to writers who influenced him. At the height of his power, in refuting the statements of one Mollien who had belittled his knowledge, the Liberator said: "Certainly I am learned neither in the philosophy of Aristotle nor in the criminal code, but it may well be that M. Mollien has not studied so closely as I, Locke, Condillac, Buffon, d'Alembert, Helvetius, Montesquieu, Mably, Filangieri, Lalande, Rousseau, Voltaire, Rollin, Berthot. . . ."

Here is a comprehensive list. Of the thirteen names, eleven are French, one English and one Italian. Yet Bolívar had an even higher opinion than Miranda of the English political thinkers. He also owed much to Humboldt, the eminent German naturalist and traveler. The founders of the United States were admired by him, but not imitated. He particularly disliked, for South America, the idea of a federal republic.

At Angostura, where he offered the draft of a constitution, he affirmed that the laws ought to conform to the topography of the country, the climate, the nature of the land, and to the kind of life led by the people and to their customs. He buttressed his arguments with quotations from Montesquieu. "Behold the code which we should consult, and it is not that of Washington!" he exclaimed. "The excellency of a government does not consist in its theory, its form; not in its

SIMÓN BOLÍVAR

A rare portrait of the Liberator as a young commander.

From the painting by Francis M. Drexel

mechanism, but in its appropriateness to the self, the character of the nation for which it is designed."

The quality of his eloquence was intensely French. He spoke at times like Danton, at times like Napoleon, very little like a Spaniard, never like an Anglo-Saxon. While the National Congress of Venezuela was debating the question of independence, Bolívar set the country afire with a speech before the Patriotic Society, where he was a dominant figure. He cried:

"They are discussing what course should be taken. And what do they say? That we should commence with a confederation—as if we all are not confederated against foreign tyranny! That we should consider the results of Spanish policy—What does it matter to us whether Spain sells her slaves [the colonies] to Bonaparte or keeps them herself, if we are resolved to be free? These doubts are the sad effects of our ancient chains. That we should prepare for great projects with calm—Are not three hundred years of calm sufficient? . . . Without fear, let us lay the cornerstone of South American Independence."

Bolívar ardently advocated democracy, but his was too creative a mind to accept current formulas in toto. He desired continuity as well as immediate reform. The most penetrating comment on his thought known to the writer is the following by Belaúnde, referring to the Angostura speech:

"Bolívar had an intuition of the real evil in pure democracy, that is, the placing of society, which is not only an organism, but a psychic entity, in the present time, which is mechanical time, and not in human time, which is the integration of the past with the present and the future; an integration produced by the synthesis of historical experience with the needs of the moment and the influence of the ideal. In this sense Bolívar resembled the great French master Hauriou, who confers only powers of control on the majority (*pouvoir majoritaire*) and leaves the business of government to a minority (*pouvoir*

minoritaire) constituted by authority based on natural qualities of competence, honor and will to command."

It would be outside the scope of this book to trace the steps
by which the nationalistic revolutions that swept the Spanish-
speaking sections of the New World achieved success. The
role of France is what concerns us.

In 1808 Napoleon compelled Charles IV to abdicate for
himself and his heirs, and elevated Joseph Bonaparte to the
throne of Spain. The loyalist opposition refused to admit
that the prince next in line could be deprived of his rights by
this transaction and, as Ferdinand VII, the inadequate son of
a weak father was proclaimed to the Iberian world. Napoleon
was confident that the oppressed colonies would prefer his
regime to that of the Bourbons. His envoys to Mexico,
Venezuela and Buenos Aires, however, were received in hostile fashion, then deported, with the approval of the municipalities, the only governing bodies in which Creoles had a
voice. Then, as always, there was no wish to substitute one
foreign sovereignty for another. Public demonstrations were
held and *juntas* formed in favor of Ferdinand VII. Presently
the municipalities, or *cabildos,* assumed control of affairs, re-
affirming their loyalty to the shadowy King, albeit hypo-
critically in most cases, while they chased his representatives
from office.

By 1810 revolts had broken out in all the important
centers. The following year came the first declaration of
absolute independence, that by Venezuela under the urging
of Bolívar seconded by Miranda.

The resulting wars lasted beyond the lifetime of Napoleon.
French volunteers joined the armies of liberation, particularly
after Waterloo, though they were not so numerous as the Irish
and English legionaries. The influence of France on this
chapter of American history was, from the beginning to the
end, moral rather than physical.

Chapter XXII

"Peace Reigned"

SLAVERY and the economic problems resulting from its abolition molded events in the West Indian colonies that remained to France after the Napoleonic Wars. Otherwise they had no political history for half a century. "Peace reigned" is the pet phrase of the chroniclers in describing Martinique, Guadeloupe and its dependencies, the half of tiny St. Martin, and Guiana under the restored Bourbons. It was the peace of reaction. The organization which had existed before the Revolution was re-established and the old names used at first. But privileges conceded by Louis XVI were taken away. Thus, the Superior Councils soon became mere courts of appeal without any political or legislative attributes. Even their representative character was weakened when it was provided by law that part of their membership must be composed of professional magistrates from France. The sullen welcome given these newcomers, the protests against the civic degradation implied, may be considered the last manifestation of the ancient colonial spirit.

There were changes from time to time, which culminated in a fixed plan. A Governor was appointed as the supreme head of each colony, with a Director of the Interior under him who inherited some of the duties of the former Intendant. These two were assisted in their executive work by a Privy Council, and in financial matters by a General Council. The members of the latter were named by the King from a list of candidates submitted by the municipalities. The General

Council had the right to maintain a representative in Paris as an agent, without a seat in the French Parliament.

This typical Bourbon structure passed with Charles X. Louis-Philippe, the "Citizen-King," who was placed on the throne by the Revolution of 1830, played true to form by giving the colonies something more liberal, yet inadequate. The General Councils became Colonial Councils, elected directly by the people, with full financial control and restricted powers of legislation in other fields.

Cane sugar had boomed briefly after the termination of the wars. There ensued a depression in all branches of agriculture and commerce, which grew steadily worse. Coffee, cocoa, cotton and indigo could not be sold profitably. The Windward Islands, and Martinique in particular, had always believed in a diversification of crops. Now they turned to sugar as the only product that could save them from bankruptcy, and this despite the fact that world prices of cane sugar were low because of the exploitation of new lands and the increasing competition of beet crystals in Europe. Between 1820 and 1840, the percentage of the wealth of Martinique invested in cane jumped from slightly under fifty per cent to eighty-seven per cent.

The plantations owed their survival at this juncture to the cheapness of slave labor. But abolition was an irrepressible issue, and the more enlightened planters knew it. During the Hundred Days, Napoleon had abolished the slave trade, and the Government of Louis XVIII had not dared to cancel the reform. The importation of blacks from Africa continued on a smaller scale, as a contraband traffic, though declared by all civilized nations to be piracy. Even without this scandal to arouse the humanitarian elements in France, slavery itself would have been doomed. The example of England was too powerful to resist. Furthermore, the institution in the French colonies had become a worse evil than it had been for longer than two centuries. This point is usually overlooked. The Code Napoleon, which in 1805, replaced the Code Noir, failed to mention the obligation of masters toward slaves, and abuses had rapidly sprung up.

In 1822 Negro rioting sufficiently serious to lead to twenty-one executions occurred in Martinique, where on account of the English regime in the 'Nineties there had never been an interlude of revolutionary freedom. Guadeloupe's recent memories of massacre and re-enslavement had left it too apathetic to take part. The following year there arose, also in Martinique, a Negro leader named Bissette whose ascendancy over the emancipated colored folk grew to be considerable. He was one of thirty-seven deported to Senegal in 1827 on the charge of spreading race propaganda, but he and two others were also given life imprisonment at hard labor. Thanks to the Revolution of 1830, Bissette was amnestied after three years, allowed to live in France, and became for the better part of a generation a sort of unofficial and privileged representative of his race there. He was a man of no culture and his talents, even as an agitator, were mediocre.

The second serious movement to free all slaves, successor to that of the Amis des Noirs, started with the accession of Louis-Philippe. Lamartine and most liberal intellectuals of the day supported it. Victor Schoelcher, who has been called the French Wilberforce, was its guiding spirit. Schoelcher traveled around the world and made himself not only an authority on slavery, but on the entire problem of the administration of colonies. His personality lacked charm. No one could deny his sincerity, his knowledge or his sense of justice, and that was what counted.

At the very beginning of the Citizen-King's reign, free men of color were given full civic rights. The Government a little later removed all restrictions on voluntary emancipation, with the results that by 1842 there were more than half as many freed Negroes as slaves in Martinique and Guadeloupe. Significantly, the manumissions were nearly all of women and children. A list, dated 1831, of slaves to whom liberty was accorded "for services rendered their masters," contained sixty-nine names, of which only two were those of male adults—one an old man of sixty, the other the betrayer of a conspiracy. It was the old story. The whites freed their concubines and illegitimate offspring, but were unwilling to lose the services of able-bodied laborers.

This did not satisfy anyone, except the immediate beneficiaries. Schoelcher reiterated the classic argument: "Slavery must be destroyed not only for the sake of the slaves, but for that of the masters, because it tortures the first and depraves the second."

England had decided to take the final step. The last shackles on men under her flag were knocked off in 1838. The news spread to the remotest plantation barracks in the French colonies, and many bondsmen tried to flee to the liberty of adjacent Dominica and St. Lucia. Some were so simpleminded as to plunge into the sea and attempt to swim the distance. Those that were caught—a majority, of course—were punished with excessive cruelty to deter the rest.

Schoelcher made full use of the emotional value of these events. The Colonial Councils, on the other hand, hurt the cause of the planters by their intolerant attitude. Arguing that any modification of slavery would ruin the sugar industry, they refused to receive or to help the committees of inquiry sent from France. Local abolitionist groups were not permitted to organize.

In 1845, a humane law was adopted by the home Government. It was not emancipation; it simply established a new type of slavery, or rather a system for the gradual suppression of slavery. By its provisions, the bondsman ceased to be a piece of property. The master's right to the labor he had acquired was all that remained of the institution. The slave might purchase his freedom at any time for cash, at a price to be fixed by the courts. One day a week, when he could work for his own profit, inalienably belonged to the slave.

The whites fumed at this device, the temporary and transitional nature of which was obvious. It would soon have been termed a malignant form of serfdom and repealed in favor of abolition. But it was scarcely in effect when the Revolution of 1848 swept it aside. This was an upheaval led by far more radical thinkers than those who had made the one of 1830. The French Second Republic emerged. Lamartine was a member of the provisional Government. Schoelcher became an under-Secretary of State. Armand Barbès, called by Proudhon the "Bayard of Democracy," a native of Guadeloupe, was released from the jail where Louis-Philippe had confined him, and elected a people's representative. Revolutionary Socialists occupied high places.

Under such auspices there could be only one answer regarding slavery. An act was rushed through in March, 1848, abolishing it without qualifications. Payment to owners was fixed at the nominal sum of 430 francs per head. The market value of a slave was then from 1,500 to 1,800 francs. The State declared that it did not feel itself obligated to cover the loss of outlawed "property," but it allowed the difference for five years between the cost to the master of keeping a slave and employing a free laborer. A single modification was conceded. Emancipation had come in the middle of the cane harvest, and to aid the planters the date was postponed to July. Naturally enough, the excited Negroes would not work and a large part of the crop was lost.

The new republican Government in France had swept away all colonial foundations. Commissaries were sent out to act as Governors. Martinique and Guadeloupe once more became integral parts of the home country. It was announced that each island would have three seats in the French Parliament, and meanwhile they would elect that number of deputies to a Constituent Assembly. Universal suffrage had been adopted, which gave the deciding voice to a huge majority of illiterate ex-slaves with no comprehension of the political issues. This reduced the election to a plebiscite on the change that had occurred.

Bissette came back from France and campaigned ebulliently for a seat. Schoelcher was nominated in both Martinique and Guadeloupe; partisans applauded his expressed hope that the blacks would be absorbed by intermarriage into the French race. The count of ballots showed Schoelcher, Bissette and a gentleman of the odd name of Pory-Papy elected from Martinique, in the order given. From Guadeloupe those returned were Schoelcher, again, and two other continentals. The reformer decided to sit from Martinique and resigned the other seat in favor of his alternate, Louisy Mathieu, a coal-black man.

It looked like the triumph of extreme democracy. Few had any suspicion of what the next three years would bring: the candidacy of Louis Napoleon Bonaparte for the presidency of the Second Republic; his fantastic victory in December, 1848; the *coup d'état* of December, 1851, and his restoration of the Empire with himself as Napoleon III. Colored leaders like Bissette had been deluded into supporting the tricky adventurer with the portentous name. After the catastrophe, they paid the price of a complete loss of influence in all quarters. We hear no more of Bissette.

The white colonials hailed the return of conservatism. Napoleon III quickly put an end to the departmental self-government that had been enjoyed briefly, and he stripped the islands of their right to elect members to the French Parliament. The regime he established bore a resemblance to that prevailing in the British Crown Colonies. There was a Governor with large powers, aided by officials from Europe, and a General Council half of whose membership was named by the Governor and half by the municipalities. No opposition party was tolerated.

But the Emperor did not even contemplate the restoration of slavery. Free labor proved increasingly undependable and restless. Many Negroes refused to work on the plantations, which they associated with their former lot. They preferred to cultivate small patches of land for the maintenance of their families, or to live in the towns by some trade. Beginning in 1852, indentured labor from Africa and Asia was introduced, supposedly voluntary recruits who signed contracts for a term of years, at a monthly salary that averaged twelve francs, and their keep. The experiment proved an unhappy one. Hindus constituted the mass of the immigrants. Some had been deceived with glowing tales of riches in America, and some had been kidnaped. They suffered from melancholia on the plantations, which reduced their efficiency, and they were unusually susceptible to yellow fever.

Central factories for the processing of sugar cane were established in the 1850's. This did away with the wasteful repetition of tasks on hundreds of small estates. It helped to ease the labor difficulty, since fewer hands were now employed in the industry as a whole. The period was marked by a lively demand in Europe for French West Indian rum, a fact which saved many planters from bankruptcy. Exports of rum from Martinique jumped from around 200,000 francs worth in 1848 to 2,183,046 francs in 1868.

Some of the trade restrictions of the archaic *Exclusif* had remained in force until 1861. All were abolished that year, and for the first time in their history the colonies were free to buy and sell wherever and whatever they pleased. In 1866, they were authorized to fix their own customs duties for the purposes of local revenue. These were the most important economic reforms obtained under Napoleon III.

But civic life remained at a standstill. It was merely a

question of whether the Governor of the moment was good or bad. The only administrator worthy of mention was Admiral de Gueydon, Governor of Martinique from 1853 to 1856. He embarked on a great series of public works, notably for the improvement of the harbor and town of Fort-de-France, which have kept alive his memory there. Gueydon also encouraged vocational education and sought to create needs among the blacks that would stimulate them to work. He ably codified the laws of the colony.

The story of Guiana had been simpler and more depressing. Nothing significant occurred there between the restoration of the Bourbons and the year 1848. On the first announcement of emancipation, the blacks walked out en masse and could not be induced to complete harvesting the sugar crop. The planters thereupon wiped their hands of responsibility, and if it had not been for the aid given by religious orders the old and infirm Negroes would have perished of want. An angry hostility possessed the whites. They treated their former slaves as they had always treated the Indians of the woods. As they found it impossible to recruit other labor, the plantation system crashed. All improvements went to ruin in a few years and the colony became an economic desert.

Napoleon III then decided to improve on the policy adopted during the French Revolution and transport there large numbers of undesirable citizens. He began in 1852 with several boatloads of convicts who had elected this course, in preference to serving out their terms. Most of them had committed serious crimes and were under long sentences. Numbering 2,220, they came as free settlers subject to certain mild parole restrictions, and pledged to remain in the colony. Other batches followed until almost 10,000 had been brought out.

The plan was not a success. Yellow Jack, the eternal enemy, again intervened. One epidemic carried off 1,057 men, and in a single year the mortality from all causes was sixty-three per cent. In addition, the settlers were apathetic and would not work. Even the life prisoners would do nothing practical to establish themselves. The great majority had but one idea—to escape and return to France.

A Governor of the period filed an intelligent report, in which he declared against penal colonization. It would never succeed with Frenchmen, he said, because it was deprived of contact with a society capable of absorbing the reformed settlers. The latter had neither the culture nor the pride needed to build a civilization of their own. He believed it would be a good idea to continue transporting criminals to Guiana, as criminals, because they could be handled there more humanely than in the crowded prisons of France. His views were not well received. But toward the end of the Second Empire the transporting of white convicts was abandoned. Only Arabs, Annamites and other colored malefactors were sent, and these proved much more adaptable to the life.

In 1855 placer gold was discovered in Guiana, a belated sign that there had been some truth in the El Dorado legend. The deposits were unimportant compared with those of other gold-bearing regions, yet the State's royalty on this commodity alone has ever since permitted the colony to balance its budget.

No account of the French in the West Indies would be complete without some mention of early relations with Haiti, leading up to recognition of that republic. Napoleon had never admitted the loss of the country. The Bourbons at first took the same stand. Malouet, Secretary of the Marine under Louis XVIII, slowly came to the conclusion that it would be necessary to compromise. He sent negotiators, while Alexandre Pétion was President in the south and Henry Christophe King in the north, to propose autonomy that would be in fact independence, but with nominal bonds favoring

French prestige and commerce. Pétion refused to discuss the matter. Christophe was equally scornful, and learning that one of the agents had been born in the island, he ruled that he was a Haitian subject and had him shot as a spy.

In April, 1825, Charles X took the remarkable step of decreeing that the ports of "Saint Domingue" should be open to the commerce of all nations, with a fifty-per-cent reduction of dues on French ships; that the inhabitants should in five years pay an indemnity of 150,000,000 francs to the former colonists; and that upon the fulfillment of these terms independence would be recognized. Jean Pierre Boyer was then President of a reunited Haiti. He found the decree utterly distasteful, but as it was accompanied by a serious threat of war he accepted it. This opened the way to recognition by other Powers. Britain, Holland, Sweden and Denmark acted promptly. It is commonly overlooked by modern writers that, owing to the opposition of Dixie, the United States did not take the same step until 1862, shortly after the outbreak of the War of Secession.

The Government of Louis-Philippe signed a new convention with Haiti in 1838, granting unconditional recognition and reducing the indemnity by half. Further reductions were negotiated later in the century. Only a fractional part of the original sum was ever paid.

Chapter XXIII

Napoleon III and the Confederacy

The only French regime which sought to meddle in the affairs of the New World, in defiance of the Monroe Doctrine (enunciated December 2, 1823), was that of Napoleon III. A passion to control Mexico, and a dream of digging a transcontinental canal at the Isthmus of Tehuantepec, the Nicaragua depression or the Isthmus of Panama, furnished the motives. These did not appeal strongly to the Government as a whole, but were personal ambitions of the Emperor and a few of his closest advisers, notably the Empress Eugénie and his illegitimate half-brother, the Duc de Morny. It was almost a family affair, and Napoleon's attitude toward the war between the North and South in the United States was profoundly affected by it. We know that he stopped short of recognizing the Confederacy, or giving it overt aid. Neither act could have been called a breach of the Monroe Doctrine. Clearly, however, he often contemplated one or both of them not for any love of Dixie, but to safeguard himself in Mexico where he was committing a flagrant violation and to render Washington helpless to oppose his schemes for a canal.

The Monroe Doctrine says that "the American continents . . . are henceforth not to be considered as subjects for future colonization by any European powers. . . . We owe it to candor . . . to declare that we should consider any attempt on their part to extend their system to any portion of this hemisphere as dangerous to our peace and safety." Napoleon III's policies looking to nullify that dictum were inextricably mixed. It seems best to devote separate chapters to the Con-

253

federacy, Mexico and canals, while allowing the two first subjects to overlap freely and carrying the third beyond the reign of Louis Napoleon.

When the Southern States seceded early in 1861, much spontaneous sympathy for their cause was evident in France. Legalists who had studied the conditions under which the Union had been founded agreed that the right to secession had been reserved. It was regarded as a war for self-determination on the part of the manifestly weaker party, and this made a romantic appeal. On account of the Negro question, the dominant class in the colonies was markedly pro-Southern. The elements which had fought and abolished slavery took the Northern side, of course. But there was no objection to the proclamation of neutrality in May, which accorded belligerent rights to the new Government. Outright recognition doubtless would have been accepted with complacency at that time.

The state of French public opinion suited the Emperor perfectly. He was still better pleased by the war itself, which threatened to break up the United States. For he had long had designs on Mexico and had been postponing them through fear of a hostile reaction in Washington. He wished to found an empire below the Rio Grande with a European prince as ruler, to maintain it under French tutelage and eventually to push its borders all the way to Panama. His consort, Eugénie, a devout Catholic, had urged him on because the enterprise would redound to the glory and power of the Church which had been roughly handled by republican Mexico. The Hapsburg Archduke Maximilian, brother of the Emperor Franz Joseph of Austria, had already been approached as the possible monarch. Maximilian's wife, Carlotta of Belgium, was as enthusiastic about it as Eugénie and had enlisted the support of her family. But Louis Napoleon's most effective supporter was Morny.

This brilliant and unscrupulous man, son of Queen Hortense by Charles de Flahaut, himself an illegitimate son of the great Talleyrand, had helped to organize the *coup d'état* and ever since had been the most formidable influence behind the throne. Some historians hold that he was the real Emperor up till his premature death. Morny lived expensively and was greedy for money. He saw opportunities to get it in Mexico. Quite willing that the venture should cost the lives of French soldiers, he wanted no disastrous fizzles, no gambles, but a sure thing. When his imperial half-brother got excited over the expeditions of William Walker into Sonora and Lower California in 1853 and 1854, and asked Morny about seizing those territories for their silver mines, he replied that the scheme was excellent economically, but that politically it was too great an undertaking for so new an Emperor. "You must be established yourself before you make Emperors for the Americas," he said.

Chaos in Mexico had been growing. A generation of revolutions culminated in the 1850's in a death struggle between the old banditry and a constitutional party led by one of the noblest of Mexicans patriots, the full-blooded Indian, Benito Juárez. Victory was slowly swinging to the side of Juárez when, in 1859, Morny was approached by a Swiss named Jecker who offered him nearly seventeen millions of Mexican national bonds at ten cents on the dollar. Jecker had advanced only a fraction of this sum in cash, but his documents permitted him to claim the whole. Juárez had repudiated the agreement made by a predecessor, and Jecker had come to Paris to find a purchaser at cut rates. Morny was interested. He helped the Swiss to get naturalization papers in a hurry, bracketed the claim with others that France was trying to collect for her citizens from Mexico, and privately formed a syndicate to buy the bonds.

Until then the French bill had been trifling. Even with the

Jecker bonds to inflate it, the total was less than a third of what Mexico owed to Spaniards and about a twenty-fifth of what she ostensibly owed to Englishmen. Nevertheless, Louis Napoleon suggested in 1860 to Britain and Spain that the three countries make a joint military demonstration against Mexico for the purpose of collecting the debts. They agreed. Action of that sort had been successful before, without enraging Washington since territorial gains had not been envisaged. But Louis Napoleon intended it as the opening wedge for his imperialistic project. It seems likely that he would have gone right ahead if Morny had not reminded him to be cautious and delay the expedition. Morny had been watching the turmoil of political happenings in the United States. He foresaw the War of Secession and preferred that it should start before the allies moved.

In January, 1861, Juárez finally crushed his enemies and was supreme in Mexico. As he had set his face against all exorbitant foreign claims, the reason for coercion grew stronger. A few weeks later the Confederacy bombarded Fort Sumter into submission and the long-awaited strife between North and South was a reality. Jefferson Davis immediately sent three commissioners to Europe to solicit recognition from Britain and France. The best-known of these was William L. Yancey, the celebrated orator and early advocate of secession. Official circles in London were cool, discouraging, those in Paris more friendly. But the Emperor and Morny waited to see if the South could win battles.

First Manassas gave what looked like a conclusive answer. William H. Russell, correspondent of the London *Times,* had called it a rout, the beaten Federal army a disorderly mob. He had expressed the belief that the Union could never be restored. That Queen Victoria's Government should take this phlegmatically was in character. John Slidell later wrote cynically that England wanted to see the North humbled, but hoped to avoid being put to any expense in the matter. Had the Confederacy lost Manassas, in his opinion, England would probably have rushed to its aid. All that this and other victories accomplished was to convince English statesmen that the South could win without their help.

But Napoleon III certainly did not have this attitude. He desired close relations with an independent South. Why, then, did he not extend recognition after Manassas? The answer lies in his Mexican obsession and the commitments he had made to England in connection with the debt-chasing foray. He must not offend England by doing for the South what she had refrained from doing. His Government, indeed, went to the length of declaring publicly that on the issue of Confederate independence and the negotiation of treaties of friendship and trade, it would act strictly in concert with Westminster.

"One morning," writes Burton J. Hendrick, author of *Statesmen of the Lost Cause,* "Mr. Seward was astonished by the appearance of Lord Lyons and M. Mercier, British and French Ministers in Washington, on a joint visit to the State Department, demanding that they be received together. Mr. Seward deftly but firmly declined to grant this startling request, but the proposal disclosed the extent to which the two Governments were carrying out an allied policy in the treatment of all American questions."

So the mission of Yancey and his colleagues inevitably was a failure, and they were recalled. Napoleon III meanwhile notified England and Spain that he was ready to go ahead with the Mexican affair. On December 8, 1861, there appeared off Vera Cruz a small squadron flying the flags of the three nations. Troops were landed without serious opposition. The proportional show of strength was deceptive in the extreme: 6,000 Spanish soldiers, 3,000 French, and 700 British marines. We must assume that, until disillusioned, Spain took the affair at its face value. England had by far the largest financial claim, yet sent only a token force. The comparatively modest French army was the one with far-reaching orders, but it could be strengthened as soon as the nations whose feelings mattered had been psychologized by events. It would have been very strange if England had had no knowledge of what the Emperor was up to.

What happened in Mexico will be told in the next chapter. The *fait accompli* of Vera Cruz seemed to improve the chances for recognition when the next Confederate commissioners arrived in Europe. These were John Slidell, assigned to Paris, and James M. Mason, assigned to London. The vast publicity of the *Trent* incident attended them. While on their way from the neutral port of Havana in an English boat, they had been forcibly removed by the commander of a Northern warship and taken to Boston. Vigorously worded protests, carrying the threat of war, had obtained their release. They were now lionized as international figures, the manner differing widely, however, in the two capitals. Mason was entertained at the homes of English aristocrats, but had only one interview with the Secretary of State for Foreign Affairs, and that an informal one. Slidell also luxuriated socially, and in addition saw the highest in the land on frequent occasions. The Emperor received him cordially at the Tuileries, Saint Cloud, Vichy and Biarritz. Morny, two successive Foreign Ministers and other officials treated him with such consideration that he was actually, if not in name, a member of the diplomatic corps.

Both Mason and Slidell had more complicated instructions than those which had been given Yancey. They must not only work for recognition, but attempt to gain lesser points and especially a ruling against the legality of the blockade which the North had clamped upon the coasts of the Confederacy. Ineffective at first, the blockade was beginning to hurt. England was a co-sufferer, since it kept cotton from the mills of Lancashire and threw thousands out of employment there. Yet France, whose trade with the South had not been of vital importance, showed greater signs of irritation, and Slidell made the most of that.

The subject had been well advertised by Captain Raphael Semmes, who had run the blockade from New Orleans early in the war in the *Sumter,* a converted passenger liner of 500 tons, and had profitably raided Northern shipping for seven months. He had called at Saint Pierre, Martinique, in November, 1861, to coal and to put prisoners ashore. A United States battleship had tried to pin him there. Semmes had waited for a dark night and quietly slipped away to continue his operations in the Atlantic, a feat which caused much excited talk on the Parisian boulevards. Subsequently, Semmes had disposed of the *Sumter* at Gibraltar and run up his flag on the *Alabama,* a cruiser built at Liverpool, the most celebrated raider in history.

Nevertheless, the Emperor could not bring himself to take a definite attitude advantageous to the Confederacy. He was torn by hesitations which revolved around his Mexican project. Even Morny failed to hold him to a consistent, firm course. The English and Spaniards had retired from Mexico. The French were alone there, but the military campaign offered no insuperable difficulties and it was obvious that Maximilian could be placed on the throne. To keep him in power would be another matter, depending largely on whether the United States survived or became two nations. If England would only act first in recognizing the South, Napoleon III was eager to follow, was willing even to send troops to the aid of the Richmond Government.

Hendricks states flatly that he needed a victorious Confederacy to be permanently successful in Mexico, and adds: "It is an interesting study to review the ups and downs of the

Mexican adventure, and to observe how each vacillation in attitude depended on events in the American Civil War." Not until Lee triumphed in the Seven Days' battles before Richmond was the Emperor convinced that it would be prudent to occupy the City of Mexico. "The possible restoration of the Union was a nightmare that haunted Napoleon's dreams."

But the reluctance of England to take any but a neutral stand bluffed him. His hesitations over Mexico were reflected in his dealings with Slidell, to whom he sometimes blew hot and sometimes blew cold.

An instructive episode occurred in July, 1862. Judah P. Benjamin, Secretary of State for the Confederacy, authorized Slidell to offer France a gift of 100,000 bales of cotton (subject to increase) if she would send merchant ships through the blockade to Southern ports. The cargoes of these ships would be admitted duty free, an immensely profitable business for the owners. The Confederacy, desperately short of certain supplies, was willing to pay high for them and also to present the cotton as a token of gratitude. The transaction would have been irregular, but it appealed so strongly to Napoleon III that he discussed it with Slidell in a private interview at Vichy. He asked bluntly: "How am I to get the cotton?"

The Confederate envoy answered that the Northern blockade was not unbreakable—particularly as France owned three ironclads, the first to be built by any navy. This was as good as inviting the Emperor to start hostilities with the North. Napoleon conceded tranquilly that his ironclads could end the blockade and with it the war, but he said there might be opposition on the part of England. The offer of cotton and free trade, according to Slidell, "did not seem disagreeable" to him; he would think about it. He went so far as to express regret that he had not recognized the Confederacy at the beginning. Now, he hinted, it might be too late.

Nothing came of this interview, and from then on it was increasingly difficult for Slidell to extract encouragement from the Emperor, or from his cabinet. The defeat at Gettysburg the next year threw a damper on *pourparlers* with recognition in view which the French Foreign Minister had tentatively proposed to Westminster. In June, 1864, when Semmes brought the storm-worn *Alabama* to Cherbourg for repairs after a cruise of nearly two years without a home port, scant official courtesies were extended. But an ovation from seamen in the harbor accompanied the raider to her valiant finale against the U.S.S. *Kearsarge* a week later.

The Duc de Morny behind the scenes persisted to the end—his end—in maneuvering to cement an alliance with the South, which in the darker days would of course have involved giving military help as well as recognition. He believed that that was the surest way of saving the Mexican affair from failure. Toward the end of 1864, the Prince de Polignac, who as a volunteer officer was commanding a division under Kirby Smith, received a significant letter from Morny. It suggested that the chiefs of the Confederate Government address themselves directly to Napoleon III. Secret agents at once started for France, to learn on their arrival in March, 1865, that Morny had just died. They would have been too late, anyway. In a month the curtain was rung down at Appomattox.

Chapter XXIV

The Mexican Adventure

When the joint expedition landed at Vera Cruz, it impressed official Mexico as being similar to a coup by the French alone twenty-three years earlier. The Prince de Joinville had occupied the port, demanding the payment of a long-standing debt, one of the items of which had been $60,000 claimed by a French baker for pastry alleged to have been stolen from him by revolutionists. On that occasion, General Santa Anna had made a surprise attack and driven the invaders back to their ships. But faced by the threat of a real war, the Mexican Government had agreed to settle in full, while trying to save face by calling the business scornfully the *reclamación de los pasteles* (the pie claim).

President Juárez wanted no repetition of that farce, and in view of the terrible civil war that had just closed he was eager to avoid more bloodshed. He allowed the allies to advance at their leisure to Orizaba, nearly a third of the distance to Mexico City. He then entered into negotiations with the commissioners of the three Powers. The justice of the financial claims was acknowledged on general principles, though Juárez reserved the right to contest certain items, such as the Jecker bonds. Cause of military action was sedulously avoided. The commissioners, on their part, had declared that their presence in Mexico was for the sole purpose of settling certain vexed questions peaceably. A prompt evacuation would have been logical.

The French stalled, however. Re-enforcements began to reach them. The Spaniards caught on to the fact that a more serious project was involved and their commander, the distinguished General Prim, found it embarrassing. Prim and the British Minister cornered Dubois de Saligny, the French Minister, and insisted on knowing his Government's intentions. They learned only that France was demanding 12,000,-000 pesos, cash down, and the subsequent settlement of her claim in full. This was preposterous, because of Mexico's bankrupt condition. The others had planned to scale down their much larger bills radically.

Saligny had been for a long time one of the chief villains in the piece. He was a protegé of Morny, and it was Morny whom he served. The reports he sent home deceived Louis Napoleon into believing that a French army would be welcomed by the people of Mexico. The Juárez liberals, according to Saligny, were plunderers of the nation and persecutors of the Church. The masses hated them. The masses realized that more than half the revenue of the country was being stolen, and they would regard a monarchy backed by France as a godsend.

Encouraged by Saligny, a delegation of Mexican reactionaries had gone to Paris and told the Emperor much the same story. The party had included General Juan N. Almonte, a former lieutenant of Santa Anna, a Roman Catholic Bishop, and other clericals. It had been joined by the fugitive ex-President Miguel Miramón, the man who had issued the Jecker bonds; and two rich exiles, José Hidalgo and Gutiérrez de Estrada, who hoped to regain their confiscated estates. The representations of these interested and fanatical persons had been the final persuasion needed to commit Louis Napoleon to the venture.

While Prim was still arguing with Saligny and taking the Mexican side rather than his own—unique role for a Spanish General—a new French army larger than the first one arrived at Vera Cruz. It was commanded by General Laurencez. He brought with him the Mexican agitator Almonte, who at once assumed the title of Provisional President. This was too much for Prim. In April the Spanish troops were withdrawn and sailed away, followed by the English.

Laurencez lost no time in announcing that he would advance on the capital, by way of the industrial city of Puebla. Less was said about the debt now. In his proclamations Laurencez spoke of liberating the country. Actually, he was not authorized to penetrate farther than Puebla unless a revolution favorable to the French occurred. The only event that could be interpreted in that light was the adhesion of Leonardo Márquez, a brutal, discredited guerrilla leader who had failed against Juárez, and a few score of his tattered riders.

Puebla was well fortified, but defended by poorly armed troops. It should have been easy for Laurencez to invest and capture the city. But on May fifth he recklessly hurled his men into a frontal attack which necessitated swarming up the steep slopes of the Cerro de Guadalupe. The French fought bravely, only to be disastrously repulsed with a loss of more than a thousand men. The day is observed as a Mexican national holiday.

Back at his old headquarters in Orizaba, Laurencez awaited orders from Paris. Before they came, one brilliant feat was accomplished by men hungry for glory. Some heights above the city had been occupied by from three to four thousand Mexican troops, and heavy guns were being moved up. A bombardment from that position would have made Orizaba untenable. The ordinary paths of approach were well guarded. One night, however, a young captain led only 150 soldiers Indian-file up a narrow goat-track, along which a woman had been seen daily carrying water to the summit. As he fell on the enemy, the officer shouted orders proper to a couple of regiments and the Mexicans broke in confusion. A general, 300 men and all the guns were captured.

A mood of caution, unusually stagnant even for him, possessed Napoleon III when he learned what had happened at Puebla. Everything had to wait until the Southern Confederacy had won some great victories. But he sent more and more troops to Mexico, 30,000 of them, under a new commander-in-chief, Marshal Elie Fréderic Forey.

The attitude of Forey was dictatorial. He forbade Almonte to call himself President on penalty of being considered unfriendly to France. He made fresh pronouncements to the Mexicans, assuring them that he had come to assist in the regeneration of their country and with no other object. The local support which had been denied Laurencez failed to materialize for him, also. He lingered at Orizaba and on the coast for seven months. The defeat of McClellan by Lee before Richmond had not been quite enough for Louis Napoleon; he waited for Second Manassas in October, for Fredericksburg in December. Then, at last, Forey received orders to subdue Mexico by force.

Moving his army into position slowly and skillfully, Forey completed the investment of Puebla on March sixteenth. The city was better equipped to defend itself than it had been the year before; the garrison was as large as the French force and the fortifications had been strengthened. But Forey did not repeat the blunders of Laurencez. He conducted a siege, his lines tightly drawn, his daily bombardments murderous, and for that the Mexicans had not been prepared. In less than two months they had expended all their ammunition and eaten their last scrap of food. Unconditional surrender followed. The French marched in, enthusiastically received by only one element of the population—the clergy.

Juárez had staked the major part of his resources on Puebla. He had about 14,000 soldiers left in Mexico City, and although he had talked of making a stand there he perceived that it would be suicide. As the French started to climb the last approaches to the central plateau, he retired to San Luis Potosí. It was an operation that the stubborn Indian would repeat many times in the next three years, until he stood at El Paso del Norte, across the river from Texas. Never did Juárez concede that he had been ejected from the presidency.

Forey made his official entry into the capital on June tenth. There had been time for the Church and the conservatives to prepare an ovation for him, and it was duly staged with a few prominent men to make speeches of welcome and thousands of hired demonstrators to cheer and toss flowers. Forey may have seen through it, but he sent a sufficiently encouraging report to Paris.

"A day or two later," writes Henry Bamford Parkes, in his admirable *History of Mexico*, "the hosannahs of the clergy suddenly died away, for Forey issued a proclamation guaranteeing the existing owners of church property, many of whom happened to be French citizens; the clergy were not to recover their treasures or their *haciendas*. It was now the turn of the Mexican clericals to discover that they had been tricked. Napoleon, it appeared, had not sent his armies across the Atlantic merely to fight in the holy cause of religion."

Forey soon showed them who was master. When they threatened to close the churches, he warned them that if they did he would blow open the doors with cannon.

The effect on the reactionaries was to redouble their ardor for the Austrian prince. His was one of the most stanchly Catholic of royal families and he might be expected, when power was in his hands, to reverse the decision of the French Marshal. The remnants of the Conservative Party held a convention, or assembly of notables as they called it, and offered "the crown of Montezuma" to Maximilian.

Dilatory tactics, ceremonious and absurd, were now practiced when lightning energy should have been displayed. If Napoleon III had urged his candidate to accept promptly, had rushed him to Mexico and established the regime with fanfare and bayonets, there would have been excellent chances of success. The Federal Union in the north had as yet won no major victory and was not in a position to resent anything that might be done in Mexico. The new empire would have become virtually an ally of the Confederacy—Morny's secret policies provided for this—and it is reasonable to suppose that they could have saved each other.

Instead, Napoleon allowed the summer of 1863 to slip by, the fateful summer of Gettysburg, while a delegation was organized to wait on Maximilian at his castle on the Adriatic and formally invite him to become Emperor of Mexico. Tall, dignified and handsome with his blond beard flowing to his chest and parted in the middle, the thirty-one-year-old archduke decidedly had an imperial presence. His Hapsburg blood made him a perfect aspirant, for among his ancestors had been Charles V, Holy Roman Emperor and King of Spain. But he was poorly fitted by temperament for the role of autocrat in a turbulent, exotic land. Maximilian was sentimental, well-meaning but irresolute, a dilettante prince who attached much importance to the social graces and whose hobby was the study of botany. The vainglory which induced him to listen to the voice of the tempter was wholly supplied by his archduchess, Carlotta of Belgium, who worshiped him and wanted extremely to be an empress.

Maximilian's honesty caused further delay when the delegation, headed by Gutiérrez de Estrada, interviewed him. He announced that he would accept only if the proposition could win approval by a free vote of the Mexican people. A free vote! There had not been one since the independence of the country. The constitutionalist, Juárez, had himself ridden the wave of a revolution. But Napoleon III did his best to oblige.

Marshal Achille Bazaine was sent to replace Forey, and he carried instructions to obtain a favorable plebiscite. The new commander, whose reputation was to be ingloriously destroyed a few years later at Metz, in the Franco-Prussian War, found that Mexico was less than half conquered. The French had occupied only the central states. Bazaine struck north-ward, driving the Juárez Government before him to Saltillo and then to Monterey. Wherever he went, he rigged up a plebiscite. At the end of a few months he had captured most of the cities and had seen to it that majorities had been regis-tered, in installments, for Maximilian. He never subdued either the far south, where the young Porfirio Diaz held the field, or the far north, which remained loyal to Juárez.

Only in April, 1864, did Maximilian formally accept the throne. He arrived with Carlotta a month afterward. They were depressed by the cool reception given them at Vera Cruz and on the road to the capital. Once they were in Mexico City, the conservatives flocked about the new monarchs and things looked better. They established themselves with florid splendor at the Castle of Chapultepec; the furniture, drapery and paintings they brought with them, their glass coach, are still displayed there as museum pieces.

As between Napoleon III and Maximilian, from then on, the honors are all on the side of the Austrian. Napoleon be-lieved that the summer of 1864 was too late for the successful founding of a Mexican Empire. The North was winning the war in the United States, and it was probable that as soon as that conflict was over there would be a demonstration on the banks of the Rio Grande by the veteran armies of Grant and Sherman. Morny still hoped that intervention might save the South; hence his last-minute message to the Prince de Polig-nac, mentioned in the preceding chapter. Napoleon, sunk in pessimism, toyed with the double-dealing and hopeless plan of bribing Washington to recognize his puppet in Mexico. He seized Confederate ships that were being built in French ports. When he learned that that would not bring results, he pre-pared to desert Maximilian. Yet he promised him faithfully that Bazaine's troops would support him until the end of

1867. Needless to say, the bill was to be paid by Mexico, at the rate of a thousand francs a year for each soldier.

The decorative victim, meanwhile, did his best to govern as a good ruler—and, amazingly, a liberal one. He declined to let the reactionaries control him, but formed a cabinet based on moderate opinion, appointed many liberals to important posts, fostered education and insisted on the passing of a law abolishing peonage. Above all, he firmly opposed the Church in the matter of its confiscated estates, which he declared had properly been restored to the nation. This got him into a quarrel that had reverberations in the Vatican, without gaining him the popular support he needed. The masses could not bring themselves to credit his sincerity.

Bazaine, who took his orders directly from France, was his sole reliance. And Bazaine, a military bully lacking even the virtue of thoroughness, a waster of public funds, unhappily was not the man to make friends for an imported regime. The Marshal in time pushed Juárez to the most distant limits of Chihuahua and captured Oaxaca in the south. Effective opposition in the field ceased. But the party was lost for Maximilian. The American War of Secession ended; soon Washington sent notes requiring an evacuation.

Napoleon, playing for time, ordered Bazaine to make a last desperate attempt to seize the person of Juárez. This failed. The Marshal advised Maximilian to abdicate, and on his proud refusal to do so the French army commenced to withdraw. The last soldier was out of the country months in advance of the deadline agreed upon. Carlotta went to Europe, pleaded her husband's cause in vain, became demented doing it. Maximilian was left alone, to resist his foes ineptly and die before a firing squad on the Hill of Bells at Querétaro.

Of all France's adventures in the New World, this was the one of which she had least reason to be proud.

Chapter XXV

Scheming for Canals

Napoleon III was in his early days the most canal-minded person in Europe, and he never lost his interest in the fascinating subject. While only a pretender and confined at the fortress of Ham, he had written a brochure on the prospects of linking the Atlantic and Pacific Oceans. The advantages of the Nicaragua route over the Isthmus of Panama were elaborately set forth by him. For a man who had never visited either locality, he showed a good grasp of his topic and many of his arguments were alluring. Through agents in England, he proposed to form a company with a capital of four million pounds. The enterprise was to be called the Canal de Napoléon. It naturally aroused some enthusiasm in Nicaragua, where one of the factions went so far as to inform Louis Napoleon that, "provided he could effect his escape," he would be backed for President of the Republic. This offer did not tempt him, but he kept in touch with his Central American supporters after his escape from Ham.

He was active in promoting the scheme during the two years that preceded the Revolution of 1848 and his return to Paris, but it did not get beyond the stage of prospectuses and the selling of a little stock. The bizarre turn of fortune that made him Prince-President of France submerged the canal idea, and when he revived it after the *coup d'état* it took the form of a national project. His Foreign Minister advocated it in 1854 as a complete proposition that needed only to be ratified by the Nicaraguan Government.

Yet almost simultaneously, Napoleon began to contemplate

the possibilities of a canal across the Isthmus of Tehuantepec, in Mexico. That the United States had a jealous eye on both regions did not disturb him.

The Nicaragua route follows the San Juan River from the Caribbean port of San Juan del Norte, or Greytown, to Lake Nicaragua, and beyond Lake Nicaragua it crosses a sixteen-mile neck of land to the Pacific. The river bed would have to be deeply excavated and the neck cut. This route, though roughly three-and-a-half times as long as the present Panama Canal, is still regarded by certain experts as the more desirable. It could be dug at sea level. There would be less danger from landslides.

What made it a dubious ambition for France in Napoleon III's time was the Clayton-Bulwer Treaty of 1850 between the United States and England, which bound those two powers "never to obtain or maintain any exclusive control" over a ship canal in either Nicaragua or Panama, and "never to fortify or exercise dominion" at the crucial points. If they were so insistent on a joint venture or none, they assuredly would not allow France to cut in ahead of them. The California gold rush had led to the founding of a transit line by boat and stagecoach across Nicaragua, and this was owned by Commodore Vanderbilt of New York. Presently the American filibuster, William Walker, entered the field and temporarily made himself master of the country. The shrewd Emperor pulled in his horns without publicly admitting that he had done so. He found it easy to prefer Tehuantepec since it was in the land of the Aztecs, the inspiration of his most grandiloquent dreams.

The Mexican isthmus is 125 miles broad, with an extreme elevation of 735 feet. It would be perfectly practicable to dig a canal there, though the cost would be higher than at Panama or the Nicaragua depression. Being farther north by several hundred miles than any other possible canal, it would offer by far the shortest westward route from Europe to the Orient. The Spaniards used it as an overland link for the transshipment of cargoes.

Late in 1859, just when Napoleon III was becoming serious about intervention and his project for a Mexican empire, the United States obtained from the Juárez liberals a perpetual, unlimited right of transit across Tehuantepec, with the privilege of bringing troops into the country to protect American property and enforce order. The price of the concession was to be $4,000,000, half paid in cash to the Mexican Government and half applied to claims against the latter by American citizens. This is known as the McLane-Ocampo Treaty. It had been extorted in return for Washington's friendly attitude toward Juárez during his struggle for power, and there had been final pressure in the form of a threat that the United States would seize Tehuantepec if any European nation showed signs of meddling with Mexico.

The French Emperor had no choice but to respect, briefly, the prior claim thus established. The War of Secession reopened the question from his standpoint, and Tehuantepec became part of his general policy concerning Maximilian. It was well understood that as soon as the Austrian was firmly established he would reassign the transit rights, either to France or to a victorious Southern Confederacy. Napoleon was willing to build the canal as a partner of Jefferson Davis. When that mirage faded, all the interested parties dropped the Mexican route. The United States Senate actually rejected the McLane-Ocampo Treaty.

Nicaragua again appeared to be the most logical setting for an American interoceanic canal, and Napoleon's ardor for it flashed intermittently. But his own fall was near, and on the eve of his passing, Suez focused the attention of Europe. He had had a finger in the gigantic promotion of that affair, too. It went ahead rapidly under the guidance of the celebrated

engineer Ferdinand de Lesseps, and in 1869 the Mediterranean and the Red Sea were joined.

Meanwhile, individual speculators had been negotiating
with the Republic of Colombia, of which Panama was then
a province. A railroad from Aspinwall (now Colon) across
the narrow isthmus had proved a most profitable venture.
Here, after all, was the site which the Spaniards had thought
of excavating since its discovery by Balboa, which Bolívar
and other great men had chosen for practical reasons, including international strategy. It was the shortest route and
probably the least expensive one.

In 1878 Lieutenant Bonaparte Wyse, an obscure French
officer, obtained from the Bogotá Government a concession
for the construction of a canal at Panama. The financial
machinations behind this deal are not very clear. Two years
earlier, the legislature had authorized in vague terms the
signing of a contract with a French company. Suspect foreigners had distributed bribes freely. But nothing positive had
come of it until Wyse emerged as the sole benefiiciary. He
did not appear to have the funds needed for so large a project,
and it is likely that he was used by backers as a dummy to
forestall De Lesseps.

For almost at once the hero of Suez launched a company in
France, which sold stock to the public on the guarantee of
enormous returns to be derived from an American canal. De
Lesseps was then seventy-four years old, vain of his success in
Egypt, and eager to crown his career with a second and
greater triumph of the same kind. He was a good engineer,
and he had ably solved the problem of cutting through desert
sands. It should be recalled, however, that the work was
known to be possible, as there had been a canal at Suez in
antiquity. Now he selected Panama over Nicaragua, and without making a personal survey of the territory he announced
that he would dig a sea-level ditch through the mountains,

forests and swamps. The perils of yellow fever and malaria do not seem even to have occurred to him. His company bought Wyse's concession for $2,000,000, and then paid the extravagant sum of $25,000,000 for the Panama Railroad, a rate of half-a-million a mile.

France was plunged into a new orgy of money madness, tinged with illusions of regaining lost ground in America. Forgetting the Mississippi Bubble of 160 years before, the Cayenne boom of 115 years before, the people invested hundreds of millions of francs in a project not fundamentally unsound, but badly managed. Their money was obtained by means of high-pressure salesmanship, re-enforced by fairy tales published in the Company's official organ, *Le Bulletin*. The glamour of De Lesseps' name counted for much. He went to the Isthmus only twice, spending less than two months there in all. The bulk of his time was devoted to social intercourse with bankers and politicians, and the making of speeches in France and the United States. Yet, on the occasion of his election to the Académie Française in 1885, Renan, who should have known better, said he had been born to pierce isthmuses and that the ancient world would have made him a god.

The scheme did not even have the merit of being a national emprise, nor would it have led to the planting of a French colony. It was strictly a commercial proposition, the plan being to charge a uniform toll for the passage of the ships of all nations. Technically, the Monroe Doctrine was not violated, though President Hayes remarked, "The policy of this country is a canal under American control." If De Lesseps had succeeded, there can be little doubt that the United States would have found a way to dominate the route so as to have special rights in time of war, precisely as England did in connection with the Suez Canal.

But he could not succeed, for three major reasons: waste and incompetence on the job, graft, and the eternal specter of Yellow Jack. Machinery and supplies of every sort were furnished lavishly, dumped on the scene before the engineers required them. This was because purchases were being made to put money into the pockets of influential men, and dishonest commissions were collected all along the line. The actual work was done by contractors who, with a few exceptions, cheated the Company brazenly, or who perhaps had paid rebates and did no more than it was privately expected they should do. They would excavate the soft earth at the stipulated price per cubic yard, then throw up their hands and go into bankruptcy to avoid having to take out the more difficult rock.

John Foster Fraser, an English observer, speaks of the "criminal expenditure of money." When more was required, the crooked financiers behind the scheme practiced every infamous trick to make the public believe that all was well and to cajole them into buying fresh issues of stock. "It is difficult to refrain from feeling that the French, fascinated with the idea, went mad. The extravagance was amazing; the salaries paid were colossal; millions of money were spent in buying things the use of which is a mystery; highest prices were paid. The Colombians, through whose property the route was cut, extracted the value of valuable town property for miserable swamp. When the greed was such that even the French, desirous though they were to conciliate the natives, had to resist, the only appeal was to Colombian law courts, and the decisions were always in favor of the rapacious Colombians."

Disease, however, was by far the greatest obstacle. The French built fine hospitals and sent out good doctors. Their nursing force was not familiar with tropical fevers, and in dealing with them at that time nursing was everything. No one had the faintest notion that the Stegomyia mosquito was the only carrier of yellow fever and the Anopheles mosquito the only carrier of malaria. Doctors could do nothing to prevent and little to cure, because they supposed that both maladies were contracted, like typhoid, by drinking bad water, or by inhaling the foul air of swamps. Yellow fever, in particular, was believed to be a "dirt disease" and to be highly contagious. The natives shared this delusion, but at all events they knew from long experience how best to treat a patient. The nuns that accompanied the French were helpless in the face of the growing calamity.

Panama had long had the reputation of being a deathtrap for the unacclimatized. De Lesseps found it to be so. His imported Chinese and colored labor from more healthful places perished almost as rapidly as the whites. The annual death rate from all causes hovered between 150 and 178 per thousand. No yellow fever epidemic of major proportions occurred. That disease did not attain the virulence of the scourge that had wiped out Leclerc's army in Saint Domingue in 1802; but it was active each year through the hot months from May to October, and more than fifty per cent of those stricken died. Malaria was always present. Nearly every newcomer caught it, and although the patient usually recovered from a given attack it killed more persons in the long run than yellow fever.

By 1886 the canal enterprise was in a bad way. De Lesseps had had his daughter turn the first sod late in 1879, when he had promised that the job would be completed in six years. There had been banquets and receptions. He had induced Sarah Bernhardt to come to Panama and give a gala performance. He had seemed a magician, and they had called him "Le Grand Français," a name of which he was inordinately proud. Anyone could flatter him by using it. Now he begged for a little more time, and set out to raise a great deal more money. The final subscriptions sent the total to beyond a billion francs, of which it has been said that perhaps ten per cent reached the Isthmus. The rest was embezzled by officials of the Company, or distributed among venal statesmen, including certain members of the Chamber of Deputies. De Lesseps, as the promoter, could not escape responsibility, but there is small evidence to support the charge that he was personally dishonest. He was merely too old for the work he had undertaken, too histrionic and too gullible.

By the end of 1887 the winds of scandal blew loud in the Chamber of Deputies, where many members had accepted tainted money and where careers were soon to be destroyed as a result. An honest group assailed the Panama venture with biting sarcasm.

"The ruin is doing well!" announced a deputy named Goirand, addressing the house. "Scarcely more than fifty per cent remains to be lost."

The false structure collapsed in 1888, and the Company had to be liquidated. Less than twenty-five per cent of the necessary excavation on the Isthmus had been accomplished. There was a fourteen-mile channel based on the Chagres River from the Caribbean to beyond Gatun, a few deep trenches in the mountains, and a partly completed, workmanlike cut at Culebra on the Continental Divide. The man responsible for the last-mentioned was Philippe Bunau-Varilla, then under thirty years of age, the only engineer to distinguish himself. Toward the end it had been realized that a sea-level canal would be impracticable and locks were being planned.

De Lesseps was tried for fraud and convicted, but never forced to serve in jail the term imposed. He died insane. A reorganization of the Panama venture under Government supervision occurred. A new company controlled by M. Eiffel, the builder of the Eiffel Tower in Paris, took over and announced that the work would proceed. It obtained an extension from Colombia until 1904. But only a skeleton force was employed, the real object being to hold the franchise until it could be disposed of advantageously. This, in effect, marked the termination of the last attempt by Frenchmen to score heavily in the New World.

The services of Bunau-Varilla had been retained. He it was who, in 1903, exercised a larger influence than any other man in bringing about the revolution that created the independent Republic of Panama, thus breaking a deadlock caused by the refusal of Colombia to agree to terms for the construction of a canal by the United States. President Theodore Roosevelt heartily approved the maneuver. Bunau-Varilla, appointed first Minister of Panama to Washington, added to his laurels as a maker of history when he and John Hay signed the treaty that transferred the canal route and bought out the French investors for $40,000,000.

Chapter XXVI

Under the Third Republic

THE Franco-Prussian War in which Louis Napoleon's empire foundered affected the colonies only remotely. They were not called upon to furnish troops, and as Prussia had no navy the old, familiar evils of bombardment, invasion and the cutting off of commerce were not repeated. The disastrous campaign ending at Sedan was so brief that men beyond the seas hardly realized what was happening. The founding of the Third Republic and the echoes of the Commune, however, aroused a good deal of emotion. There was one Negro riot in Martinique as a demonstration in favor of democracy. The white planters and merchants bemoaned the change as one that would almost certainly have the result of lessening their influence. They pointed to current events in Dixie under Reconstruction as examples of what might be expected from a Negrophile republic. But there was no talk of resistance.

Promptly the imperial forms were swept away and the colonies were treated as French departments. As in 1848, they were invited to send representatives to an emergency Assembly. The constitution of 1875 confirmed their new status, and from then on Martinique and Guadeloupe each had one senator and two deputies, and Guiana one deputy, in the legislature of France. Strictly speaking, local administration should have been confided to prefects under the Minister of the Interior, with sub-prefects for each *arrondissement,* but it was felt that this would lead to complications in territories so out of touch with Paris. Governors were appointed, instead, and given Privy Councils to assist them. Everything else was as in Europe. The towns elected mayors and councils. Ruling by decree became taboo. Ordinances to regulate special problems could be adopted on the spot by an elective General Council. Law-making was the prerogative of the national Parliament. Magistrates were assigned through the French Ministry of Justice.

The passionate interest in politics now taken by the colored population astonished some observers. But the reasons for it were logical and simple enough. A peasantry of small landowners and renters had come into existence. A second generation had reached maturity since 1848, and it had the rudiments of education which its slave parents had lacked. The eighteen-year, mild dictatorship of the Second Empire had given men plenty of time to brood, while allowing them no voice in the government of the colonies. It was small wonder that, finding themselves eligible to any elective office, the mulattoes and Negroes should rush to participate. Their ideas about their civic duties remained primitive for several decades. Leadership and office-holding appealed to them. The franchise seemed less interesting. It was easy to get crowds to manifest wildly for a popular candidate, but hard to induce them to cast their ballots. The immense preponderance of colored voters made it possible, none the less, to round them up and elect a large number of Negroes from the start.

Visitors from France in the late nineteenth century delighted in poking fun at West Indian politics. The serious-minded bemoaned the scandals that arose. The writer Victor Meignan spent a few weeks in Martinique and took a hasty glance at Guadeloupe, in 1881. He published a fairly superficial book the following year, in which he remarked that he had found island elections to be "always a question of the color of the skin, and I fear that the decisions of juries are influenced in the same manner." The choice of a mulatto general councillor by a total of forty-two votes in a district where there were 5,000 electors on the lists horrified him. He repeated the probably apochryphal story of a contest in Guadeloupe when no voters appeared at the polls. The polls were re-opened the following Sunday. A candidate who had had no expectation of victory chanced to meet nine of his employees on the road and asked them to vote for him. He was elected by precisely those nine ballots.

Yet the system produced some able statesmen. The most important offices were those of the senators and deputies. Because of their status in France, these men exerted much influence over the Governor, who often complained that he dared not act without their approval. In Martinique and Guadeloupe, by tacit agreement over a long period, one deputy was white and one colored. French senators are chosen by indirect vote, and the members from the islands generally were white. It became a commonplace in Paris that the senators from Martinique and Guadeloupe were superior to the average run of their colleagues from rural departments.

In 1877, France reacquired St. Bartholomew from Sweden. This was a sentimental transaction, as the islet had no natural wealth and was barely self-sustaining. A plebiscite was held to determine the wishes of the inhabitants, 350 ballots out of 351 being cast in favor of French sovereignty. The sum of 400,000 francs was paid to Sweden. A professor at the Naval College, Joannès Tramond, wrote that it was "most certainly the last operation of the kind" that would ever take place between two European nations in the New World, and thus far he has proved to be correct.

The swift rise in the Negro population of the colonies during the second half of the nineteenth century seemed to confirm the theory that the slaves, in the old days, had been infertile because they were slaves. New problems now developed. The peasantry found it increasingly hard to obtain land on which to settle as cultivators. Their holdings had tripled by 1900 and the total acreage for the first time exceeded that of the sugar plantations. But they could not be extended farther unless the large estates were broken up. Many of the young people were forced to solicit wage labor. The shortage of hands of which the planters had complained after emancipation turned into an overplus. The harvesting of cane was seasonal, and the sugar centrals could not begin to absorb the unemployed.

Furthermore, the small agriculturists did not build up commercial prosperity, since native foodstuffs had no foreign market. There was a return in part to coffee and cocoa, grown as accessory crops by the more enterprising Negroes, the driblets of produce being collected by commission merchants. Pineapples were added, with fair success. Capitalists encouraged by the Government naturalized the vanilla vine in Guadeloupe and created a minor industry.

The period was one of a slowly stagnating economy, which was not helped by the fact that the old white families tended to give up the struggle and emigrate to France. Tramond ascribes this to the emergence of a mulatto ruling class, with numbers on its side and with nothing to prevent it from exercising a decisive influence politically, though the whites were still in possession of a large part of the property and of the technical direction. "The tenderness and pride with which the Creoles regarded their little *Patrie*," he says, "could not hold out indefinitely against changes which exposed them to vexations, real or imaginary." Yet the defection was gradual, and on the other hand a good number of the whites took the course of intermarrying with the mulattoes and helping to form that composite race which Schoelcher had predicted.

Everything considered, Martinique and Guadeloupe became happier communities than they had ever been. The demon of race warfare had been exorcized. If a low standard

THE EMPRESS JOSEPHINE
Born in Martinique, she became the consort of Napoleon.

of living prevailed for the majority, at least starvation was impossible in the luxuriant tropics. The nature of the colored people under French influences was amiable, more artistic than is usual among Negroes, pleasure-loving yet easy to please with little things. It took a cataclysm, the eruption of Mont Pelée in 1902, to bring the period to an end. Before we consider that terrible event, let us glance at what was happening in Guiana.

The Cinderella colony on the northeast coast of South America was the scene of important discoveries by two noted French explorers, and it attracted further unfavorable attention as the land of the "dry guillotine." The work of Dr. Crevaux and Professor Coudreau. Devil's Island, where the innocent Alfred Dreyfus was imprisoned. Such were the contrasts offered to the world.

Crevaux, a naval physician with a passion for natural history, made his first journey into the interior in 1877. He mounted the Maroni River, between the French and Dutch Guianas, then roamed the wild hinterland to the Andes, accompanied only by a Negro servant called Apaton. Crevaux explored rivers till then but vaguely indicated on the maps and discovered many of their tributaries. When he reached Pará, Brazil, in 1879, his name was classed with those of the greatest modern travelers. He made two other voyages, pushing farther and farther southwest toward the Bolivian frontier. He was murdered by Indians in the Gran Chaco in 1882.

Henri Coudreau, a member of the staff of the College of Cayenne, decided to take up the work of Crevaux, which had been partly devoted to finding a solution to the age-old boundary disputes between France and Holland on the one side and France and Brazil on the other. He enlisted the Negro, Apaton, started in 1889, and between that year and 1896 he conducted five expeditions. He kept closer to the environs of French Guiana than Crevaux had done. He was the less scientific of the two and the more political-minded. In 1888 the controversy over the Surinam border had been decided against France by the Czar of Russia, to whose arbitration it had been submitted. Coudreau was eager that the more valuable territory of Counani to the southeast should be definitely acquired over Brazil's claim to it. This led him into strange adventures.

A number of Frenchmen, including Coudreau, proclaimed Counani as the Republic of Independent Guiana, with a publicist named Jules Gros as President. They hoped to gain recognition by the Powers, and then apply for annexation to France. The district was more than 100,000 square miles and had an estimated population of 17,600. Gold was discovered there in 1893, and both French and Brazilian prospectors rushed in, followed by detachments of soldiery. Desultory fighting occurred. France denied that she had sponsored the "republic." In 1897 she accepted the Swiss President as sole arbitrator, and three years later she was again declared the loser.

In the 1890's increased use was made of Guiana as a penal station. Newcomers were placed on islands off Cayenne, one of which is Devil's Island. Good behavior earned for the majority the privilege of being transferred to the mainland, in and about Saint Laurent on the Maroni River, where they lived and worked under light restraint. Desperate cases and prisoners deemed to be of unusual importance stayed on the islands. Dreyfus, a Jewish army officer who had been falsely accused of selling military secrets to Germany, was thus confined for several years. The charges against him eventually were reopened and he was acquitted. He aroused universal sympathy. The stories of escaped convicts helped to make Devil's Island a synonym of horror. But while the regime in Guiana was archaic, at times cruel, it was not so barbarous as outsiders were led to believe. Dreyfus suffered more from solitude than anything else; he had a hut to himself, and hard labor was not required of him. The slum rats who composed the ordinary run of convicts loathed their strenuous, regimented existence under a tropical sun, but, save for the incorrigibles, they were treated more gently than they would have been in a European penitentiary.

Saint Pierre, Martinique, was a city of 26,011 inhabitants in 1902, situated on the Caribbean coast in a fold of the rocky buttresses of Mont Pelée, the volcano which forms the northern head and summit of the island. No one has described the city better than Lafcadio Hearn, who saw it first in 1887. The following is from his *Two Years in the French West Indies:*

"Saint Pierre, the quaintest, queerest, and the prettiest withal, among West Indian cities: all stone-built and stone-flagged, with very narrow streets, wooden or zinc awnings, and peaked roofs of red tile, pierced by gabled dormers. Most of the buildings are painted in a clear yellow tone, which contrasts delightfully with the burning blue ribbon of tropical sky above; and no street is absolutely level; nearly all of them climb hills, descend into hollows, curve, twist, describe sudden angles. There is everywhere a loud murmur of running water—pouring through the deep gutters contrived between the paved thoroughfares and the absurd little sidewalks, varying in width from one to three feet. . . .

"A population fantastic, astonishing—a population of the Arabian Nights. It is many-colored; but the general dominant tint is yellow, like that of the town itself . . . rich brownish yellow. You are among a people of half-breeds—the finest mixed race of the West Indies."

Of Mont Pelée, 4,500 feet high, Hearn remarked, "For the moment, it appears to sleep." The volcano had given no sign of activity from its discovery until 1851, when a convulsion rained ashes over the roofs of Saint Pierre and gouged a huge cup in its own summit, which filled with water and became the Lac des Palmistes. Twenty years afterward occasional mutterings were heard. But no one would believe that the mountain was dangerous.

In April, 1902, occurred warnings: earthquake shocks felt even out at sea, jets of gas and cinders from fissures in the peak, the bubbling up of mud in the rivers causing them to overflow. Several telegraphic cables snapped as the earth quivered. A factory by a stream in the village of Prêcheur was destroyed by the sudden rising of hot, sulphurous water.

The people of the entire section took fright and began to flee. The authorities sought to calm them. M. Mouttet, the Governor, set an example by coming to Saint Pierre with his family. He declared that there was nothing to worry about, and he refused to postpone the elections which were to have been held during the day of May eighth. That morning broke clear and warm. In the early forenoon Mont Pelée exploded like a thunderclap and overwhelmed the city with a storm of flaming lava in less than one minute. All the ships in the harbor were burned, except one which broke its chains and reached Castries, St. Lucia, half its crew sprawled on the decks suffocated. A few persons who had thrown themselves into the sea from other vessels were picked up by a French cruiser which arrived at two o'clock. A Negro prisoner locked in an underground cell was the city's sole survivor.

Saint Pierre and its environs had been reduced to an immense chaos of debris, blazing at first, then smoldering until it seemed that the very stones were being disintegrated. The lava from Mont Pelée had surged down in well-defined zones, on either side of which the area was intact. Many victims had succumbed only because they had not had the time to leap across the edge.

The Soufrière volcano in the near-by island of St. Vincent blew off at approximately the same time, and was shortly followed by the Soufrière of Guadeloupe. The St. Vincent disaster was relatively as serious as that of Martinique, though no important town was destroyed; the one in Guadeloupe was milder. Further eruptions of Mont Pelée occurred, and on August twentieth the flow of lava was formidable enough to sweep several localities in the northwest of the island and cause a thousand more deaths. The aspect of the summit was considerably modified. The Lac des Palmistes had disappeared, and in its place had risen an enormous peak, or dome, a mass of red-hot rock which crumbled in contact with the atmosphere and was reduced in the course of months from a much greater height to about 400 feet.

One-fifth of Martinique had been devastated, its topography changed, the rivers turned from their courses, the entire section covered with wreckage and a thick blanket of cinders. The finer ashes fell at distances of a thousand miles and more. The loss of life had been about 40,000, roughly 26,000 in Saint Pierre, 4,600 in Prêcheur and the rest scattered. All animal and vegetable life took months to reappear in the ruined countryside.

This was the worst natural calamity ever visited on a Caribbean island. It proved intensely interesting to scientists, whose analyses of it are as yet by no means complete. France promptly sent out a commission headed by Alfred Lacroix, who ascribed it to *nuées ardentes*—flaming dense clouds. He rated this a phenomenon which was until then unknown and which the Mont Pelée eruption made it possible to study in all its details. Lacroix defined it as a sudden freeing of an enormous quantity of vapor composed of gas and water subjected to a tremendous pressure and raised to an excessive temperature, carrying with it a mass of burning slag and debris. He called the discharge an "emulsion" of matter giving the whole a solidity that prevented it from dissipating into smoke and which overthrew and incinerated everything in its path. There appeared to be no phenomena of asphyxiation of victims, but an abrupt raising of the temperature which no life could resist.

The false peak upthrust in the crater was regarded by Lacroix as characteristic of the unique volcanic activity which took place. The material which went to form the peak had been serving as a sort of cork preventing the normal escape of vapors. This was the opposite of what usually happens, and to it was attributed the exceptionally violent nature of the explosion and the *nuées ardentes,* which gave the disaster its individuality as a "cosmic cataclysm."

Chapter XXVII

Franco-American Louisiana

DURING the decade preceding the Louisiana Purchase, New Orleans and the near-by parishes were greatly influenced by the influx of refugees from Saint Domingue. Many came penniless. Others had escaped with gold, jewels and furniture, and were even accompanied by slaves who had chosen to cling to them. They stimulated, among other things, the development of sugar plantations. They brought expansive, tropical conceptions of luxury, as well as some of the fruits of civilization which had been discouraged under Spanish rule. As early as 1794, Louis Duclot, a Saint Domingue refugee, founded the first newspaper ever published in the province. It was a weekly in French, *Le Moniteur de la Louisiane,* and it appeared for twenty years. On the other hand, the West Indian slaves are believed to have spread the voodoo cult, and in a short while it was ruled that no more Negroes from Saint Domingue could enter.

A celebrated *emigré* was General Jean Robert Marie Humbert, he who had served in Leclerc's ill-fated expedition. He was considered one of the handsomest men in the army. Humbert returned to France as the escort of the widowed Pauline Bonaparte Leclerc, and fell into disgrace with Napoleon because of her obvious partiality for him. An extreme republican, he joined the Mexican revolutionists against Spain, then settled in New Orleans and spent the rest of his life there. Perhaps the most famous native of Saint Domingue to make Louisiana his home for a while was J. J. Audubon, the naturalist.*

Following the Purchase in 1803, the French inhabitants of the Territory, soon to be the State, of Louisiana obtained the adoption of the Code Napoleon under the name of the *"Progée,"* as the basic law. Numerous modifications have since been made, but it is still a fundamentally Latin code differing widely from that of any other State in the Union. The equal standing of French and English in legislative and court procedure, obligatory French texts of public documents, long prevailed. This was dropped bit by bit, until in 1914 it was wholly abandoned. But in 1936 an act was passed requiring that the texts of civil law be printed in the two languages.

Settlers from the north and east poured into Louisiana once the American flag had been raised. During the period from the transfer to the War of Secession in 1861, however, the French better than held their own politically and socially. New Orleans became twin cities, the Vieux Carré, or quarter within the old ramparts, remaining Gallic and enjoying the greater prestige, while a new Anglo-Saxon town, the activities of which were mainly commercial, sprang up on the other side of Canal Street. The majority of the early mayors were Creoles. State offices were shared. The list of Governors shows French and English names alternating pretty regularly. A. B. Roman, who served two non-consecutive terms in the 1830's, is perhaps the best-remembered Creole chief executive.

In the Acadian parishes, American supremacy made little or no progress for fifty years and has not succeeded in fully

---

* It is now established that Creole, as applied to native-born white persons of Latin blood, did not come into general use in Louisiana until after the arrival of the Saint Domingue refugees. The word is from the Spanish *criolla,* meaning as an adjective indigenous, or domestic. It was the formal term for French Colonial islanders. British West Indians, the descendants of Anglo-Saxons and Celts, also call themselves Creoles. Nowhere in the Caribbean region does the name imply an admixture of Negro blood.

dominating to this day. The people held stubbornly to their language and their customs. Yet they accepted the change of sovereignty in good spirit. Acadian volunteers fought under Andrew Jackson at the battle on the plain of Chalmette that saved New Orleans from the English in 1815. They were consistently active in State politics.

The secessionist movement made a strong appeal to the French of Louisiana. A sense of nationalism which the Federal Union had never aroused in them now manifested itself for the Southern region. Their interests were identical with those of the citizens of the other seceding commonwealths. They, too, were slave-holders and their economy depended on sub-tropical agriculture. The aristocrats of Virginia and the planters of the cotton belt were comprehensible types to them, and the descendants of the New England Puritans incomprehensible. The States' Rights idea meant little to the French, who wanted Louisiana in the Confederacy for emotional reasons. Some were moved pridefully by the destiny they foresaw for New Orleans as the maritime metropolis of the new nation.

The race threw its man power without reserve into the war. Its *amour-propre* was flattered by the immediate prominence of one of its own, General Pierre Gustave Toutant Beauregard, the victor of Fort Sumter and the First Manassas. Another brilliant Creole leader was General Alfred Mouton, who fell at the Battle of Mansfield in the Red River campaign while leading a division composed largely of Acadians. His command devolved on that blue-blooded volunteer from France, the Prince de Polignac, and the survivors were among the last Confederates to lay down their arms with Kirby Smith.

Armies of both sides had surged back and forth over the Acadian country and left it ravaged. The prolific, hardworking strain soon restored their material losses. But the plantation owners and the urban families whose slaves had been taken away from them were harder hit. Some never recovered. Charles Gayarré, the historian, who had supported secession as an irrefutable right and who had been ruined financially, wrote in 1865:

"Louisiana was then [1861] in as high a state of prosperity as any land was blessed with, but with sublime imprudence she did not hesitate to stake the whole of it on the cast of a die, at what she conceived to be the call of honor and duty. Four years have now elapsed; she is now the seat of desolation."

Morally the Louisiana French as a whole had endured a blow which caused lasting injury to their self-esteem. Not that many of them did not fight back during the grim days of Reconstruction. Few American journals have equalled and none have surpassed, in the literature of invective and pungent satire, the weekly *Le Carillon* published and edited in New Orleans from 1869 to 1875 by Forester Durel. It scourged with ridicule the "black and tan" legislature, which it called the *"Sénat Radicanaille"* and whose members it gave the names of animals. A series of articles dealing with this body each opened with a variation of the formula: "The Jackal on his perch, fifty beasts being present, the Nickel Calf delivered a prayer. To what God can these animals pray?"

Judge Alcibiade de Blanc had founded the order of the Knights of the White Camellia at Franklin, St. Mary's Parish, in 1867, with the mission of defending the rights of white Southerners. Its effectiveness in New Orleans had been crippled by spies. Later the White Leagues took up the work, and *Le Carillon* did its utmost to help. Five thousand League members and sympathizers attacked the militarized police at the foot of Canal Street, New Orleans, in the "September

14 Battle," 1874. Thirty-two men were killed and seventy wounded on that occasion. A monument marks the scene. The Leagues eventually played the principal role in overthrowing the tyranny of the carpetbaggers.

Nevertheless, the War of Secession and Reconstruction left the French pessimistic, doubtful of their ability long to maintain their traditions against Anglo-Saxon pressure. When the State regained its sovereignty, a general decline of their influence occurred. They no longer got an equal, or even a proportional, share of high offices. Occasionally, a French Governor or senator would be elected. More often, they had to be contented with smaller rewards, such as the lieutenant-governorship or seats in the lower house of Congress.

They began to give way on their language. French was not taught in the primary schools, was only an optional course in the high schools; no serious protest resulted. The younger generation learned to speak it from their parents without formal instruction, but except in the remote parishes exhibited a tendency to use English for everyday transactions. French-language newspapers died a lingering death.

Just as the bayou folk at one end of the social scale held out, intellectual circles at the other end prevented the process from becoming complete. Historians like Gayarré and Alcée Fortier did much of their work in the old tongue. French novels and poems were published. French dramas were produced in New Orleans. The best of these are all dated prior to 1901, and in the present century Louisianians of both races have made their important literary contributions in English.

A number of cultural organizations have been active for the past sixty years, and it assuredly is not negligible that their combined membership is now about 30,000. There are ample signs of a renaissance. The First World War stimulated the old pride in France. In the 1930's a movement to renew relations between the Acadians and the French of Canada developed. Pilgrimages were made to Nova Scotia and Quebec, and the visits were returned. A new society aimed at youth was formed. Its members take a vow which is worth quoting:

"I shall learn the French language because it is the language of my fathers; I shall learn it because it is the language of my religion; I shall learn it because it is the language of reason."

Acadians and those of part-Acadian blood in the State today are estimated at 400,000. Certain families have almost incredibly far-flung ramifications. There are 4,200 Moutons by birth or marriage, "the largest flock of *moutons* (sheep) in the world," as the jest goes. Similarly, there are 3,800 Broussards.

The present war, naturally, has caused anguish of spirit to the Louisiana French. Many of them support the De Gaulle movement. They take some comfort from the fact that in the general flight of the intellectuals of Europe to the United States, New Orleans has attracted a small but increasing group of highly desirable French immigrants. The clubs and circles are able to feature the names of lecturers who three years ago could have been heard only in Paris.

In the opinion of the writer, the war gives Creoles a unique opportunity to make New Orleans once more a center of Gallic culture. A city within a city is all they could expect to maintain, but that would suffice. Enthusiasm for the idea exists. Certain local authorities—all of Anglo-Saxon origin, be it said—have been emphatic in declaring that this is not so; they regard the young generation as solidly standardized on the American pattern. To them, the efforts of the French societies are artificial respiration which will fail to revive the corpse. The writer cannot agree. Gaelic was thought to be a hopelessly submerged language in Ireland prior to the Sinn Fein agitation; it had no international prestige, no modern literature, from which to draw strength, but it came back. French is deeply implanted in southern Louisiana and will not perish, because of its native vitality and because world conditions furnish reasons why admirers of the parent culture should help to build new centers for it on existing foundations.

André Lafargue, President of the Athenée Louisianais, says: "It is a matter of pride with us, and rightly so, that we should have remained bilingual under most adverse circumstances. . . . The prospects are promising and seem to belie those who predict that the French language within the near future will no longer be spoken in Louisiana." He used to be considered an extremist. Today those who share his views travel on a rising tide.

Chapter XXVIII

All Around the Caribbean

FRENCH influence has been widely exerted in many parts of the Caribbean region, outside of the Republic's existing colonies and of Louisiana. The reasons are manifest. Islands like Dominica, St. Lucia, Grenada and Tobago have on various occasions belonged to France, and some settlers remained despite the change of flags. A certain number of immigrants seeped from the earliest times into countries held by Spain, notably Mexico, Panama, Venezuela and the island of Trinidad, which last is now an English possession. During the slave insurrection in Saint Domingue, the exodus of refugees was not wholly to North America; thousands went to near-by Cuba and Jamaica, while others scattered. Finally, the infiltration of French thought and culture, which played so large a part in the revolts of the Spanish colonies, continued to the point where it may be said that up till the present war Paris, rather than Madrid, was the spiritual capital of Hispanic America. French finance and commerce have been additional factors.

The writer has noted elsewhere that the little islands which once were French bear a stamp that generations of English rule have not effaced. This is strongest in Dominica, on account of its location between Martinique and Guadeloupe, and weakest in Tobago at the southern end of the archipelago. The Dominica *patois* is mainly Gallic, with English, African and Carib words interlarded. Carnival and Catholic feast days are observed, often without a clear notion of their origin. But overlapping of customs explains only in part why these islands have never been fully anglicized. There is among the colored inhabitants, a subconscious drift toward the warmer, more unconventional ways of the French. Art and letters scarcely exist. However, the work of one Dominican poet, Daniel Thaly, who writes in French, should be known to a larger audience.

In the 1780's, Spain made an exception to her ancient policy of exclusiveness and invited foreigners of all nations to settle in Trinidad. This rich island had been feebly exploited by Spaniards, the chief use to which they had put it having been as a jumping-off place for expeditions to find El Dorado. Hence the liberal ruling in the reign of Charles III. The majority of those who took advantage of it were Frenchmen. As remarked in a previous chapter, a mass removal of the immigrants to Venezuela took place after the English had seized Trinidad in 1797. Some had remained, and others drifted back to join them when the times grew tranquil. The town of Port-of-Spain had a curious attraction for the French, and its polyglot civilization today has a tinge contributed by them.

Eastern Cuba and Jamaica were the places the fugitives from Saint Domingue could reach most easily during the years of terror. The Spanish Government let down practically all bars, and a good many mulattoes as well as whites crossed the narrow Windward Passage to seek new fortunes. Sugar and coffee plantations were started in the vicinity of Santiago-de-Cuba by the refugees, who managed them so efficiently that they brought prosperity to that end of the island. The sugar holdings are now largely in the hands of American corporations, but descendants of the original families still grow coffee. The French colony became important with the passing years. Among those who joined it was Dr. F. Antommacchi,

Napoleon's physician at St. Helena. He interested himself in the study of yellow fever.

The English in Jamaica did not welcome the Saint Domingue refugees quite so hospitably, because they feared that some of them would introduce republican doctrines. Gardner says that the landing of the first arrivals was considered a "grievance." The Governor did all in his power to awaken sympathy for these people, but with little success at first. "Their presence, and especially that of their slaves, was declared to be dangerous. The latter had been heard to sing Jacobin songs, and were not respectful to white people. Great numbers both of planters and slaves were sent away and only about two hundred were allowed to settle, and from these some of the most respectable families in the island have descended."

Lady Nugent, wife of the succeeding Governor, tells in her sprightly *Journal* that hundreds more French—she does not give the exact figures—landed from Saint Domingue in 1803 immediately after the final triumph of Dessalines. Her concern was with their social standing. As she was in a delicate state of health, she decided to postpone visting any of them until they had established themselves and it could be seen clearly to what class they belonged.

French names persist in Jamaica, often strangely corrupted. The language did not take root. Seeing how near this island is to Hispaniola, it is extraordinary that only a few words have crept into the dialect of the common people. The refugees, to be sure, had to buy slaves on the spot and to learn to give orders in the patter spoken by them, rather than teach them a new tongue that would not be generally useful. Those who decided to remain as settlers simply gave up French. Some were birds of passage, whose nostalgia eventually drove them to seek a more familiar atmosphere. The Du Quesnay family, for instance, after spending years in Jamaica and rearing children there, transferred to New Orleans, where members of the young generation won renown as littérateurs, musicians and priests.

Mexico attracted French adventurers during its revolutionary period. They were fascinated by the undeveloped wealth of that great country and built up a colony of merchants and speculators running into the thousands. Napoleon III's project to install Maximilian as emperor and exploit the land under his aegis resulted, although a failure, in additional Frenchmen taking root. Many from Marshal Bazaine's army remained. They ended by becoming a popular group, better liked than peninsular Spaniards. José Yves Limantour, the celebrated finance minister under Porfirio Diaz and leader of the *cientificos,* was descended from French immigrants.

De Lesseps' scheme for an interoceanic canal, another failure, left a residue of engineers and businessmen in Panama. None of the Central American republics or Colombia has a French colony relatively as strong. But Venezuela has been hospitable to Gallic infiltration, which began before the time of Bolívar. Carlos Soublette, one of the Liberator's trusted lieutenants and Vice-President of Venezuela under him, was of French parentage. The dictator Guzmán Blanco, as the nineteenth century waned, was a devotee of the Gallic manner, did his utmost to place its stamp upon Caracas and encouraged immigration. He divided his favors equally between intellectuals and concessionaires. The major part of his own leisure was spent in visits to Paris. When his daughter married the eldest son of the Duc de Morny, Guzmán Blanco felt that life had little more to offer.

The effects of the French mind upon all the Latin countries of the region have a deeper significance than the groups of Frenchmen fortuitously present under various flags. Simón Bolívar died in 1830. That same year occurred the street revolution in Paris which eliminated the restored Bourbons, and modern liberalism was thereby stimulated. To a remarkable extent, the constructive Spanish American leaders who came after Bolívar were inspired by French liberal ideas. They were particularly moved by the men who made the Revolution of 1848, men whose beliefs were colored by the new social philosophy which gave prominence to the interests of the working class.

Alphonse de Lamartine was the chosen master of the young generation. "From 1848 to 1858 he was a demi-God, a second Moses," according to one authority. The fact that Lamartine was both religious and romantic appealed strongly. He had said that democracy was "in principle, the direct reign of God." He defended all the liberties, and he advocated the program of the equalitarian republic because he held it to be Christian. "We can understand what enthusiasm this eloquence, impregnated as it was with idealism and the love of humanity, must have produced in America," writes F. García Calderón.

Guizot, the historian and conservative statesman, whose championship of the propertied interests had helped to bring on the Revolution of 1848, also had his disciples. The reactionaries of Spanish America resembled the liberals, in that they turned to a Frenchman for guidance. The influence of France was supreme.

The trend persisted. Victor Hugo was idolatrously praised for his thunderous polemics against Napoleon III, his advocacy of the Third Republic. This seemed the well-nigh perfect structure for the practice of democracy, winning much more admiration and respect than the United States. Léon Gambetta assuredly was preferred to Ulysses S. Grant, Jean Jaurès to Grover Cleveland, Georges Clemenceau to Theodore Roosevelt and Raymond Poincaré to Woodrow Wilson. The First World War increased the affection for France, and it has only been since her collapse in the present conflict that

Spanish Americans have begun to waver with regard to her.

The literature created in the countries under review has not been quite so powerfully affected. Since they wrote in their mother tongue, the local novelists and poets at first took the Spanish masters as models and changed with the changing fashions of Madrid. They soon became extremely responsive to the schools that grew up in France, notably the romantics, the parnassians, the decadents. Naturalism and symbolism made less appeal. Rubén Dario, the Nicaraguan, greatest of Spanish American poets, strikes diverse notes which can be traced to Hugo and Verlaine, yet achieves originality. The supreme flattery, however, is paid by José Maria Heredia the younger, born in Cuba in 1842, who made his home in France and adopted the language to such effect that his impeccable style in the *Trophées* and other books of verse founded a school. He was elected a member of the Académie Française.

The present generation of Latin-American novelists is producing works in both the Spanish and Portuguese tongues which, at last, are realistic and purely native.

To quote García Calderón again:

"France is the modern heir of the genius of Greece and Rome, and in imitating her, even to excess, Ibero-Americans have assimilated the essential elements of the antique culture. We find in the Gallic spirit the sense of taste and harmony, the *lucidus ordo* of the classics; the love of general ideas, of universal principles, of the rights of man, and a hatred of the mists of the north and the too violent light of the south; rationalism, logical vigor, emotion in the presence of beauty, and the cult of grace. France has been the teacher of social life and letters to the American democracies; her influence is already of no recent date. . . . She has here created a new variety of the Latin spirit."

But these republics are marked by the well-recognized

weaknesses of their dominant race, not least of which is an exaggerated individualism in public affairs. Clemenceau, on visiting South America, observed "a super-abundant Latinism; a Latinism of feeling, a Latinism of thought and action, with all its immediate and superficial advantages and all its defects of method, its alternating energy and failure in the accomplishment of design." It was a judgment passed by an intelligence too keen to permit itself to be warped by adulation.

CHAPTER XXIX

The Twentieth Century, to 1942

THE Mont Pelée disaster is regarded in the islands as a great turning point, with social as well as material consequences. Guadeloupe had been far less seriously damaged than Martinique, but it had depended to some extent upon the city of Saint Pierre as a commercial center. Nearly all the rum distilleries had been located there and every one of them had vanished. Other concentrated sources of wealth had been destroyed. The rebuilt distilleries were scattered over both colonies, a plan favorable to future prosperity. Indeed, after a brief depression, a larger foreign trade than before was being carried on. A radical change in the control of business had occurred, however. The whites had suffered the heavy losses, which insurance did not begin to cover, and this was the final blow that drove many of them into exile. With the aid of absentee capitalists in France, mulattoes and Negroes obtained an industrial grip which they had never had previously.

Politically, also, the colored people acquired more power. It came to them, so to speak, by default; for although they had sought it and no doubt eventually would have got it by sheer force of numbers, the self-elimination of so many whites hastened matters. Stephen Bonsal, an unsympathetic observer, saw it as follows in 1912, in his *The American Mediterranean*:

"Since the destruction of Saint Pierre, which was the center of the white population and the seat of culture in the French islands, the equilibrium between the whites and blacks, which for several decades had been maintained, with each year increasing difficulties, has been rudely upset. The deputies chosen since the disaster have been almost without exception men of the lowest social position, and of most radical politics. The idea of a perfect equality between the races has long since been abandoned as antiquated, and upon the stump in the islands at least, if not in the Palais Bourbon in Paris, the Negro deputies demand the supremacy of the blacks. These tribunes of the cane fields and the port cafés rule the unfortunate Governor of the hour with an iron hand."

There was, of course, the affair of Legitimus, a Negro, who while serving as Mayor of Pointe-à-Pitre, was elected in 1909 to the Chamber of Deputies. An auditing of the municipal accounts showed large sums unaccounted for, and a warrant for the arrest of Legitimus was issued. He hid in the woods, accompanied by female admirers, until it was time to sail for France, which he did surreptitiously. Immediately after being admitted to the Chamber, he offered himself for trial, was found guilty and punished. The newspapers of the Anglo-Saxon world expressed their horror. But it is absurd to be scandalized over such an episode because the politician in question happens to be black. Parallel cases are not rare in white American communities.

Against Legitimus should be set the able colored deputy from Guadeloupe, Candace, who once sat in a French cabinet. At least one island Governor was native-born and of mixed blood. In their *Trois Siècles d'Histoire Antillaise,* Alfred Martineau and Louis-Philippe May comment:

"Political struggles in Guadeloupe, as well as in Martinique, have consistently played an important but not a preponderant part. It is remarkable, in fact, that the Antillean representation in France, although the offspring of a very mixed population, in which the white race does not dominate, has almost always given proof of sagacity. One sometimes regrets that our Antilles, and Guadeloupe especially, do not have more inhabitants so as to be still more useful to the country; neither their remote origins nor their present aspirations are an obstacle to this collaboration."

The slowly improving commerce of the islands averaged 35,000,000 francs for Martinique and 30,000,000 francs for Guadeloupe, including exports and imports, during the decade ending in 1914. But public receipts were never equal to expenditures, and the French Government paid a subsidy each year to make up the deficit. This sum ranged between 500,000 and 150,000 francs for Martinique, and between 800,-000 and 400,000 francs for less productive Guadeloupe. France's sentimental attachment to her last footholds in the Caribbean accounted for her generosity; they no longer appeared to have strategical importance. Only the slender yield of the Guiana gold fields prevented that colony, also, from being a burden.

Universal conscription was applied to the islands for the first time in 1912. It caused no protest. The law had scarcely begun to be operative when the First World War broke out. A native of Guadeloupe, General Charles Louis Marie Lanrezac, enjoyed a brief moment of fame in the early days. He had been professor of military history at the War College. On the eve of the outbreak of hostilities, he entered the Superior War Council and replaced Gallieni as commander of the Fifth Army. Lanrezac fought the Battle of Charleroi as a delaying action during the German rush to the Marne. He gave way before Von Bülow, and was removed from his post. Joffre is said by French critics to have "sacrificed him on the demand of the English, with whom he could not get along."

Martinique called up 14,755 men for military service, of whom 1,637 were killed, wounded or missing. The figures for Guadeloupe were approximately the same. The actual conflict did not come near these colonies. On the other hand, they benefited by a greatly increased demand for their products. Sugar exports more than doubled and rum quadrupled, while prices boomed to unheard-of levels. A couple of years after the war, the general crash which involved all sugar countries, and particularly the West Indies, was severely felt. But rum held up, its net value as an export exceeding that of sugar.

In 1928, the whole island of Guadeloupe was devastated by a hurricane followed by a tidal wave, 1,500 persons being killed and 15,000 injured. It was one of the notable calamities of its type in the Caribbean, yet little has been written about it. Half a billion francs had to be raised in France to repair the material damages, the Government voting one-fifth of the sum outright.

The colonies made no history, otherwise, between the two great wars. American statesmen and journalists occasionally ventilated the idea that they should be ceded in part payment of France's debt to the United States. The same thing was being said about the more important British West Indies, and in neither case was it meant very seriously. Frenchmen riposted with noble sentiments. "One does not cede one's family," wrote Tramond, and added that no circumstances could possibly arise which would induce France to part from one square foot of this ancient territory. Such are the perils of prophecy. It remained true that the military significance which Fort-de-France acquired between 1939 and 1942 was difficult to imagine at an earlier date. That the Grande Terre, the fairly flat eastern half of Guadeloupe, has the best large undeveloped landing fields for airplanes between Puerto Rico and Trinidad is a realization only of yesterday.

By the middle 1930's foreign trade was again flourishing. Sugar won back first place over rum. Bananas appeared on the list as the third largest export. The franc had depreciated to about a fifth of par, but even so a business twice as large as that of 1914 was being done. The countryside around Mont Pelée had wholly recovered. A town of 3,000 inhabitants had been built on the lava-crusted site of Saint Pierre. The islands were a contented backwater of the French Empire, a population that was rising too rapidly being the chief menace to their future happiness. There are 662.3 persons to the square mile in Martinique, 353.2 in Guadeloupe and its dependencies with a much greater density in Guadeloupe proper. The condition should be borne in mind. Among Caribbean units only Puerto Rico and Barbados, where the economic problem is acute, have more inhabitants to the square mile than the French West Indies.

On September 1, 1939, Adolf Hitler attacked Poland, ostensibly to settle the question of Danzig, and two days later France and England declared war. The speed with which a crushing victory was won by Germany's mechanized divisions over her eastern opponent demonstrated to military experts that a new technique of warfare had been evolved, but on the allied side they were slow to learn the lesson. There followed the dismal "sitzkrieg" of the winter of 1939-1940, when France waited behind the supposedly unbreachable Maginot Line, and England to all intents and purposes fought with her navy only. The British expeditionary force on the Continent was inadequate.

This phase of the struggle affected the French Caribbean colonies less closely than the First World War had done, for although their man power was mobilized it did not go abroad. Men dreamed complacently of a fresh boom in cane sugar, seeing that most of Europe's beet fields had been thrown out of production.

Then came the debacle. Denmark, Norway, Holland and Belgium were overrun in swift succession. The Maginot Line was turned at Sedan and France invaded. The sweep of

abysmal calamity that ended for the English troops at Dun-
kerque, and for the Army and Government of France in the
woods of Compiègne, left small tropical outposts dulled with
incomprehension. There was no Martinique poet to compare
the charge of the Teuton horde with the burning death that
had flowed from Mont Pelée. The realities of war, however,
were soon to be brought home to these islands.

A cruiser, the *Jeanne d'Arc,* and several lesser ships, including the auxiliary cruiser *Belain d'Esnambuc,* constituted a
patrol squadron based on Fort-de-France. They had little to
do, for the British attended zealously to the matter of rounding up the few German craft that tried to break into the
Atlantic from neutral Caribbean ports where they had been
lurking.

When the collapse of France became a certainty toward the
middle of June, the aircraft carrier *Béarn* had already started
from Halifax, Nova Scotia, with 105 planes obtained in the
United States. A few were second-hand machines consigned
to Belgium, the rest brand-new fighters for France. Halfway
across the ocean, the *Béarn* received instructions by radio to
go to Martinique and stay there indefinitely. She completed
her detoured voyage without let or hindrance.

Meanwhile, the Banque de France had emptied its vaults
and sent a shipment of gold of unannounced value to Brest.
The fatal crumbling of resistance on the Somme was the signal for loading the treasure aboard the cruiser *Emile Bertin,*
one of the fastest boats of its class in the world, which sailed
for Halifax and arrived at that port on June eighteenth. The
Captain found orders awaiting him to proceed to Martinique.
Canadian officials, well aware that an armistice was in the
wind, notified him that an armored train guarded by troops
was waiting at the end of the pier to take the gold to Montreal.

A battle of wits and bluff ensued between Captain Robert
Batet, of the *Emile Bertin,* and the Canadian commander.

Batet declared that he must check up with Paris, and that if there were any attempt to force him into action before he received a reply he would shoot his way out of the harbor. British warships stood by in sufficient strength to make his threat empty. Instead of shooting, Batet slipped the second night between two of the watchers, took to the open sea and outdistanced a belated pursuit. The gold was safely stored in the archaic Desaix fortress on the inland side of Fort-de-France, when the armistice between France and Germany went into effect on June twenty-fourth.

Martinique at once lost its immunity. Britain became intensely interested in it and sent two cruisers attended by minor craft to hover about its shores. Within a week of the surrender by Marshal Pétain, British agents including a high colonial official and a naval commander came ashore at Fort-de-France and tried to negotiate for the control of the colony. The Governor refused to surrender his powers. A naval blockade was then ordered, for the avowed purpose of preventing the French warships and planes from leaving and passing, voluntarily or involuntarily, under the control of Hitler. That the gold was Britain's main preoccupation is hardly to be doubted. The fighting craft could almost surely have been captured or destroyed if they had left the island. Bullion could be smuggled out if there was the least laxity. So it was made a rigid blockade. All importations of food were cut off. Even mail was stopped from entering. The cable to St. Thomas was cut. A somewhat less paralyzing watch was kept on Guadeloupe, also.

The value of the gold that caused these *demarches* has been variously stated. John Gunther, in *Inside Latin America,* puts it at $250,000,000. Stephen Trumbull, a newspaper correspondent, who went to Martinique and investigated, asserts categorically that the store consists of 14,000 sacks of coins and bars, each weighing sixty kilograms, with a total value of

$945,232,344. It is still there. So are the planes, which stand ashore in the open; they are covered with tarpaulins and their motors are oiled and tested once a week.

If Britain had not been so hard pressed herself in June, 1940, she might have occupied Martinique after the rebuffing of her agents. She had just established a precedent by landing soldiers in Curaçao and Aruba, to "protect" the oil refineries. But she hesitated, and it is reasonable to assume that Washington, which had not objected to the move into the Dutch islands, was unwilling to see the French gold sequestered by Britain and sharply disapproved of a British occupation of the invaluable harbor of Fort-de-France which might have become permanent.

Under pressure of the somber events in Europe, there was held the following month in Havana the most important Pan-American conference that has ever occurred. The problem was what the twenty-one republics would do in case Germany were completely victorious and a change in the sovereignty of European colonies in the New World were proposed. It was the fixed policy of the Governments represented by their Foreign Ministers that no transfers from one European power to another would be tolerated. The Congress of the United States had passed a resolution to that effect, redefining and strengthening the Monroe Doctrine. Proof of American solidarity, as well as a clear-cut decision on the steps to be taken, were the chief objectives of the conference.

There resulted the Act of Havana. It provides that a colony which has lost its allegiance, or where democratic institutions are imperiled, may be occupied by one or more of the republics and administered under the guidance of a super-commission representing all of them. An organic law must immediately be established for the natives of the region after consultation with the people in whatever manner possible. The initial period of administration is limited to three years, and if renewed it may not be for longer than ten years. An occupied territory is assumed to have the right of independence when fit for it. However, it may be restored to its former rulers if that is compatible with the security of the Americas.

The Act says: "If a non-American State shall directly or indirectly attempt to replace another non-American State in sovereignty . . . over any territory located in America . . . such territory shall automatically come under the provisions of this convention." But the transfer of areas from a European to an American nation, no matter what the terms may be, is not prohibited by the Act.

The point last-mentioned soon took on greater import than the hypothetical emergency with which the conference had dealt. England had seemed close to invasion and rout during the hot summer weeks while the conference debated at Havana. In September the prospect had changed. Hitler had been unable to cross the Channel, except with airplanes. England had shown herself capable of withstanding a siege. France had not been asked to make over her colonies to the Nazis. It was no longer a question of providing impromptu government, perhaps overnight. Instead, as the American policy of aiding Britain became more definite, more implemented, President Roosevelt announced the bases-for-destroyers deal with Winston Churchill. The United States acquired sites in Bermuda, the Bahamas, Jamaica, Antigua, St. Lucia, Trinidad and British Guiana on ninety-nine-year leases.

Martinique immediately became a pawn of another color. Lying midway of the curve of the Lesser Antilles, possessing in Fort-de-France a far better natural base than Antigua to the north of it or St. Lucia to the south, this island could not fail to loom large in America's plans for the defense of the Panama Canal. Rights could not be obtained there from the Vichy Government, because Germany would refuse to sanction the action. Britain, on the other hand, no longer needed to have a Caribbean policy in the military sense and was willing to yield the responsibility of watching Martinique. The latter could have been brusquely seized by the United States without offending the other democracies. But this step would have caused a diplomatic rupture with France and driven Marshal Pétain further into the German camp. It was vital to encourage him to maintain the greatest possible measure of independence.

Events followed a slow and ambiguous course. Early in November, the British blockading cruisers sailed away and American warcraft took their places. A naval attaché landed, and he and the United States consul at Fort-de-France became the unofficial advisers of Admiral Georges Robert, recently appointed High Commissioner for the French Antilles. Economic conditions had by then reached a serious pass. Martinique has never produced enough meat for its needs, and all flour comes from abroad. The peasantry have depended since the days of slavery upon cheap salt fish from Newfoundland, Nova Scotia and the French-Canadian islands of Saint Pierre and Miquelon.

The British blockade had driven prices up to from three to five times the pre-war figure. Salt fish advanced from three francs a kilogram to fifteen francs. Fortunately there had been considerable stocks of flour, but this is a commodity which does not keep well in the tropics. When the Americans came in November, there had been no bread for four days. Also, a serious shortage of medicines existed. Serum to counteract snake-venom is an important item in Martinique, where an average of twenty field workers are stung monthly by the deadly fer-de-lance serpent. The clinics were completely out of anti-venom.

This state of affairs was alleviated at once by admitting supplies from near-by islands. Purchasing power in the United States was nil, because French dollar credits in American banks had been frozen. In the general readjustment that followed, sufficient funds were released by Washington to finance cargoes of meat and flour at regular intervals. The good will of the people of Martinique was earned by the first merchantman that appeared with the Stars and Stripes painted on its side.

In December, President Roosevelt made a tour of the Caribbean and inspected most of the bases leased from Britain. Calling at Fort-de-France, he pointedly failed to receive Admiral Robert. But the President and the Admiral left the island within an hour of each other, Robert returning the next day. There is ample reason to suppose that they conferred at sea. The French authorities then openly assented to a United States destroyer patrol to cover all their possessions in the Lesser Antilles, the declared object being to prevent German infiltration in any form whatsoever. The two warcraft which have since hovered offshore were nicknamed by the people of Fort-de-France the "guardian angels"—for they did not halt foodships as the British had done. A scouting plane has arrived daily in the harbor to check up, departing after a stay of about an hour.

A small commerce with France had been resumed as the year 1941 opened. Ten vessels had sailed for Europe in the preceding two months. The English stopped some of these in the Atlantic and confiscated at least one which was taking goods to Marseilles and had 1,500 soldiers aboard. This episode heightened the anti-British feeling of the islanders, smoldering as a result of the recent blockade.

Politically, Martinique and Guadeloupe have been in a state of suspension since the armistice. The General Councils no longer function, though they have not been suppressed. Local administrators go to the military for orders. Public opinion decided at the start for Vichy as against the movement led by General Charles de Gaulle. There has been no talk of independence as an outcome of the present situation. An intense French nationalism prevails. The mulatto and Negro leaders assert that there would be a rising *en masse* to oppose any armed invasion, whether by Nazis, De Gaulle forces, or even the United States. Yet they freely accept the idea that part, if not all, of Martinique and Guadeloupe is likely to pass under American rule before the war ends. They profess to dread the change because of the color question, while admitting that it offers the best hope of curing their economic ills.

In late May and early June, 1941, a scare developed. It was alleged that German officers had gone to the Caribbean by airplane, that some had landed in Martinique and some in French Guiana, to set up branches of the armistice commission and to control exports from the two colonies. This must be rated a canard. A few espionage agents may have got through. Almost simultaneously, the British searched a ship bound from Marseilles to Fort-de-France and discovered German and Austrian "tourists" aboard her. The rumor spread that the United States would proceed to an occupation. Cordell Hull quashed it with a series of statements in which he accused propagandists of trying to stir up trouble. He interposed the Act of Havana: "Any action contemplated will accord with the agreement reached with the other American republics at the Havana Conference."

Two underlying facts had telling weight at that time and for the next six months. (1) A base at Fort-de-France and landing fields on Guadeloupe were perceived by the experts to be not merely desirable, but necessities in the general scheme of hemisphere preparedness. (2) It was impolitic to insist upon having them because Vichy was apparently functioning as an independent French Government within the intent and spirit of the Monroe Doctrine and of the Act of Havana.

Fort-de-France harbor comprises fifteen square miles of landlocked deep water. There are many substantial piers and a drydock there, as well as machine shops equipped to serve the needs of a large fleet. Against these advantages, stack the truth about St. Lucia and Antigua in the immediate vicinity. Britain has not surrendered Castries, the best port in St. Lucia, but has leased to the United States Gros Ilet inlet, where it is doubtful whether an anchored seaplane could live in stormy weather. As for Antigua, Trumbull points out that the most effective comment is to be found in the United States Navy's hydrographic publication, *Sailing Directions for the West Indies,* which states: "Almost the entire island is surrounded by dangerous reefs. . . . The coast should be approached cautiously, with the lead going constantly."

The British use the port of St. John's, Antigua, where only craft smaller than destroyers can enter the inner harbor. The United States got the inferior and unimproved Parham Sound. Had it been possible to install modern armaments at Fort-de-France in 1941, St. Lucia and Antigua would have been reduced to their proper status of outposts of the Martinique base.

But the sovereignty of France, uncontrolled in her West Indian possessions whatever it may have been in Europe, created an impasse. The administration at Washington was not disposed to flout an ancient friendship and adopt violent measures without the best of reasons for doing so.

The last week of November, the picture began to change. Pétain, obviously yielding to the demands of Germany, removed the anti-Nazi General Maxime Weygand as proconsul in North Africa and embarked on secret negotiations with the oppressors. He had an extremely suspect personal talk with Hermann Goering in occupied territory. Hull promptly announced that American policy toward France was being reviewed.

A few days afterward, United States troops landed in Surinam, or Dutch Guiana, with the endorsement of the Netherlands government-in-exile and of Brazil. The declared object was to guard the mines which furnish American industry with more than sixty per cent of the bauxite needed in the manufacture of aluminum. Military strategy also was advanced. The armed forces of the United States were brought that much closer to the perilously narrow ocean gap between the Brazilian bulge and Dakar, Africa. A full-fledged base at Paramaribo is a probability for the near future.

Nor was the Surinam move disassociated from events in France. The writer believes that it was the first of several moves which will round out the bulwarks looking eastward. Tom Connally of Texas, chairman of the Senate Foreign Relations Committee, informed the press:

"I approve the action of the President in taking steps to protect the security of our basic war materials [specifically bauxite]. I think we shall have to take over Martinique and French Guiana, if Vichy continues to succumb to Nazi influence."

Senator Connally's words are supported by the logic of the circumstances with which the democracies are faced in 1942. France is less of a free agent than she has been at any time since the armistice. She cannot be forced to deliver her New World colonies to Hitler, for the Atlantic Ocean makes that impossible. But the strategic points she owns should be fortified against surprise attacks, should play an all-out American role instead of stagnating in a false neutrality. The eastern border of French Guiana is another two hundred miles nearer to Dakar than is the eastern border of Dutch Guiana. The importance of Martinique and Guadeloupe on the arc of the Caribbean bow has already been emphasized in the preceding pages.

Japan's treacherous blow at Pearl Harbor on December seventh forced the United States into war with all the Axis Powers. The defense mechanism of the Western Hemisphere became a more vital problem than ever. That the three French colonies will be left out of it much longer appears improbable. At the time of writing, the indications are in favor of their being detached from the Vichy regime by March fifteenth. What steps will be taken to effect this cannot be predicted, because they will depend on the drift of the Franco-American relations in the meanwhile. The De Gaulle movement may contain a clue to the enigma.

On Christmas Eve Vice-Admiral Emile Muselier, obeying secret orders from the Free French leader, captured the islands of St. Pierre and Miquelon, near Newfoundland, and got the overwhelming support of the inhabitants in a snap plebiscite. This was officially disapproved and termed "arbitrary" by the State Department, which had just renewed a neutrality accord with Robert in the Caribbean and did not want Vichy antagonized. But no action was taken to expel Muselier.

Prior to the St. Pierre and Miquelon coup, De Gaulle had been studiously correct in his attitude toward Washington's sphere of influence. However, he dropped a few meaningful hints. In the autumn of 1941 he declared, "If America goes to war, Free France will gladly and freely give any bases within our power." He could not have been thinking—at that time— of territories he controlled in the South Pacific. He meant bases in this hemisphere, where he foresaw that he might be able to expand.

Should the United States break off diplomatic relations with Vichy, General Charles de Gaulle doubtless will be recognized as the head of a provisional government, and his forces may then be allowed to take over the French Caribbean islands and Guiana. This would mean armed clashes with the garrisons, though it is unlikely that the resistance would be more than perfunctory. There would be no popular uprising, despite the threats of agitators. The coming of the Free French would assure a return to the lenient democracy of the Third Republic which the colored masses found very much to their advantage.

A managed revolution in the name of De Gaulle would leave the national status of the territories unchanged, so far as the twenty-one American republics are concerned. If this course is not permitted, the Act of Havana doubtless will be invoked and civil administration set up according to its provisions, with eventual independence a possibility.

In either case, military, naval and air bases will be established without delay. These will be under the United States flag, presumably on ninety-nine-year leases, as in the British possessions. Tenancy for that length of time is equivalent to an outright cession. History, at all events, does not know the difference, for it has never furnished an example of land being returned to the power that yielded it upon the expiration of such a long-term agreement. Often a wholly unforeseen disposition has been made of the lease at an earlier date; it has stuck otherwise.

The United States, therefore, seems destined to be a permanent influence in these lands that have been French for longer than three centuries. It is a grave social responsibility. Material help will have to be given, to rehabilitate the colonies after the present war which has so impoverished them. On the spiritual side, their beginnings of negroid culture should be encouraged without seeking to Americanize it. The colored people of Martinique, Guadeloupe and French Guiana, like those of Haiti, respond best to the Gallic genius.

THE END

A SHORT BIBLIOGRAPHY

Belaúnde, Victor Andrés, *Bolívar and the Political Thought of the Spanish American Revolution.*

Boyer-Peyreleau, E. E., *Les Antilles Françaises.*

Charlevoix, Père P. F. X., *Histoire de l'Isle Espagnole ou de S. Domingue.*

Davis, H. P., *Black Democracy.*

Dutertre, Père Jean-Baptiste, *Histoire Générale des Antilles Habitées par les Français.*

Edwards, Bryan, *The History, Civil and Commercial, of the British Colonies in the West Indies.*

García-Calderón, F., *Latin America.*

Garran-Coulon, J. P., *Rapport sur les Troubles de Saint Domingue.*

Gayarré, Charles Etienne Arthur, *History of Louisiana.*

Hearn, Lafcadio, *Two Years in the French West Indies.*

James, Cyril L. R., *The Black Jacobins.*

King, Grace, *Sieur de Bienville.*

Labat, Père Jean-Baptiste, *Voyages aux Isles de l'Amérique (Antilles).*

Lacroix, Général P. A. de, *Mémoires pour Servir a l'Histoire de la Révolution de Saint Domingue.*

Lauvrier, Emile, *Les Français en Louisiane.*

Martineau, Alfred, and May, Louis Philippe, *Trois Siècles d'Histoire Antillaise.*

Means, Philip Ainsworth, *The Spanish Main.*

Meignan, Victor, *Aux Antilles.*

Mims, Stewart L., *Colbert's West India Policy.*

Moreau de Saint-Méry, Méderic Louis Elie, *Description de la Partie Française de Saint Domingue.*

Phelps, Albert, *Louisiana.*

Poyen, Colonel H. de, *Les Guerres des Antilles de 1793 a 1815.*

Raynal, Abbé G. T., *Histoire Philosophique des Deux Indes.*

Roberts, W. Adolphe, *The Caribbean: The Story of Our Sea of Destiny.*

Schoelcher, Victor, *Des Colonies Françaises.*

Stoddard, T. Lothrop, *The French Revolution in San Domingo.*

Tinker, Edward L., *Les Ecrits de Langue Française en Louisiane.*

Vandercook, John W., *Black Majesty.*

Vaissière, Pierre de, *Saint Domingue (1629-1789).*

Anonymous, *Histoire des Désastres de Saint Domingue.*

ACKNOWLEDGMENTS

THE author gratefully acknowledges the facilities placed at his disposal by the Howard-Tilton Memorial Library and the Louisiana State Museum Library, New Orleans, and by the Consulate General of France in the same city. He thanks Miss Elsie Benjamin for friendly assistance rendered, Mr. Philip Ainsworth Means for making fruitful suggestions, and the Rt. Hon. Lady Decies and Mr. Lyle Saxon for kindly lending pictures for use as illustrations.

His grateful appreciation is expressed to Harper & Brothers for their permission to quote from Lafcadio Hearn's *Two Years in the French West Indies;* to Houghton Mifflin Company for their permission to quote from Henry Bamford Parkes's *History of Mexico;* to Little, Brown & Co. and Atlantic Monthly Press for their permission to quote from Burton J. Hendrick's *Statesmen of the Lost Cause;* and to Stephen Bonsal for permission to quote from *The American Mediterranean.*

INDEX

INDEX

Abbadie, Philippe d', in Louisiana, 161-163

Acadians, in Louisiana, 290-291, 294; Gayarré quoted on, 164-165

Act of Havana, the, 310-311, 314-318

Alabama, the, Semmes on, 259; battle with the *Kearsarge*, 261

Alexandre, called Bras-de-Fer, a buccaneer, 48

Alexander VI, Pope, bulls of 1493, 13

Ailhaud, commissioner to Saint Domingue, 202

Almonte, Juan N., Mexican reactionary, 263-265

Amazon River, La Ravardiere visited, 24

American Revolution, the, effects of, 123, 171

Amis des Noirs, Société des, 183, 188, 190

Anguilla, the English in, 35

Ango, Jean d', preyed on treasure ships, 15-16

Antigua, the English in, 35-36

Antommacchi, Dr. F., in Cuba, 297

Arawâks, in the Lesser Antilles, 32; cruelty of Spaniards to, 150

Artibonite valley, Boudet in the, 217

Aspinwall, (Colon) railroad from, 273

Athenée Louisianais, 295

Attakapas, La., Acadians at, 164

Aubry, Philippe d', in Louisiana, 163, 165-168

Audubon, John James, in Louisiana, 290

Auger, Governor, defense of Guadeloupe, 97

Aux Cayes, buccaneers at, 70; mulattoes at, 203

Baas, Jean Charles de, Marquis de Castelmore, Governor-General of Martinique, 74; quoted on slavery in Martinique, 151

Barbados, annexed by the English, 31; "planting" of, 34; compared with Saint Domingue, 69

Basse-Terre, Guadeloupe, 34

Basse-Terre, St. Christopher, Esnambuc at, 33-34, 39

Basse-Terre, Tortuga, 62, 70

Batet, Capt. Robert, of the *Emile Bertin*, 308-309

Baton Rouge, La., taken over by England, 162

Bazaine, Achille, in Mexico, 267-269

Béarn, the, at Martinique, 308

Beauharnais, Marquis de, Governor of Martinique, 121, 145; first husband of Empress Josephine, 145

Beauregard, Gen. Pierre Gustave T., in the War of Secession, 291

Belain d'Esnambuc, the, at Martinique, 308

Belaúnde, Victor Andrés, quoted on Nariño, 237; quoted on Bolívar, 241

Belzunce, Vicomte de, in Saint Domingue, 137

Benbow, Admiral John, fought Ducasse, 76, 88

Benjamin, Judah P., and gift of cotton to France, 260

Bernhardt, Sarah, at Panama, 276

Biassou, Negro revolutionist, 196-197, 200

Bienville, Jean-Baptiste le Moyne, Sieur de, expedition to the Mississippi, 99-105; character of, 100-101; founded New Orleans, 110; pleaded cause of loyalists in Louisiana, 163-164

Billaud-Varennes, Jacques Nicholas, imprisoned at Guiana, 228

Biloxi, fort at, 99; capital of colony, 110

Bissette, Negro leader, 245, 248

Blanc, Alcibiade de, and the Knights of the White Camellia, 292

Blanchelande, Governor-General of Saint Domingue, quoted, 191

Blanco, Guzmán, dictator of Venezuela, 299

Boisseret, Marquis de, in Guadeloupe, 42

323

France, Government of—*continued*
16; new war with Spain (1552), 17; death of Henry II, 19; regency for Charles IX, 19; Wars of Religion, 19; Henry IV, 23-24; regency for Louis XIII, 24-25; Cardinal Richelieu, 26-29, 37; Mazarin, 41, 57; Louis XIV, 57-106; war with England (1666), 58; Treaty of Madrid, 65; success of French colonization and colonial administration analyzed, 66-69; War of the Spanish Succession, 102, 118; interest in Mississippi (Louisiana), 98-116; Seven Years' War, 120-122; part in the American Revolution, 123; interest in French Guiana, 148-149; the Code Noir of Louis XIV, 152-157; Louis XV, 163; Louis XVI's challenge to English naval supremacy settled, 171-181; revolution and effect on colonies, 182-192; Louis XVI beheaded, 203; war with England, Spain, Holland, 203; peace with Spain, 205; Napoleon, 209-242; Louis Philippe, 245-248, 252; the Second Republic, 248; Napoleon III, 256-272; Napoleon III and Mexico, 256-269; and the Panama Canal, 270-278; Franco-Prussian War, 279; The Third Republic, 279; World War I, 305; World War II, 307; collapse of France, 308; *see also* Free French movement and Pétain, Marshal

France's Wars, with Spain (1542), 16; with Spain (1552), 17; of Religion, end of, 23; of the Austrian Succession, 119; Seven Years' War, 120; with England, 223; *see also* Free French movement

Francis I, of France, expeditions to America, 13-14; character of, 14; founded Le Havre, 15; death of, 17

Franco-Prussian War, the, effects of, 279

Fraser, John Foster, quoted on the Panama scandal, 275

Free French movement, 313-314, 317-318

Freemasonry in Saint Domingue, 136

French books prohibited in Spanish colonies, 235-236

French colonies, list of, in 1679, 89

French Guiana, first French colony in the West Indies, 25, 27; Chanvallon

French Guiana—*continued*
in, 148-149; the Code Noir in, 156; Acadians in, 165; the "dry guillotine" in, 228; abolition of slavery in, 250; penal colony in, 250-251, 284-285; discovery of gold in, 251

French Hispaniola, *see* Saint Domingue

French language in Jamaica, 298; in Louisiana, 290-291, 293-295

French loyalists, in Louisiana, 163-164

French Revolution, the effects of, on the colonies, 182-192

Galbaud, General, in Saint Domingue, 204

Gardner, W. J., quoted on slavery in Jamaica, 156-157

Gatun, 277

Gaulle, Gen. Charles de, Free French movement, 313-314, 317-318

Gayarré, Charles, Louisiana records of, 159; quoted on Acadians, 164-165; quoted on Louisiana, 292

Germany, World War II, 307, 314-316

Gibraltar, l'Olonnois at, 63

"Gibraltar of the West Indies," 124

Glorieux, the, in the Battle of the Saintes, 178-179

Gold, French, shipped to Martinique, 308-310

Gonaïves, 70

Gourgues, Dominique de, avenged massacre by Menéndez, 21

Graff, Laurens de, attack on Vera Cruz, 71-72; at Campeche, 73; with the Iberville expedition, 99

Grammont, François, at Campeche, 74

Grande Anse, the, planters of, 203, 205

Grasse, François Joseph Paul, Comte de, in the Lesser Antilles, 123, 172-180; in Chesapeake Bay, 173; at the Battle of the Saintes, 174-181

Graves, Admiral Thomas, at Chesapeake Bay, 173

Grenada, claimed by the French, 36; massacre in, 55; taken by the English, 121; annexed by England, 122; taken by the French, 123; raided by Hugues, 227

Grey, Sir Charles, took Martinique, 224

Greytown, *see* San Juan del Norte